Photographer's Resource

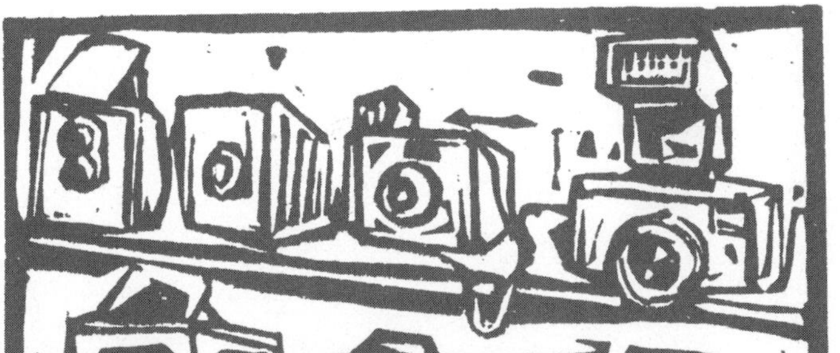

Photographer's Resource

The Watson-Guptill Guide to

- Workshops
- Conferences
- Artists' Colonies
- Academic Programs
- Digital Imaging Programs
- On-the-Road Programs

Stuart Cohen

Getting Your Act Together™

Produced for Watson-Guptill Publications by
David Emblidge — Book Producer

Watson-Guptill Publications
New York

Getting Your Act Together™

Series Concept: David Emblidge

Series Editor: David Emblidge

Researchers: Keri Gleason, Barbara Zheutlin

Database design: Chris Blair, Stuart Cohen, David Emblidge

Copy Editor: Katherine Ness

Book design & icons: Bill Cooke

Page makeup: Robin O'Herin

Illustrations: Roy Germon

Photographs: See credits with each image.

Indexer: Letitia Mutter

The text of this book was created in Microsoft Word and Q&A for Windows, and pages were subsequently designed in Quark XPress. Program descriptions were imported from the database using the X-Data extension. Display typefaces used include Frutiger and Officina Sans. Veljovic is used for the main text.

Library of Congress Catalog Card Number: 97-060100

10 9 8 7 6 5 4 3 2 1
Printed in the United States

Contents

7 **Foreword**

9 **Introduction**
- How to Use This Book
- Definitions
- Acknowledgments

PART ONE
Photography, The Greatest Job in the World

18 **On Becoming a Photographer**
- A Career in Photography
- The Decision to Become a Professional
- The Decision to Remain an Amateur
- Getting Your Act Together

PART TWO
Photography Programs in North America Today

26 **Joining Up**
- Associations and Organizations for Photographers

30 **Selecting a Program**

33 **Photography Programs**
- State by State: Workshops, Conferences, Residential Programs, Academic Programs, Digital Imaging Programs, On-the-Road Programs

PART THREE
The Business of Photography

148 **Equipped to Do the Job**

150 **Selling Pictures vs. Selling Yourself**

152 **Doing Business in a Businesslike Manner**

155 **Money, Money, Money**

156 **Business Planning**
- Sole Proprietorship and Taxes
- Incorporation
- Investing for Your Future

158 **Feeding Your Soul**

PART FOUR
Bibliography & Resources
Index

162 **Bibliography & Resources**

164 **Index**

176 **About the Author**

176 **About Getting Your Act Together™**

Foreword

AS A YOUNG BOY GROWING UP in Florida, I was first introduced to the fascinating world of photography by my grandfather, who loved to photograph the changing weather patterns and cloud formations that swept across the beaches near our home. Beautiful changes of color and light would play across the sand and surf, and time would seem both frozen and endless, as he worked with his camera. Later, we would examine the transparencies with a weekly slide show on Friday nights. This ritual established my future direction as a photographer and editor.

Today, I look back on the years that have stretched between then and now. I see the evolution of my photographic tastes and editorial skills not only as a result of my own efforts and experience, but also as the product of fortuitous encounters with mentors along the way. From the beginning, I was able to share my love of photography with others who could teach me much about its art and craft. These same mentors were also able to infuse in me a passion for the process of photography, whose end result can be shared with others as the gift of memory.

I can still vividly recall all-night printing sessions on deadline for the high school yearbook and newspaper. Such sessions often began with the coaching of my student advisor and the town's veteran newspaper photographer, each regaling the other with stories of assignments past and photographic solutions to thorny problems handled by improvised equipment or improbable encounters. Later, as the night progressed, they would retire to leave me to my labors. Yet somehow the infectious joy they had communicated was inspiration enough to keep me at my task.

Over the years, I have realized many things about photography and learned many important lessons about coaxing top performance from myself and others. I think it is essential that gifts be developed in an atmosphere of respect and enthusiasm. Talents can flourish only when people learn with the freedom to make mistakes. Generally, such encounters come when enthusiastic students encounter passionate teachers willing to share their experiences and their being.

Photography is a gift, for both the artist and the viewer. It is a transaction where the sight of the human mind, heart and eye is fully engaged to observe and document the world, producing a physical artifact that can be shared with others. The sharing is the reward for both parties, regardless of the venue or the type of photography involved. Obviously, the more developed the vision and the clearer the photographers are about their motives, the more likely it is that the communication will be something delightful and worthwhile to look at. Photographs are mysterious. While they are often documents about highly specific situations and experiences, simultaneously they can be transcendent statements expressing a higher, universal truth. Honing their talents to produce or recognize such work has been the task of most professionals I've known over the years. Most of these professionals will concede that learning is a lifelong experience. Many have taught photographic workshops, and all will admit that in them they learn as much as they teach.

While it was always easy for me to understand and value the educational process, it was sometimes hard to obtain it or to measure its impact. As a young man, I was often far from the photographic centers of the world. Later, as a beginning newspaper photographer, I hungered for feedback and for the kind of criticism that would mold my talents and make me a better communicator. I realized that aptitude and interest were not enough without talent development, including the trials of the field and meaningful feedback from critics whose insights and judgments I could trust.

The beauty of this book is that it lays out a clear path to such experiences. Regardless of your own photographic goals or level of present experience and ability, you can use this book as a resource to find the experiences you are seeking. I applaud Stuart Cohen and Watson-Guptill for creating this invaluable guide and for making it available to the public. I am sure that you who use it will find your own photographic journeys more pleasant and more fruitful.

Thomas R. Kennedy
Director of Photography, National Geographic Society

Introduction

Welcome to *Photographer's Resource,* a compendium of information and ideas for the photographer—from serious amateur to working professional—who wants to move ahead.

Whether you want to improve your skills, develop your personal vision or learn new techniques, this book offers dozens of opportunities at your level and either in your region or in a location you would love to visit.

Before you get down to particulars, flip through the pages. Photography programs come in all shapes and sizes, including some that focus on areas you may never have considered. Imagine yourself studying with someone whose work you have always admired. Perhaps you would like to try a completely new approach or to enter a comprehensive training program. Besides the program listings, Part Three, "The Business of Photography," and a number of informative sidebars will enhance your understanding of what it means to be a photographer today.

We wish you all the best.

How to Use This Book

Use this book as your personal research assistant. Let it help you decide how to proceed with your quest to expand your horizon as a photographer.

An enormous cross-section of programs is listed here. You might want to check out the details of those in your home region first: perhaps what you seek is offered nearby. You can use the index to locate programs that teach whatever photographic genre suits your personal style, and then see which of them may be worth a phone call or a visit.

Is there a particular instructor you want to study with? Many prominent instructors offer workshops and classes under their own names, so you can look them up directly. If you have known a favorite photographer to teach under the aegis of a larger organization, you will be able to get in touch with them to inquire about upcoming courses. Not sure how to proceed? Take your time and look around. You will find in these pages a host of institutions and organizations that offer a broad selection of learning opportunities.

Fine artists may choose either the instructional path—studying with a particular teacher—or the independence of an artists' colony. These retreats, some of which accept artists at all levels of experience, provide a quiet time in which a creator can focus on artwork with a minimum of distraction. The descriptions in this book will help you find one that may be right for you.

Students who are considering training for a career in photography have a number of specialized schools and university programs from which to choose. For those who seek to learn the latest digital imaging technology, there is a wide selection of photography-related computer courses in major cities across the country.

Part One, "The Greatest Job in the World," provides guidance on how to think about your personal path in photography. How important is making pictures to you, and how large a part do you want it to play in your life? Are you in it for love, or for money, or for some combination of the two? Part Three, "The Business of Photography," is a short course on the issues you would need to consider in setting up and running a for-profit photography operation. You will find it valuable whether you are committed to photography as a career or simply want to understand how the industry works when you sell pictures for publication or take on assignments.

Sandwiched in between, Part Two, "Photography Programs in North America Today," makes up the bulk of the book. It begins with a brief listing of associations and organizations you may want to join. After that, we switch to gazetteer format, moving state by state through descriptions of Workshops, Conferences, Residential Programs (artists' colonies or retreats), and some of the best Academic Programs. This is also where you will find special listings of organizations that teach the high-tech digital imaging products that are having such an impact on the world of photography.

Definitions

Six icons make it easy for you to navigate through the book and locate what you are seeking.

Workshop

A Workshop is any gathering of a limited number of photographers under the tutelage of one or more advanced photographer/teachers for the purpose of enhancing participants' vision, technique and skill. The majority of listings in this book fall under this broad category.

Many of the workshops listed here are presented by one or two professional photographers who simply love to teach. Others are offered by large organizations whose business is to serve the needs of photographers like you who seek to improve their knowledge and their images. A workshop may comprise a few days to a few weeks of instruction, and may take place in a classroom, darkroom, a studio or in the field.

Workshop topics are as varied as the photographers who teach them and may include scenery, wildlife, black & white fine art technique, photojournalism, portraiture and a variety of commercial skills.

Conference

A Conference is a large gathering of photographers for a day or several days to meet with colleagues and learn about the state of the industry or of their own area of specialization. Some photography conferences include a series of workshops and seminars on individual topics, and some may be combined with an equipment-oriented trade show. A number of the photography organizations listed in Part Two under "Joining Up" have their own annual or biennial conferences.

Residential Program

A Residential Program is designed to offer photographers and other artists a place to live and work for periods of time ranging from a week to several months or even a year. Typically, artists have a great deal of freedom to follow their own inner voice and create new artwork. The social milieu can vary from total seclusion to a highly interactive mixing of all the resident artists. Some residencies include regular supervision and critiques by advanced professionals. Most but not all residencies that accept photographers are equipped with darkrooms.

Academic Program

Academic Programs include the colleges and universities that teach photography as a course of study leading to a BA, BFA, MA or MFA degree. In addition, several specialized photography schools offer excellent certificate or diploma programs. These courses of study range from several months to two years, and provide photographers with the skills and knowledge they need to be able to seek employment as a photographer or to open a freelance business.

Because of the sheer numbers, only a few of the very best college and university degree programs could be listed here. If you are interested in an academic photography program in your area, consult your local higher education institution. State-supported universities and community colleges often combine photography and liberal arts education at a terrific bargain price. In addition, most art-education schools and institutes around the country permit students to specialize in photography.

Digital Imaging Program

The birth of digital imaging technology, which refers to the capture of images on digital media and the use of computers to alter images, is changing the face of how photographs are taken, transmitted and used. And while it will be a long time before film is completely supplanted by electronics, many photographers are eager to learn the ins and outs of digital photography.

Most organizations that teach digital imaging base their courses on the industry's dominant computer software, Adobe Photoshop. These organizations, primarily such photo-oriented businesses as color labs and broad-based computer-training facilities, teach Photoshop and/or other software, mostly on the Macintosh platform, to anyone who is interested. Most introductory courses, though, barely scratch the surface of what these sophisticated programs can do. For those interested in more than simple retouching, the learning curve is quite long. Photographers who take a two-day beginning course will still require many hours of trial and error before they can produce flawless, commercially acceptable digitally manipulated or morphed (combined) images. Advanced classes may help. Long-term practice is the key to success.

Several sidebars in the book address other issues concerning digital imaging.

On-the-Road Program

Many of the programs in the book take place exclusively at or near their home address. Others travel to locations across the country and around the world. The On-the-Road icon indicates that a program, usually a workshop, is not limited to the town, or even state, in the listed address. So if you live in Texas and want to take a workshop in the Rocky Mountains, do not restrict yourself to looking under Montana and Colorado. You may find exactly what you want from a workshop organization based in New York or Washington.

Workshop groups and individual instructors tend to vary their destinations from year to year. This book, compiled in 1996 and released in 1997, could not begin to anticipate where photography programs might visit in 1998 or 1999. So if you want to travel, as most photographers do, and you find an organization that appeals to you and/or an instructor you want to study with, call, fax or e-mail them. They might be going just where you want to be.

How the Information Is Displayed

Every program listing has two components: the information block and the write-up.

In the write-up, you will find one or more paragraphs of description. Short write-ups generally signify smaller or simpler programs. More important or complex programs merit more detail and take up a larger space.

In the information block (right), most items are self-explanatory, but a few of the categories bear further description.

Icons:

= Workshop

= Conference

= Residential

= Academic

= Digital Imaging

= On-the-Road

International Center of Photography

For photographers at all levels

Upper Fifth Avenue, Manhattan — 1130 Fifth Ave., New York, NY 10128 **Voice:** 212-860-1776, ext. 156 **Fax:** 212-360-6490 **Contact:** Registration **Founded:** 1974 **Admission:** Some courses require portfolio review or other prerequisites **Cost:** $250–$325 for weekend workshops; $385 for 10-week evening classes; slight discount for members; $7,500 plus $600 lab fee for yearlong program **Financial Aid:** Work/Study **Size-Attendees:** 12–15 **Degree or Certification:** Two 1-year certificate programs; MFA program in association with NYU

Addresses: The on-site mailing address where the program is based and where it may take place is listed as the primary address. If a second address is given, it is usually where the organization has asked for applications or other mail to be sent.

Country: Always the U.S. except for those few in Canada.

Contact person: The one to ask for if you want well-informed, up-to-date information. Sometimes it may not be possible to get to the head of a given program, but it is always worth a try. Many programs have coordinators, admissions people or administrative assistants who can answer most questions.

Web site: The explosive growth of sites on the World Wide Web section of the Internet continues. Some of the Web sites listed here are extremely thorough and informative, so that you can learn about individual instructors, find out current schedules and even print out an application or registration form directly. We strongly recommend that you check out the Web site of any program that seriously interests you.

As you read this, many more of the organizations may have acquired Web site addresses. You might want to look for them using a good browser and any of the Internet search engines.

Open: Exact program dates tend to vary from year to year. We give the likely time period.

Admission: Almost all programs call for some kind of application or registration form, but beyond that the requirements vary. In some you just sign up, pay up and go. Others, especially more advanced programs and residencies, ask to see a portfolio of your work and may request a resume. Generally speaking, the more stuff they want in advance, the more selective they are. Artists' colonies that cover all expenses and offer a stipend are likely to have a lot more applicants per opening than pay-as-you-go programs.

Application fees are common for programs offered by academic and nonprofit organizations. Besides covering the cost of administering a large number of applicants, fees tend to screen out half-hearted hopefuls. Most application fees are modest. If you are put off by the fee, call for more information to see if you really want to apply to the program.

Deadlines: Deadlines are simply an administrative reality in some programs, especially where financial aid is requested. While some program directors like to keep the door open a crack for especially qualified late applicants, it is a good idea to get all the paperwork in well before deadline, just in case.

Cost: We have done our best to give you a fair picture of what things cost. The first number in any listing is the program fee, or at least the fee for some of the more popular programs this particular institution may offer. Lodging, meals and materials are generally not included in the fee; where they are included, we have so indicated. Certain travel workshops (such as overseas) are the exception: all expenses (besides airfare) are included in a single fee. When a single organization offers a number of similar programs whose costs vary, we have provided you with a range of costs and as much detail as was practical to mention, including the occasional discount policy.

These numbers are accurate as of one point in time, and should not be expected to go down if they do change.

Financial Aid: The larger, more academically and artistically oriented organizations are more likely to offer financial aid than are other programs. If you plan to request financial aid, mention that when you ask for an application, and get all the necessary forms in as early as possible, before available funds are gone. If you desperately want to enroll in a particular program that you cannot afford, call the director and ask if a special provision might be made or a work/study or payment schedule arranged.

For the most part, you will be better off if you can wait to take a program until you can afford it, or until you can arrange a loan from a friend or family member. Some organizations that offer limited tuition discounts asked us not to mention it in our listing so as to not encourage too many requests. Our advice: be bold and ask.

Group Size: The number of participants can vary greatly from one program to another. We indicate the average (or maximum), and where applicable, the number in the larger group—for example, "250 total; workshops 20."

Handicapped Access: Programs at institutions receiving federal tax dollars are likely to have handicapped-accessible facilities. We report "Handicapped Accessible" only when the program itself makes this claim. Many programs that do not say so are in fact accessible to participants with varying levels of disabilities. Those who need special facilities should always call ahead for details and to reserve what may be a limited number of spaces.

How the Information Was Gathered

It would have been fantastic to visit every program and spend a few days with every workshop group or instructor, but that would have delayed the publication of this book for years. Instead, we called program directors and chatted about their offerings—what they considered special about their courses and how photographers could benefit. We perused brochures and catalogues, being careful to read both what they said and what was tucked between the lines. We spoke to graduates of some programs, followed up on referrals, and contacted arts administrators. We scoured photographic publications and the Internet for education and training opportunities, large and small, that deserved to be listed in this book. We kept our ear to the ground.

Of course, the landscape changes constantly. New programs are born; others disappear. That is why we plan to update this book every two to three years. Be sure you have our most recent edition.

How You Can Participate

Readers are invited to respond. Please correct our mistakes, offer your perspectives and let us know what else you'd like to see in the next edition. Please tell us where you bought or borrowed this book.

Write to: Editors, Getting Your Act Together™, c/o Watson-Guptill Publications, 1515 Broadway, New York, NY 10036.

Acknowledgments

We could not have produced this book without the assistance of the many program directors and administrative assistants who sent us information and answered our detailed questions. I am especially grateful to researchers Barbara Zheutlin and Keri Gleason, who made so many of the phone calls, left so many messages on answering machines and followed up until the information was received. Copy editor Kathie Ness corrected the vagaries of my creative punctuation and prodded me to clarify those paragraphs that made perfect sense to me when I wrote them but were otherwise inscrutable. Photo researcher Marcy Ross tracked down pictures from all over the country and cajoled their creators to let us reproduce them in the book. Sincerest thanks to both of them.

David Emblidge, the Series Editor, gave me guidance when I needed it and turned me loose the rest of the time. He was always cheerful and pleasant to deal with. Without the framework he provided, this book would have been a mishmash of disconnected bits of information.

Sam Merrell and Katrin Eismann helped with the research on digital programs.

I could not have done any of this without the cooperation and support of my wife, Anne Lucas.

PART ONE

Photography, The Greatest Job in the World

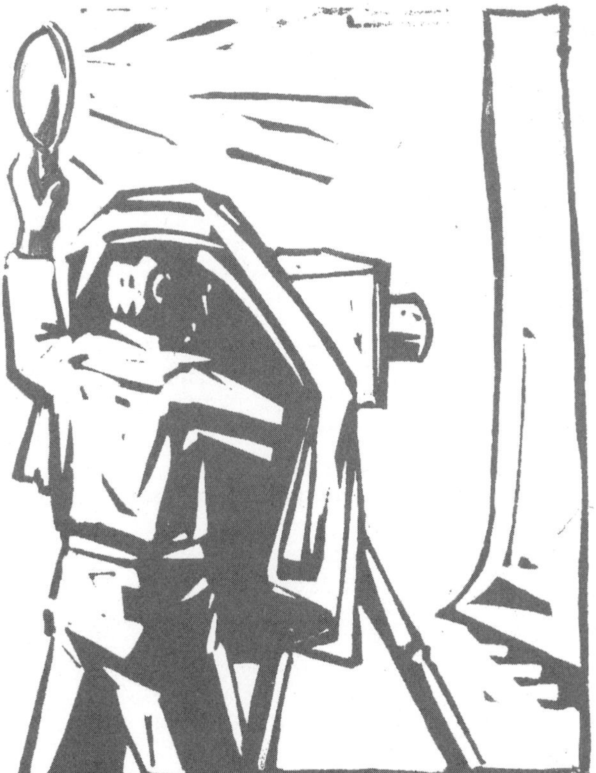

On Becoming a Photographer

MANY PHOTOGRAPHERS can recall the exact moment the inner spark ignited that led them to become photographers. For some the moment occurred upon seeing a picture they had taken, a vision of the recent past that stopped time, preserving forever people, places and feelings. For others it was in the darkroom, when a blank sheet of paper floating under a dim amber light suddenly sprang to life with a familiar image. Still others were enthralled the first time they peered through the viewfinder of a metal and plastic box filled with dark mystery and promise: a camera.

Photography has that magic. It calls people to participate. It offers the chance to grab an instant out of the fluid passage of time and space, transforming it into an image to keep, hold and show to others.

Photographs are the icons of our time. In magazines, newspapers and electronic media they acquaint us with people we have never met and reveal places we can never hope to visit. From the days of the early "shadow catchers," photographers have become the eyes of an entire society, exploring the world and rendering it, wordlessly, to the public.

No wonder the practice of photography is so attractive. Photographers get to speak, loudly, without making a sound. They tell stories and share feelings with a broad audience and never have to repeat themselves. Many who are drawn to become photographers do so because of the unique opportunity for creative self-expression. Still others come to photography through wanting to live what they perceive to be the photographer's life.

At some point, the novice photographer becomes serious about the art and craft of taking pictures. Then a whole new set of choices unfolds. What do you want to do with it? How big a part of your life do you want it to be? What do you want to accomplish with your pictures, and for whose benefit? Perhaps you want your photographs to tell stories or to express your deepest emotions. You might prefer to focus your lens and your attention on recording faces, illustrating themes and ideas or simply recording the experiences of your life. Is that enough to satisfy you? Will you be content just making beautiful pictures of sunsets and flowers?

Eventually, many lovers of photography face the big question, the career question: Do you want to become a professional? Is your relationship with photography such that you desire to earn some or all of your living with your camera?

In order to make this decision, you need a lot more than just the hunger to make photographs. You need to know how photographers work and what it is like to be a professional. A decision of this importance requires the very best information you can get and a sensitive ear to the murmurings of your heart.

The best way to find out what photographers do and how they live is to talk to experienced pros about all aspects of their work. Talk to people at different levels in their careers and in different specialties to get the most complete view. Ask all the questions you can think of. At the very least, you should know what options you have in stepping up to the ranks of the professional, and be able to imagine yourself living and working that way.

A Career in Photography

Choosing a career in photography is a bold step. As a profession, photography is alluring but also fraught with perils. It can yield great personal and professional rewards, but the demands are high. For every glamorous, expenses-paid assignment there are a dozen cranky clients, shooting days spoiled by bad weather, and technical problems with film and equipment. Along with every perfectly composed, beautifully lit picture come ten or a hundred or a thousand that are not quite right or just plain awful.

Each photographer faces a series of choices on how to proceed with a photographic career. What kind of work will produce the results you desire? What will bring you personal satisfaction, recognition, financial gain? Photography is a diverse profession with many specialties and niches. While it is possible to take many different kinds of pictures, all career photographers must concentrate their efforts on a limited range of subjects and styles. There are simply too many variations on photography for any one person to do all at once. Career photographers must settle on what they love to do best, and can do well enough to succeed.

What follows here is a partial list of the avenues a photographer might choose, and a brief description of what each type of photography entails.

Photojournalism/news

The news photojournalist is employed by a newspaper, magazine or media service to photograph breaking news stories, features and people or to illustrate articles in publications. Typically, a news photojournalist is referred to as a "staff photographer," is paid a salary plus benefits and works on regular daily or longer-term assignments. The great majority of locally generated photos that appear in the newspaper every day are shot by staff photographers They may include pictures of local politicians and business leaders, newsworthy events of all types, such as the scene of an accident or fire, local sports teams and personalities, and photo illustrations of themes to accompany human interest stories.

A magazine staff photojournalist also works on salary but may be required to travel to cover the longer stories or personal profiles that are typical of magazines. A photographer who works for a media service (what used to be called a wire service) covers local or regional news or sports for a national audience, or travels to cover larger stories, such as a war or political campaign.

Photojournalism/freelance

The freelance photojournalist does exactly the same kinds of photography that the staff photojournalist does. The difference is that the freelancer is self-employed. A magazine will hire a freelancer to shoot a certain photo or series of photos. Payment is based on a contractual agreement that may reflect the amount of time spent (a day rate) plus additional payment depending on how the photos are used in the publication.

Freelancers may work as contract photographers, or "stringers," for a magazine or media service. Stringers have contracts for a longer-term relationship, which spells out how much work the photographer will do and under what terms. Contract photographers remain self-employed: they are responsible for their own businesses, equipment, health care, taxes and insurance. An important plus to freelancing is that in most cases, freelancers retain the copyright to their images. They own "intellectual property rights" to every picture they take as soon as they take it. The freelancer who captures an extraordinary moment, such as a world leader being assassinated, stands to garner all benefit from worldwide sales of the picture.

Corporate and Industrial

The corporate and industrial photographer may be employed by a corporation or may be freelance. In most cases, only corporations with the resources and quantity of work to keep a photographer occupied full-time can afford to hire a staff corporate photographer.

Corporate photography involves shooting pictures of company operations, such as plants and facilities, people at work, executives and customers using the company's products. These pictures are used in annual reports, sales brochures and presentations, for public relations, internal communications and general record-keeping. A corporate photographer for a large or multinational organization may be required to visit facilities in many different places.

Staff corporate photographers, like newspaper photojournalists, give up ownership of copyright to the employer. They are subject to the organizational formalities and politics that any other corporate employee faces. Besides receiving the benefits of employment, they do not need to purchase their own sophisticated equipment. The company pays for and owns it all. Freelancers, by contrast, own their own gear and work on the basis of a contract, for either a single job or a longer-term body of work.

Corporate photographers must be able to produce top-quality pictures under a wide variety of circumstances. They need to understand advanced lighting techniques and should be as good at dealing with people as they are at setting up a complex shot. As modern companies begin to create digitized photographic archives of all corporate imagery, it becomes more and more important for today's corporate photographer to understand how to work with images on computers.

Advertising

Advertising photographers take pictures of things, people and situations used in advertisements in magazines, on billboards and elsewhere. Most have large, well-equipped studios in which they may set up a simple product on a tabletop or create an entire room environment, with furniture, models and a painted backdrop to simulate a view of the outdoors through a window. Many advertising shoots are done on location as well, which requires transporting lights and a crew to a destination the client likes.

Advertising photographers command high fees for pictures that are reproduced widely in expensive advertising campaigns. They also have high overhead, maintaining a studio with a lot of equipment and a professional staff. The advertising photography business is particularly sensitive to rises and falls in the economic cycle.

Fashion and Glamour

Fashion and glamour photographers take pictures of people, especially celebrities and professional models. The most successful of these photographers tend to have a higher profile than many other types of photographers because of the highly visible people they work with. The few among them who reach the top levels are well paid and can become celebrities in their own right.

Catalogue

Photographers who shoot catalogues, by contrast, labor in anonymity. On location or in large studios, they shoot hundreds or thousands of images that will appear in mail-order catalogues and store circulars. They may be employed by a single company that needs new photography on a regular basis, or they may work for a particular catalogue "house." Of all the branches of the profession, catalogue photography has been the quickest to embrace filmless electronic cameras, to save on film and processing costs and to reduce turnaround time.

Stock

Stock photographs are all those millions of images found in photo agencies, picture libraries and individual photographers' files that are available to all kinds of buyers for print and electronic publication. When buyers need a certain picture and cannot or do not want to assign a photographer to shoot it, they can call a source of stock photography and request pictures that fit their demands. Stock photographers today actively shoot, at their own expense, thousands of pictures that they think someone will pay for at some later date.

Stock photography is especially alluring to the beginning photographer because it sounds as though you can simply go out and shoot whatever you like and sell the images later. But it is the single most competitive area of photography, and difficult to break into unless you are represented by a stock photo agency that markets the images aggressively. Highly specialized photo collections tend to do better than general subjects, which are already well covered by other photographers.

Freelance Commercial and Editorial

"Freelance" is a catch-all term for all those photographers who work independently for a variety of clients. Commercial photographers shoot primarily for advertising or corporate purposes, where the object of the picture is to convey a specific idea or inspire a course of action. Editorial photographers gravitate toward magazines, public relations and educational materials, where pictures deliver information and tell stories. In practice there is considerable overlap between the two, and many freelancers do both in addition to shooting stock.

The nature of the photography business tends to lead individuals to specialize in one area or the other, particularly in the heightened competition of a crowded urban environment. Freelancers in smaller communities are more likely to be generalists who shoot all kinds of subjects.

Wedding and Portrait

Wedding and portrait studios can be found in every decent-size community in the U.S. Unlike advertising or corporate photographers, who work for companies, these men and women serve the needs of the local citizenry, documenting their families and celebrations. Wedding and portrait photographers usually run their own small studios and may also take on commercial work for local businesses.

Fine Art

Very, very few people have lucrative careers in fine art photography. There are just too many excellent artistically conceived and rendered images to support those photographers who create pictures exclusively for the fine art market. Most working photographers of all types spend a certain percentage of their time on personal work, solely for the purpose of fine-tuning their vision and creating art. They may hang these pictures on their own walls or try to sell them through galleries and exhibitions. Photographers who want to make a career of specializing in fine art should have another way of making a living for as long as it takes to establish a reputation and a market value for their photographs.

Digital Imaging Specialist

The digital imaging specialist is part photographer, part graphic designer, part computer wizard. Photographs or other images are scanned into digital form and loaded into a computer. The digital imaging specialist then manipulates, alters or combines the images on the computer to create a completely different class of image that may or may not be recognized as photography. Digitally manipulated images have many uses in print and electronic publishing, and may also be created as fine art.

Other Specialties

Subspecialties of the categories listed above are practiced by a number of photographers who concentrate exclusively on a narrow range of subjects. These may include legal and forensic, architectural, medical, aerial, underwater, wildlife, food, photomicrography and other very specific areas of photography.

Many photographers never make a formal decision to specialize in one kind of photography versus another. The process just happens. They start taking pictures because they enjoy it or feel they have something to say photographically, and their personal styles evolve. In time they find themselves gravitating toward one type of photography or another. This form of self-selection is a healthy way to discover your own best path. You end up doing the kind of photography to which you are best suited by dint of skill, preference and personality.

The Decision to Become a Professional

In choosing to become a professional photographer, you elevate your commitment to the medium. It is no longer an infatuation but more like a marriage, complete with responsibilities and sacrifices. It begins to shape the way your life unfolds. In exchange for that heightened commitment, you expect to reap rewards in terms of financial gain, social benefits and personal satisfaction. All these are possible. But in photography, as in many professions and all marriages, the good stuff does not always come easily.

Photography is competitive. For many of the same reasons you might want to make a career out of being a photographer, plenty of other people do, too. And while the demand for images is growing in these graphics-conscious times, there will always be more people who want to make a living taking photographs than there will be paying markets to support them. In time, the less talented, less passionate, less highly motivated photographers will drop away and take up other work. The desire of every new professional is to be one of those who can weather the competition and build a successful career.

The demands on professional photographers are quite different from those on even the most gifted amateurs. Professionals need to be able to create photographs that fulfill the demands of the clients who pay for them. In the best of situations, that means photographers finding clients who love the way they see and shoot pictures and are happy to pay them to do what they love. Many times, though, it is not that simple.

Professionals must produce top-quality work on every assignment, no matter how they feel or what logistical limitations they face. It does not matter if the client's art director breathes fire or the bride has acne. Professionals produce professional-grade photos. No client, upon seeing a picture that exceeds expectations, will ever ask you how you got it. A fine restaurant's reputation is based not on a few fabulous meals but on a consistent string of excellent ones. The same holds true for photographers.

Photography is one of those fields that calls so strongly to some people that they never actually work through the process of making the decision to become professionals. They know right from the beginning that they are and always will be photographers. They have a love affair with the medium that leaves them no other choice. Establishing a career is simply a manifestation of the inevitable.

For most of us, though, the decision to become a professional needs to be carefully considered.

Do not become a photographer by accident. Do not take up professional photography just because you find picture-taking enjoyable and cannot think of anything else to do. It is too challenging a career. The decisions you make deliberately and carefully, rather than just fall into, will ultimately yield greater satisfaction.

The Decision to Remain an Amateur

The root meaning of the word "amateur" is "lover." The amateur gets to do what he or she loves, without having to answer to anyone else. Many of the most passionate photographers prefer to remain amateurs all their lives rather than sacrifice their deep personal relationship with the medium to the exigencies of earning a living. They have a career, an occupation, elsewhere and spend their weekends and vacations pursuing their truest love, making photographs. Amateur photography offers many opportunities, including the chance to have photos published in major publications on a freelance basis and to make some money in the process.

Serious amateurs may be as skilled as professionals. They may have the technical expertise and personal vision for which clients would gladly pay. Instead they stay amateurs to preserve their precious relationship with photography. Anyone who loves photography should think carefully about what will be lost by becoming a professional, as well as what will be gained. It would be a shame to have your love affair with photography ground down by the need to turn pictures into cash.

Getting Your Act Together

Whether photography is for you a career or an avocation, your desire to use this book shows that you take it seriously. You recognize the need to hone your skills and learn new ways. You see how technological advances, from autofocus cameras to sophisticated lighting and metering systems to computers, have changed the way photographs are created and delivered.

In picking up this book, you seek to expand your knowledge about photography, to acquire specific skills or to advance your vision. This guide catalogues hundreds of different ways in which to advance your photographic life, whether you choose to make photography your profession or to pursue it as an amateur. You will find workshops and training facilities for all types of photography, plus organizations of and for photographers, artists' colonies, specialized photography schools and academic institutions that have strong photography programs.

All photographers thrive on the satisfaction of taking really good pictures. It is our wish that what you find here helps you to become the photographer you want to be.

PART TWO

Photography Programs in North America Today

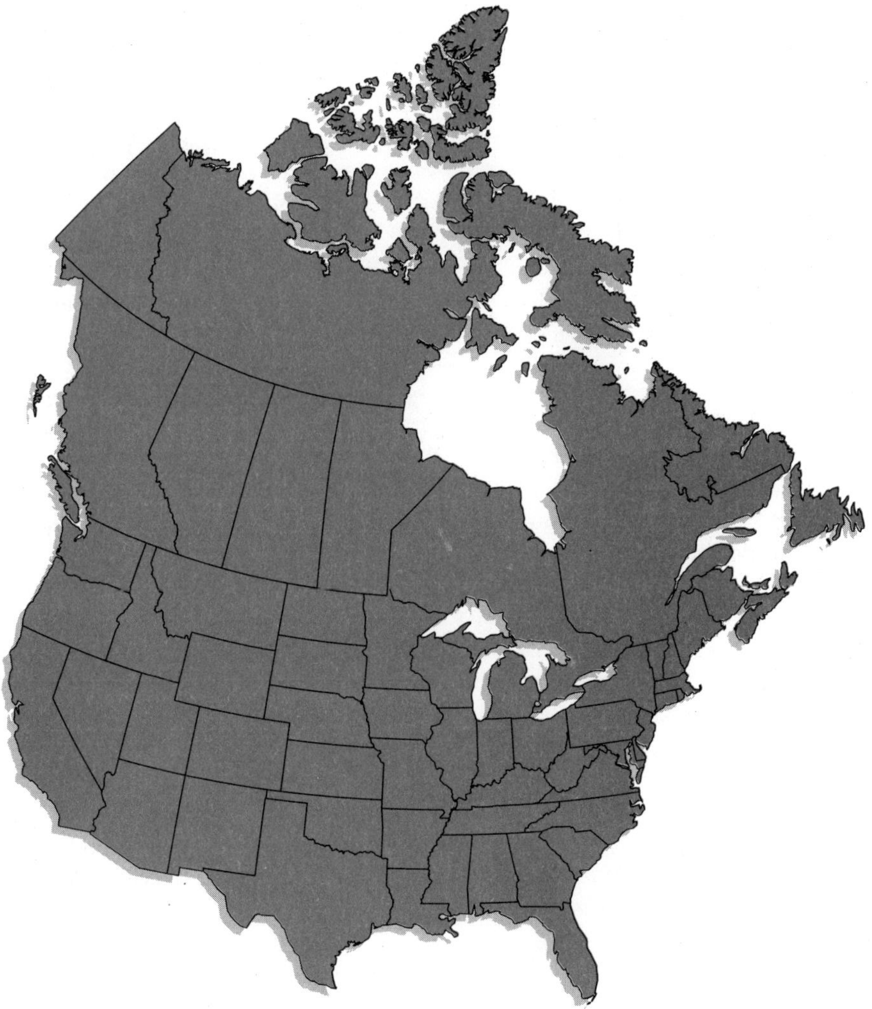

Joining Up

Associations and Organizations for Photographers

Organizations are especially important for photographers because we tend to work by ourselves. The act of looking, seeing and recording an image on film is personal and intimate, taking place only within each person's eye, mind and heart. But for a photographer to grow and learn, to make images that satisfy an ever-more-sophisticated eye, you need to associate with other photographers. As in any profession or art form, we have a lot to learn from each other.

The organizations listed below include avocational interest groups, not-for-profit supporters of the arts and professional associations. Some of the groups are open to anyone; others have specific requirements that prospective members must fulfill in order to join. Some address the broad universe of photography; others concern themselves with narrowly focused subdivisions within the field. All have something of value to offer certain photographers. Some of them may be right for you.

The benefits of belonging to the right organization of photographers are many. Most publish monthly, quarterly or annual newsletters or magazines that keep members apprised of developments in the field, from new equipment to legal issues. Some offer group insurance policies, standardized business forms and information on sound business practices. The larger ones have annual gatherings, where you can fertilize your creativity by spending a few days listening to presentations by experts or simply jawing with contemporaries from distant places. Local organizations and local chapters of national organizations have regular meetings where images and new ideas are presented.

Membership gives you a sense of belonging. Members of some groups receive special promotional considerations or discounts on supplies or programs.

As you look through the list of associations and organizations, evaluate carefully if a particular one is right for you, and worth the membership fee. An organization geared to those below your level of ability will prove boring and repetitive. One aimed at more advanced photographers has a certain appeal, though you may find the information too specialized for your needs and the other members short on attention for someone of your stature. Memberships in all but the most restrictive professional associations are modestly priced, usually under $50. If one appeals to you, why not sign on? You can always drop out after a year if it fails to address your needs.

This list contains mostly national organizations, plus those few local ones that have a national presence. For many photographers, the best group to join, at first anyway, is a local camera club. Camera clubs give you a chance to show your work and view the photos of others, and to meet photographers in your area. These clubs are a terrific resource for getting personal recommendations on a workshop you may want to try. Any full-service camera store should be able to help you locate a camera club in your area.

Advertising Photographers of New York

Who: About 500 commercial photographers, their assistants, art directors, art buyers, stylists, students and educators. **What:** This trade organization is devoted entirely to advancing the interests of advertising photographers in the New York area. Besides providing a forum for photographers to meet and exchange ideas, APNY maintains an active dialogue on behalf of photographers with clients and municipal authorities. It offers insurance and financial planning programs, technical and legal advice, business forms and educational services for the specialized needs of the advertising photographer. Multiple categories of membership allow students and photographers' assistants as well as working professionals to attend meetings. **Contact:** APNY, 27 W. 20th St., #601, New York, NY 10011; 212-807-0399 **Membership:** Annual dues.

American Society of Media Photographers

Who: 5,500 members who are among the top commercial, industrial and editorial photographers in America and around the world. **What:** ASMP was founded in 1944 to protect and promote the interests of photographers whose work is for publication, promote high professional standards and ethics, and cultivate friendship and mutual understanding among photographers. ASMP considers itself a clearinghouse of photographic information for the industry. It publishes a monthly bulletin plus a series of white papers on significant issues, and distributes guides to good business practice and a collection of standardized business forms. It maintains a legal support fund for the membership and is active in legislative lobbying on matters that concern the interests of photographers. A media licensing agency for the electronic distribution of photos is in the works. Thirty-six regional chapters hold regular meetings, and the association hosts a national gathering every other year. **Contact:** ASMP, 14 Washington Rd., Suite 502, Princeton Junction, NJ 08550; 609-799-8300; e-mail: 76020.3231@compuserve.com; Web site: http://www.asmp.org **Membership:** Annual dues. Eligibility requirements.

American Society of Picture Professionals

Who: Over 700 members, including photographers, photo researchers, editors and stock photo agents. **What:** ASPP is the only organization created to serve as a meeting place for both buyers and sellers of pictures. Members work primarily in the editorial marketplace, on educational materials and consumer publications. Five regional chapters hold regular meetings that present material of interest to the cross-section of its membership. **Contact:** ASPP, 2025 Pennsylvania Ave., #226, Washington, DC 20006; 202-223-8442 **Membership:** Annual dues.

Center for Photography at Woodstock (NY)

Who: 2,000 members, including photographers, students, individuals and families who support photography. **What:** CPW is a community-based support organization for photography in the Catskill region. Its official mission is "to provide an artistic home for contemporary photographers with programs in education, exhibition, publication, fellowships, and services that create access to professional workspace, nourishing responses, and new audiences." It publishes a quarterly magazine that deals with more esoteric aspects of photography than the regular press. The center maintains a library and permanent print collection and acts as a clearinghouse for photography-related employment in the area. Fellowships are awarded to eligible upstate New York artists. See *New York* for workshop information. **Contact:** CPW, 59 Tinker St., Woodstock, NY 12498; 914-679-9957 **Membership:** Open to all. Annual dues.

Evidence Photographers International Council

Who: Civilian and law-enforcement photographers whose pictures serve as evidence in criminal, civil, insurance and related cases. **What:** EPIC is the only organization specifically geared to forensic photography. Its publications, seminars and workshops instruct photographers on how to take effective photos and operate properly in this highly specialized field. Members learn techniques and the legal ramifications of all aspects of evidence photography. **Contact:** EPIC, 600 Main St., Honesdale, PA 18431; 800-356-EPIC or 717-253-5450 **Membership:** Annual dues.

The Friends of Photography

Who: 4,000 members, including photographers, patrons and gallery owners. **What:** The Friends of Photography, founded in 1976, is devoted to presenting, interpreting and supporting photography in all its facets and dimensions. It supports the Ansel Adams Center for Photography, a museum and bookstore in San Francisco, and offers educational programs, lectures and seminars. Members receive the quarterly publication *See* and are eligible for discounts on books and programs. The Friends of Photography was created by some of the luminaries of American photography—Brett Weston, Wynn Bullock, Beaumont and Nancy Newhall, as well as Ansel Adams—to foster understanding of the medium. It maintains the high standards set by its founders in traditional photography, video and other imaging media. **Contact:** FOP, 250 Fourth St., San Francisco, CA 94103; 415-495-7000; e-mail: seefop@aol.com **Membership:** Open to all. Annual dues.

National Press Photographers Association

Who: More than 10,000 members, including professional print and broadcast photojournalists and students. **What:** The premier organization supporting the professional needs and interests of photojournalists. The association promotes a code of ethics for photojournalists and sponsors several kinds of workshops and conferences, including the weeklong Electronic Photojournalism Workshop and one-day NPPA Flying Short Course (see *North Carolina*), the three-day Northern Short Course (see *New York*), a weeklong TV newsvideo workshop in March, an annual Digital Photography Conference in February and a Women in Photojournalism Conference in April. NPPA is a sponsor of the annual Pictures of the Year competition, runs an ongoing series of photography contests for news photographers and maintains a job bank. Eleven chapters around the country hold local meetings and programs. **Contact:** NPPA, 3200 Croasdaile Dr., Suite 306, Durham, NC 27705; 800-BUY-NPPA or 919-383-7246 **Membership:** Annual dues. Open to professionals and students.

North American Nature Photography Association

Who: Photographers and others concerned with nature photography **What:** NANPA was created in 1993 to advance serious nature photography both as an art form and as a medium of communication. It counts among its members some of the world's leading nature photographers, including Galen Rowell, Frans Lanting and George Lepp. NANPA provides educational information and supports professionalism and the essential dignity of this photographic specialty. Publishes a bimonthly newsletter and sponsors an annual forum each winter. **Contact:** NANPA, 10200 W. 44th Ave., #304, Wheat Ridge, CO 80033; 303-422-8527 **Membership:** Annual dues (discount for students).

Photographic Society of America

Who: Primary membership is amateur photographers, especially those belonging to camera clubs. **What:** PSA is a large organization that welcomes all levels of photographers. It distributes a monthly newsletter, provides educational and evaluation services and sets up exhibitions for members' work. Its eight specialty groups afford each photographer the chance to get to know and learn from others who share a particular photographic interest. PSA sponsors several tours and national and regional conferences annually. **Contact:** PSA, 3000 United Founders Blvd., Oklahoma City, OK 73112; 405-843-1438 **Membership:** Open to all. Annual dues (discount for youth).

Professional Photographers of America

Who: The majority of PPA's nearly 15,000 members work in communities across America as wedding and portrait photographers. **What:** PPA provides this diverse group with many kinds of programs designed to enhance their professional and business skills. Among the services offered are several publications, including a worldwide directory of members, the Winona School and an annual convention (see *Georgia*), equipment and liability insurance, lobbying and advocacy activities and a network of local chapters. Members are kept abreast of developments in the industry, as regards business, technique and the new technologies. **Contact:** PPA, 57 Forsyth St. NW, #1600, Atlanta, GA 30303; 800-786-6277 or 404-522-8600 **Membership:** Annual dues. Membership is available to working professional photographers and their employees, and to aspiring professionals. New members are required to sign the PPA code of ethics as part of the application process.

Society for Photographic Education

Who: Three-quarters of the members are photography teachers. **What:** Founded in 1963, SPE promotes the understanding of photography in all its forms and fosters the ongoing development of photography and photographic teaching, scholarship and critical analysis. Publications include *Exposure*, a journal of criticism and scholarly insight, and the SPE newsletter, which catalogues current exhibits and solicits work for upcoming ones and lists workshops and employment opportunities. The national conference, held in each spring, addresses issues that concern working photographic artists and educators. **Contact:** SPE, P.O. Box 222116, Dallas, TX 75222; 817-273-2845; e-mail: socphotoed@aol.com; Web site: www.arts.ucsb.edu/SPE/ **Membership:** Annual dues (student discount).

University Photographers' Association of America

Who: Institutional and individual members. **What:** UPAA is devoted solely to those photographers who work for institutions of higher learning around the U.S. and Canada. Through publications and the annual Technical Symposium, UPAA members stay in touch with colleagues and learn about the latest developments that affect photographers working on a broad array of assignments in a university environment. Publications exhibit the diverse work of member photographers. **Contact:** UPAA, SUNY College at Brockport, 350 New Campus Dr., Brockport, NY 14420; 716-395-2133; Web site: http://www.adm.uwaterloo.ca/infoupaa/index.html **Membership:** Annual dues.

Wedding & Portrait Photographers International

Who: 4,000 professional photographers. **What:** Founded in 1973, WPPI aims to improve the artistry and business of its members. The organization publishes a monthly newsletter with a "how-to" philosophy and provides lots of sound business advice, including market research on weddings and trends within the industry. An annual convention/trade show offers a series of seminars and workshops on aesthetic, technical and business matters. Members receive group insurance and may participate in print competitions. **Contact:** WPPI, 1312 Lincoln Blvd., P.O. Box 2003, Santa Monica, CA 90406; 310-451-0090; Web site: http://www.wppi-online.com **Membership:** Annual dues.

Selecting a Program

IF YOU ARE READING THIS BOOK, you are interested in taking some kind of course, class or workshop in order to become a better photographer. In the section that follows, you will find about 250 choices covering the gamut of options from one-day seminars, to around-the-world photo tours, to distant artists' retreats. If you know what you are looking for, you can use the icon system to locate the kind of program you have in mind, then search for the one that suits you best. For example, if you want to learn to be a professional photographer, look for the academic programs, from the intensive photo schools to major colleges and universities. If you can spare only a week and have always wanted to photograph the Grand Tetons of Wyoming, you will find any number of workshops and courses that specialize in nature and travel photography in the American West. Need the seclusion of an artists' colony? There are dozens here, from simple local ones that support emerging artists to the famous national ones whose alumni list includes luminaries from around the world.

We have tried to describe what it would be like for you to spend time in any of these programs. But we have not met all the instructors personally and cannot swear to their patience, understanding and teaching ability. That is why it is best for you to narrow down your choices to the ones that appeal to you most, then call and ask the contact person what you really want to know. Do not accept superficial answers.

Besides the obvious resources of your time and money, a photography program engages your inner creative force. By supplementing what is written here with your own self-knowledge and your personal gut feeling, you should be able to select the program that will best serve your interests and your life as a photographer.

Photography Programs

Workshop

Conference

Residential Program

Academic Program

Digital Imaging Program

On-the-Road Program

Alabama

Center for Nature Photography

For nature and landscape photographers *Natural settings and botanical gardens in U.S. — 3519 Glenwood Ave., Birmingham, AL 35222* **Voice:** 205-595-5665 **Contact:** Allen Rokach **Founded:** 1983 **Open:** Apr.–Oct. **Cost:** $1,000 for weeklong workshops (lodging and most meals incl.) **Group Size:** 12–15

ALLEN ROKACH, former photo director for the New York Botanical Garden, leads a series of weeklong and weekend landscape and flower photography workshops around the country. Rokach has vast experience with this kind of image making and has been teaching for many years. His workshops promise instruction in photographic seeing, the effects of light on form, and developing a personal aesthetic, as well as essential camera technique.

Workshop programs include 2 field trips and personal critiques daily, and slide lectures in the evening. Rokach is co-author of Amphoto's *Field Guide* books on photographing landscapes, trees, birds and flowers.

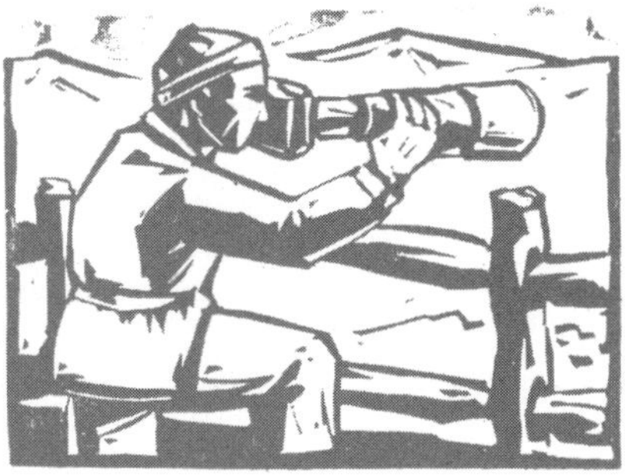

Alaska

Katmai Coastal Tours

For nature and wildlife photographers *SW coast — P.O. Box 2939, Homer, AK 99603* **Voice:** 907-235-8796; 800-871-7871 **Fax:** 907-235-0714 **E-mail:** seebears@alaska.net **Web Site:** www.alaska.net/~seebears/katmai.html **Contact:** Capt. Michael Parks **Founded:** 1992 **Open:** June–Sept. **Cost:** $2,395 for 4 days/3 nights in peak season (late June–early Aug.), $425 per extra day; $1,645 for 3 days/2 nights in shoulder season, $325 per extra day; 10% discount for full boat (6 people) **Group Size:** 6

THIS CUSTOMIZED WORKSHOP/tour offers a chance to see one of the most extraordinary places in America—the breathtaking volcano-scarred landscape of the Katmai National Park and Preserve. Brown bears are the principal attraction, although other forms of wildlife—otters, sea lions, foxes, eagles and puffins—abound. Participants live aboard the 73-foot research vessel *Waters* with Captain Michael Parks and his crew, but spend most of the endless daylight hours with an experienced photographer/guide exploring the park and looking for wildlife.

Each group books its own dates and duration. Those who reserve early have the widest choice of dates and length of trip with this friendly, environmentally oriented group. The fee includes a $1\frac{1}{2}$-hour seaplane flight from Homer, outboard accommodations, and gourmet meals.

Steve Gilroy's Alaska Photo Tours

For nature and wildlife photographers *Scenic areas in Alaska, southern Chile, Argentina, Hawaii, Africa — P.O. Box 141, Talkeetna, AK 99676* **Voice:** 907-733-3051; 800-799-3051 **Fax:** 907-733-3052 **Contact:** Steve Gilroy **Open:** June–Sept. **Cost:** $1,795–$3,895; most fees include meals and lodging **Group Size:** 8–12

STEVE GILROY'S 1- to 2-week forays into the spectacular natural showcase of Alaska provide ample opportunity to photograph the 49th state. Each of the 9 or 10 trips is led by a resident Alaskan photographer/naturalist.

Some of the trips concentrate mostly on scenery, from coastal fjords to inland mountains. Others are designed around photographing wildlife, especially brown bears. Though summer in Alaska provides many hours of sunlight in which to photograph, the weather can be harsh, which may limit photographic possibilities. No film processing is available in the wild.

Alaska Photo Tours is beginning to offer similar trips to Patagonia in South America during the winter months.

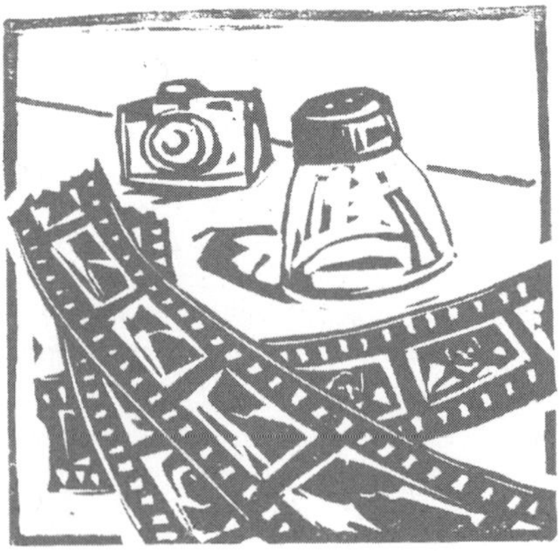

Arkansas

Matt Bradley Photography Workshops

For nature and landscape photographers *Ozark Mountains — 15 Butterfield La., Little Rock, AR 72212* **Voice:** 501-224-0692 **E-mail:** 76503.1622@compuserve.com **Contact:** Matt Bradley **Founded:** 1978 **Open:** Spring and fall **Cost:** $400 **Group Size:** 12–15

WELL-TRAVELED photojournalist Matt Bradley calls his workshops "The Creative Image" because he instructs his students in more than just how to take pretty pictures. There is a way of thinking, he says, that leads photographers to consider the visual statement each photograph makes. According to Bradley, photographers who understand how photographs convey information and emotion will consistently produce photos that are well composed and visually appealing.

The 3-day workshops, open to photographers at all levels, take place in a remote setting in the Ozarks, and include home-cooked meals and log cabin accommodations.

California

Academy of Art College

For student photographers and other visual artists *Central San Francisco — 79 New Montgomery St., San Francisco, CA 94105* **Voice:** 415-274-2200; 800-544-2787 **Fax:** 415-546-9737 **Contact:** Admissions or Graduate Studies Office **Founded:** 1929 **Admission:** Application ($50), transcripts, statement of intent for graduate students **Cost:** $15,000 undergraduate; $19,000 graduate; room and board incl. **Financial Aid:** Scholarship **Degree or Certification:** BFA, MFA

This urban arts college trains photographers, fine artists, designers, filmmakers and others for professional careers in the arts. The undergraduate curriculum includes courses in the full gamut of photographic styles and specialties. Graduate students choose to specialize in fine art, documentary or commercial photography.

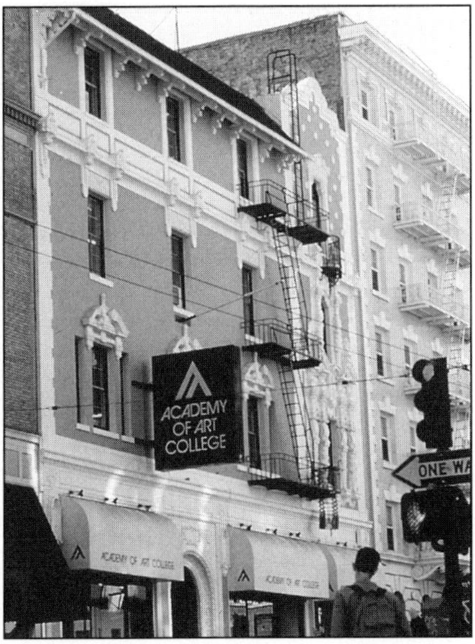

ACADEMY OF ART COLLEGE

Academy of Art College, San Francisco.

The college has committed itself to teaching the newer computer-based photographic technology, as well as traditional methods.

Non-degree students may take individual courses without credit to meet their particular interests and career needs.

Al Weber

For nature and fine art photographers *California and the Southwest — 145 Boyd Way, Carmel, CA 93923* **Voice:** 408-624-5963; 408-624-5535 **E-mail:** alweb@aol. com **Contact:** Al Weber **Founded:** 1962 **Open:** Spring and fall **Cost:** $95 for 1 day; up to $450 for full week

Al Weber has been leading workshops in landscape photography and photographic craft for over 30 years. These days he conducts only 6 to 10 workshops per year, ranging from a single day's exploration of the view camera to a weeklong sojourn to the canyons of northern Arizona and New Mexico. One of his weekend events is simply a chance to gather with other photographers and present work, swap prints and talk about matters photographic and otherwise.

Weber's orientation runs exactly counter to the slickly packaged and promoted workshop series format. His knowledge of the medium and its intricacies, however, is expert. His annual newsletter/workshop agenda meanders through many aspects of the photography world (book reviews, prints and equipment for sale) and is worth a read for anyone even considering joining him for a course.

American Film Institute

For photographers and other visual artists *Hollywood Hills — 2021 N. Western Ave., Los Angeles, CA 90027* **Voice:** 213-856-7690; 800-999-4234 **E-mail:** ccraig@afionline.org **Web Site:** www.afionline.org **Founded:** 1968 **Open:** Year-round **Cost:** $595 for Adobe Photoshop class **Group Size:** 14 **Handicapped Access**

THE AMERICAN Film Institute's primary purpose is to "advance the art of the moving image." It also opens its doors to the general public for a series of courses in digital imaging technology. Basic and advanced courses in Adobe Photoshop, suitable for but not expressly directed at photographers, run for 3 days and are offered 6 or more times per year. AFI also offers a 3-evening overview, "Photography in the Digital Era," for $295.

Art Center College of Design

For student photographers and other visual artists *Northern suburb of Los Angeles — 1700 Lida St., Pasadena, CA 91103* **Voice:** 818-584-5114 **Fax:** 818-405-9104 **Contact:** Tim Bradley, Chair **Founded:** 1930 **Admission:** Application ($45), 12 b&w prints, letter of intent for graduate students **Cost:** $7,800 per semester; $3,000 per year for materials **Financial Aid:** Scholarship; Work/Study **Group Size:** 1,200 total **Degree or Certification:** BFA, MFA

THE ART CENTER College in Pasadena is one of the premier arts education institutions on the West Coast. The photography program is grounded in an arts orientation, although it includes courses in commercial techniques and encourages students to become familiar with modern computer imaging technology. Early classes stress the mastery of technique so that students can devote ample time to developing their own unique voice.

Proximity to the creative bastion of Los Angeles and affiliation with a sister institution in Switzerland provide students with a broad choice of options concerning artistic and professional development.

Bodie Photography Workshops

For outdoor photographers *Eastern Sierras near Mono Lake — P.O. Box 515, Bridgeport, CA 93517* **Voice:** 619-647-6445 **Contact:** Bodie State Historic Park **Founded:** 1981 **Open:** Summer **Cost:** $200–$465 for 3-day workshop **Group Size:** 8

BODIE, ONCE A mining boomtown, is today a well-preserved ghost town, maintained as a historic site. Several times per summer, photography instructors lead groups of photographers into Bodie for several days of exploring and picture taking. Contact the Park for information about dates and the names of instructors, who must be contacted directly for workshop information.

Brooks Institute of Photography

For student photographers *801 Alston Rd., Santa Barbara, CA 93108* **Voice:** 805-966-3888 **Fax:** 805-565-1368 **Contact:** Inge Kautzmann **Founded:** 1945 **Open:** School year **Admission:** Application ($25), transcript **Cost:** $13,500 per year plus $6,000 for supplies; $2,250 for 7-week "special status" participation **Financial Aid:** Scholarship; Work/Study **Group Size:** 400 **Degree or Certification:** 3-year BA, 1-year MS **Job Placement:** Yes

BROOKS INSTITUTE has been training photographers for over half a century. Founded by photographer and educator Ernest Brooks Sr. in 1945, it continues to offer one of the most intensive, complete career-oriented photography programs anywhere.

Brooks operates on the principle that a thorough understanding of photography from the inside out is essential for a successful career. Brooks takes a 3-pronged approach to photographic education, blending art, science and business within a liberal arts curriculum. Two of Brooks's 3 separate campuses in Santa Barbara are devoted exclusively to still photography. The third is for film, video and multimedia. The Montecito campus, on the outskirts of the city, is a lovely old adobe estate, reconfigured to house classrooms, darkrooms and studios. Commercial and digital facilities are in the converted Jefferson elementary school overlooking the city center. Because of travel between campuses and opportunities to photograph in the surrounding area, students need their own cars.

Lower-division courses, taught in the first year-and-a-half period, focus on basic photographic and lighting skills. The emphasis: self-discipline and attention to detail. Upper-division students (the second year and a half) major in Commercial Photography, Illustration/Advertising, Industrial/Scientific, Portraiture, Media or Color Technology.

Established photographers also take advantage of Brooks's faculty and facilities. Qualified non-degree students ("special status" students) can take most 7-week advanced courses. The graduate program is designed for working professionals who want a deeper theoretical understanding of photography. Graduate-level classes are held on weekends to permit students to work and study in the same period.

Brooks's greatest sources of pride are its faculty and alumni. Nineteen full-time teachers are responsible for primary photography and liberal arts courses. Another 2 dozen working photographers teach more specialized subjects. The alumni association, a worldwide network of graduates working in photography, provides a valuable resource to all Brooks students. Previous graduates traditionally make a special effort to help new graduates build their own careers.

Santa Barbara, renowned for its pleasant climate, offers ocean, mountains and historic sites: a rich visual backdrop for photography. Students should own 35mm cameras and are responsible for their own accommodations and meals.

PETER SKINNER

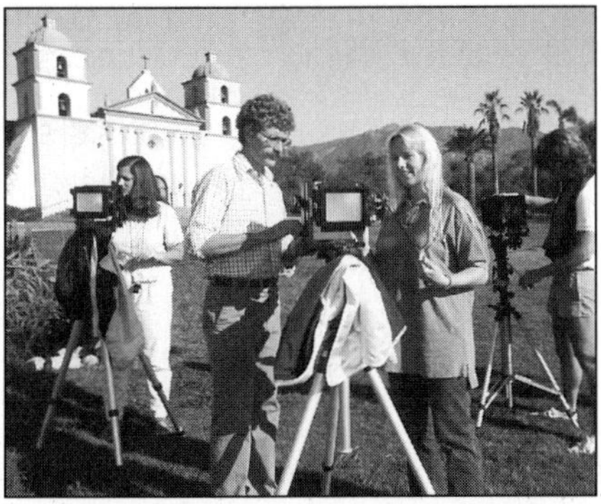

Large-format cameras at Brooks Institute of Photography, Santa Barbara.

California Natural Wonders Photographic Workshops

For outdoor and nature photographers *P.O. Box 457, La Canada, CA 91012* **Voice:** 818-954-0933 **Fax:** 818-954-0810 **Web Site:** www.apogeephoto.com/calwonders.html **Contact:** Noella Ballenger **Founded:** 1988 **Open:** Varies **Cost:** $200–$300 for 4- to 5-day workshops

Noella Ballenger leads photographers to some of California's outstanding attractions — including Mono Lake, the ghost town of Bodie, Death Valley and the Sierras — for 4- and 5-day workshops. Her teaching emphasis is on good photographic composition and technique. She also conducts a series of 1-day events in Southern California, specializing in flower photography. Prices for all her workshops are quite reasonable (food and lodging are not included).

Clayton Fogle's Hummingbirds

For nature photographers *P.O. Box 471, Santa Barbara, CA 93102* **Voice:** 805-898-0711 **Fax:** 805-898-0711 **E-mail:** cfogle@aol.com **Web Site:** www.apogeephoto.com/clayton_fogle.html **Contact:** Clayton Fogle **Founded:** 1988 **Open:** Arizona: Aug.–Sept.; Trinidad and Tobago: Apr.; California: varies **Cost:** $200 for 2-day workshop; $2,100 for Caribbean week (airfare from Miami, meals and lodging incl.)

CLAYTON FOGLE does hummingbirds. Smitten with the magical little birds since childhood, he conducts workshops that specialize in hummers and other exotic birds in Arizona, California and the islands of Trinidad and Tobago.

Fogle's 2-day intensives in Arizona's mile-high Ramsey Canyon teach his specially developed techniques and show students how to work with close-up equipment and flash to record hummingbirds' color and motion. Classes are limited to 6 students to afford personalized attention. The weeklong Caribbean trip takes up to 10 photographers to a lush location and introduces several unusual bird species. Local courses in the Santa Barbara Zoological Gardens and at the San Diego Zoo are also available.

Creative Computer Workshop

For photographers and graphic artists *145 Hamilton Ave., Palo Alto, CA 94301* **Voice:** 415-328-5048 **Fax:** 415-965-9355 **E-mail:** creativecw@aol.com **Founded:** 1994 **Open:** Year-round **Cost:** $300 for 4-week class; $175 for 2-week class **Group Size:** 8

BEGINNING CLASSES in Adobe Photoshop take place in the heart of downtown Palo Alto every month in 4 evening sessions over consecutive weeks. Intermediate Photoshop classes and courses in graphics and word processing software are also available, as is rental time on advanced Macintosh computers.

Creative Studio Lighting

For commercial studio photographers *Marin County, just N of San Francisco — Jay Daniel Associates, P.O. Box 151232, San Rafael, CA 94915* **Voice:** 415-459-1495 **Fax:** 415-459-3021 **E-mail:** jaydaniel@aol.com **Contact:** Jay Daniel **Founded:** 1985 **Open:** Twice per year **Cost:** $150 **Group Size:** 6–16

ANY PHOTOGRAPHER who hopes to make a living shooting commercially needs to understand how to use artificial light to feature, shape and dramatize subjects. Commercial photographer Jay Daniel teaches a 1-day studio lighting course that covers many different types of lighting equipment and techniques, including light ratios, broad versus narrow source illumination, the use of gels and so on.

Daniel also occasionally teaches a half-day seminar in Polaroid transfers for $75.

Djerassi Resident Artists Program

For photographers and artists in selected other disciplines *2325 Bear Gulch Rd., Woodside, CA 94062* **Voice:** 415-747-1250 **Fax:** 415-747-0105 **E-mail:** drap@djerassi.org **Web Site:** www.djerassi.org **Founded:** 1979 **Open:** Apr.–Oct. **Admission:** Application ($25), samples, project proposal **Deadlines:** Feb. 15 **Cost:** Transportation only **Group Size:** 8–12 artists at a time

WHERE THE Ohlone Indians lived in the hills between the bay and the ocean, Djerassi today is one of the most renowned artists' retreats in America.

The program seeks applicants on 2 levels: emerging and mid-career artists who can most benefit from the month-long residency, and established artists with national reputations. Each artist receives a room, a studio and meals, all at no cost. Photographers stay and work in the 12-sided barn, which also houses a color darkroom.

Residents enjoy plenty of solitude among the 600 acres of rangeland and redwood forest of the Djerassi estate. There is also ample time for mingling and interchange with artists in other disciplines. Created by Dr. Carl Djerassi in memory of his daughter Pamela, this program is an important support for the arts in Northern California, providing the gift of time to deserving artists.

Dorland Mountain Arts Colony

For photographers and artists in selected other disciplines *Nature preserve 60 mi. NE of San Diego — P.O. Box 6, Temecula, CA 92593* **Voice:** 909-676-5039 **E-mail:** dorland@ez.net **Contact:** Karen Parrott **Founded:** 1988 **Open:** Year-round **Admission:** Application, resume, statement of purpose, 6 slides **Deadlines:** Mar. 1 and Sept. 1. **Cost:** $300 per month

SHHH! DORLAND Mountain is so quiet that residents communicate by passing notes rather than talking. The primitive conditions—woodstove heat, no electricity—are designed to afford artists absolute privacy and tranquility in which to create.

Residents live and work, usually for about a month, in simple cottages with propane-fueled appliances. As a trade-off for modern conveniences, they get to enjoy 300 acres of virgin Southern California terrain, which until recently was managed by the Nature Conservancy. While not for everybody, Dorland Mountain's ultimate peace and privacy can be the perfect atmosphere for communing with your deepest artistic spirit.

Exfoditions, Journeys beyond Photography

For outdoor and nature photographers *Southwestern U.S.; also Patagonia — 1755 Correa Way, Los Angeles, CA 90049* **Voice:** 310-471-2845 **Fax:** 310-471-5711 **E-mail:** epop@earthlink.net **Web Site:** www.exfoditions.com **Contact:** Eric Poppleton, Dir. **Founded:** 1994 **Open:** Varies **Cost:** $125 per day (special gear incl.) **Group Size:** 10

ALL EXFODITIONS trips stress pushing the limits of your personal and photographic relationship with the outdoors. From forays through the urban landscape to whitewater rafting, Eric Poppleton and his instructors want participants to become enmeshed in the place they are visiting. Only by going beyond habitual ways can photographers bring a new vibrancy and vitality to their work. Workshops explore such terrain as the Arizona Canyonlands and Death Valley, and visit a Native American powwow in Idaho. Some trips involve backpacking and mountain biking as part of the experience. On-site color processing is provided during workshops lasting more than 3 days, and follow-up critiques are available to photographers in the LA area.

Poppleton also offers a black & white darkroom printing workshop twice a year, and is planning a foray beyond the natural world, into virtual reality photography for Web and multimedia applications. Attendance at some workshops may require a portfolio; some, a certification of physical fitness.

Frank Balthis Photography Workshops

For wildlife and nature photographers *West Coast from Baja to Alaska — P.O. Box 255, Davenport, CA 95017* **Voice:** 408-426-8205 **Fax:** 408-426-1623 **Contact:** Frank Balthis **Founded:** 1982 **Open:** Varies **Cost:** $2,000 for 1- to 2-week voyage **Group Size:** 25 maximum

Frank Balthis's nature images have been seen in many magazines and over 300 greeting cards. Besides being a photographer, he is a geographer, author, naturalist and sometime college instructor. Whales, seals, sea lions and dolphins are Balthis's special field of interest and the subject of his oceangoing photography workshops. He leads trips to some of the more remote areas off the West Coast to observe and photograph these animals in their natural habitat. Photographers may come to learn about this kind of wildlife or to shoot pictures for their stock files. Other scientists occasionally join in and share their knowledge of these fascinating species.

For the not-so-seaworthy, Balthis also leads a few land-based photography workshops with a natural history emphasis in the Monterey Bay area.

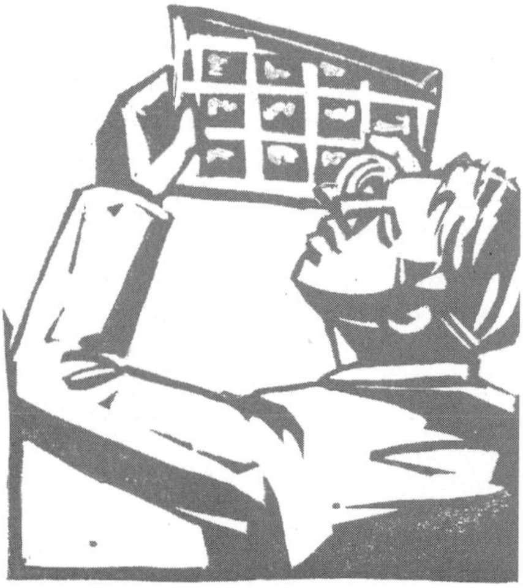

Golden Gate School Professional Photographic Workshops

For wedding and portrait photographers *Belmont — P.O. Box 187, Fairfield, CA 94533* **Voice:** 707-422-0319; 800-442-0319 **Fax:** 707-422-0973 **Contact:** Jim Inks **Founded:** 1983 **Open:** 1 week in June **Cost:** $525; $400 for PPA (or affiliate) member; $325–$365 for housing and meals; some classes have supply fee **Financial Aid:** Scholarship **Group Size:** 150 total; classes 21 maximum

The Golden Gate School, a PPA/Winona-affiliated workshop series (see *Georgia*), offers 6 to 8 concurrent workshops for wedding and portrait photographers from the Bay Area and elsewhere. Experienced professionals teach photographic technique, business and marketing, and related subjects, including digital imaging applications. Each student chooses 1 workshop for the entire week.

The workshops take place at the College of Notre Dame, 10 miles south of the San Francisco airport. The week is designed to mix study and socializing, with a big party on Saturday night.

Headlands Center for the Arts

For photographers and other artists in all media *Just N. of Golden Gate Bridge — 944 Fort Barry, Sausalito, CA 94965* **Voice:** 415-331-2787 **Fax:** 415-331-3857 **E-mail:** headlands@artswire.org **Contact:** Kathryn Reasoner, Exec. Dir. **Founded:** 1987 **Open:** Feb.–Dec. **Admission:** Letter describing residency plans, resume, up to 15 slides **Deadlines:** Early June **Cost:** Transportation only **Financial Aid:** Stipend **Group Size:** 25 residents each year

The Headlands Center occupies a series of old military buildings in the vast Marin Headlands area overlooking San Francisco Bay. Each year some 25 artists are invited either for 11-month live-at-home art residencies or for 4- to 12-week live-in situations. The Headlands Center differs from other arts organizations in that its primarily purpose is to stimulate artistic research and investigation, especially as concerns art's larger role in social, cultural and political issues. Completing individual works of art is not required.

Live-in residents live communally in a 4-bedroom house and receive a studio, 5 dinners per week, and a $500 monthly stipend. Live-out residents from the Bay Area get a studio and a $2,500 stipend. No one is required to exhibit or donate work.

All residents share the magnificent 13,000 acres of the Golden Gate National Recreation Area, with its hills, beaches and fog.

In addition to the residents, about 35 local artists rent studio space from HCA.

Residencies are available to residents of particular states and countries; call for current eligibility requirements.

Hidden Worlds

For photographers at all levels *CA and Bali — 1774 Capistrano Ave., Berkeley, CA 94707* **Voice:** 510-845-5754; 800-647-8807 **Fax:** 916-389-2167 **E-mail:** Arachnel@aol.com **Contact:** John Cooke **Founded:** 1994 **Open:** Varies **Group Size:** 6–8

John Cooke leads weekend workshops on high-speed photography and close-up (macro) techniques in the Sierras for small groups of photographers.

Cooke runs a tour company under the name "Bali Beyond the Guidebooks," which specializes in the culture, natural history and photography of Indonesia. Each trip is custom-designed according to the participants' needs. Prices vary with the level of accommodations.

International Center for Earth Concerns / Nature Photography

For nature photographers *Los Padres National Forest, 70 mi. NW of LA — 2162 Baldwin Rd., Ojai, CA 93023* **Voice:** 805-649-3535 **Contact:** Karen Collins **Open:** May **Cost:** $275 for weekend; $165 for 1-day workshop

The ICEC puts on a couple of weekend and 1-day photo workshops, including one with well-known nature photographer Robert Glenn Ketchum, at their nature preserve in the foothills of the Topa Topa mountains in Los Padres National Forest. Besides a typically Southern California ecosystem, the preserve includes Australian and South American botanical gardens. These workshops are suitable for anyone interested in learning to photograph the natural landscape.

Jean Michel Cousteau/Project Ocean Search

For underwater photographers *Fiji and waters off Hawaii, the Caribbean, the Galapagos and Micronesia — 1933 Cliff Dr., Santa Barbara, CA 93109* **Voice:** 805-899-8899 **E-mail:** jmcousteau@aol.com **Web Site:** www.jmcfir.com **Contact:** Tom Ordway **Founded:** 1983 **Open:** Varies **Cost:** $3,325 for POS; $2,100–$4,000 for 7-day trips **Group Size:** 10–20

The JM Cousteau organization offers both boat-based diving and photography trips and Project Ocean Search, a 10-day immersion vacation in Fiji in the South Pacific.

Project Ocean Search, Cousteau's luxurious and environmentally sensitive Fiji Island resort, blends photography, discovery and relaxation with learning about land and sea ecology. Participants may explore the underwater world off Cousteau's new dive boat *L'Aventure* one day and hike through an exotic rain forest the next. Visits to Fijian villages and a series of lectures provide a rich experience of the culture of this tropical paradise. Photographic instruction, using some equipment provided by Nikon, is included in addition to a full resort vacation.

The weeklong boat-based adventures use the well-equipped Aggressor fleet, which covers many of the world's tropical waters and is well known for its dive trips. A professional photographer provides instruction on those trips that feature underwater picture taking.

"Diving is a means, not an end, to the adventure of the oceans. To completely experience nature we must become aware of the interactions between oceans, land and people. By attaining a higher level of empathy and understanding, we enjoy a higher quality of life." —Jean Michel Cousteau

John Sexton Photography Workshops

For art and landscape photographers, fine art b&w printers *Carmel area and other natural locations in West — 291 Los Agrinemsors, Carmel Valley, CA 93924* **Voice:** 408-659-3130 **Fax:** 408-659-5509 **E-mail:** johnsexton@cis.compuserve.com **Web Site:** www.apogeephoto.com/john_sexton.html **Contact:** Laura Bayless **Founded:** 1985 **Cost:** $600 for 1-week workshop **Group Size:** 12–15

John Sexton is one of the world's premier black & white landscape photographers, working in the large-format tradition associated with Ansel Adams and Edward Weston. Sexton's workshops emphasize craftsmanship and strong personal vision. Each one addresses a slightly different aspect of fine art photography of the natural world. Topics include learning to see common subjects in a fresh way, approaches to landscape photography, and fine black & white printing.

Sexton teaches or co-teaches all the workshops, personally encouraging students to explore their "photographic souls." Students work with view cameras in black & white, though color images may be included for critiquing. Most of the 3- to 6-day workshops are run from Sexton's Carmel Valley studio. A few take place in other natural areas of the American West. Photographers interested in participating should call for a catalogue by late January (they sell out fast) and should apply immediately.

"As photographers, we need not only to be looking for opportunities to make exposures on an emulsion of film, but also to be observing, sensing, indeed hearing at all times—listening to the message of the light, the voice of the subject." —John Sexton

Lepp & Associates

For outdoor and nature photographers *High Sierras — P.O. Box 6240, Los Osos, CA 93412* **Voice:** 805-528-7385 **Fax:** 805-528-7387 **Open:** Late June **Cost:** $600 (local transportation incl.) **Group Size:** 10

Renowned nature photographer and author George Lepp leads 2 concentrated 5-day workshops in the Mono Lake area in the high Sierras of eastern California in late June. Photographers shoot birds from a blind, the tufa formations on Mono Lake at sunrise, and landscapes, wildflowers and perhaps mammals. This workshop is extremely intensive, with 3 instructors devoting all their attention to guiding just 10 participant photographers.

Lepp is one of the most sought-after photography instructors in America.

Macro Tours Photographic Workshops & Tours

For nature photographers
Around the U.S. — P.O. Box 460041, San Francisco, CA 94146 **Voice:** 415-826-1096; 800-369-7430 **E-mail:** Bertcam@aol. com **Contact:** Bert Banks, Dir. **Founded:** 1983 **Open:** Year-round **Cost:** $260 for weekend workshops; up to $1,100 for weeklong travel workshops (lodging incl.); $50– $70 for 1-day events

NATURE PHOTOGRAPHY is the primary focus of Macro Tours' programs. These travel workshops range from a single day in Northern California to a week or more photographing wildflowers in Yosemite, the canyons of Arizona, autumn in Vermont and other magnificent natural places.

JENNIFER ERICKSON

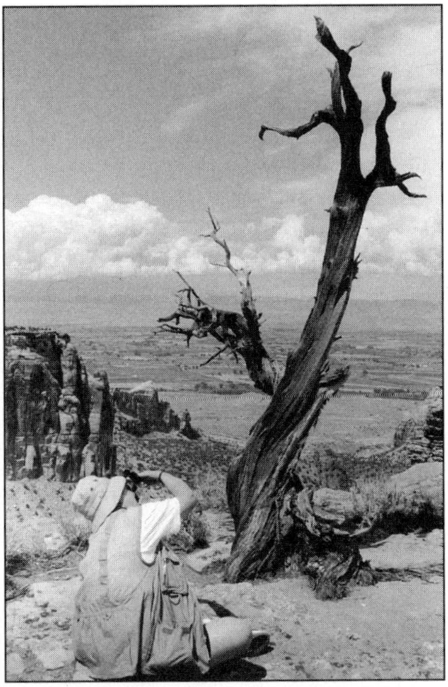

In the wilds with Macro Tours Photographic Workshops.

Small groups ensure plenty of individualized attention.

Macro Tours' genial founder, Bert Banks, also teaches an intimate class in printing color slides in his San Francisco darkroom.

Every December, participants from all the workshops are invited to contribute to the Macro Tours annual photo exhibition.

Maria Piscopo

For commercial photographers and graphic artists *2038 Calvert Ave., Costa Mesa, CA 92626* **Voice:** 714-641-7900; 714-556-8133 **E-mail:** mpiscopo@aol.com **Contact:** Cindy Brenneman **Open:** Varies

AN ARTISTS' AND photographers' representative for 20 years, Maria Piscopo leads seminars with such provocative titles as "How to Get Paid What You're Worth" and "How to Find Clients and Get Them to Call You." She is all business, and offers terrific advice on how commercially oriented visual artists should promote and market themselves to buyers.

Piscopo's seminars are given around the country, usually sponsored by arts and professional organizations, with fees set by the sponsoring organization. Call to find out the schedule.

Individual consultations and a series of books and audio tapes are also available.

Photo Metro Digital Workshops

For photographers and digital artists *South of Market district — 17 Tehama St., San Francisco, CA 94105* **Voice:** 415-243-9917 **Fax:** 415-243-9919 **E-mail:** jo@photometro.com **Web Site:** www.photometro.com **Contact:** Jo Leggett **Founded:** 1991 **Cost:** $400 for Photoshop basic; $350 for advanced and Digital Photographers workshop **Group Size:** 8 **Handicapped Access**

PHOTO METRO HAS been one of the pioneers in teaching digital photography techniques in the Bay Area. Its 3-day introductory and 2-day advanced courses provide full 8-hour days of hands-on computer time. New introductory classes are offered as often as every 3 weeks.

A monthly 2-day Digital Photographers workshop (as of this writing taught by legendary photographer Judy Dater) addresses creative and aesthetic issues for the photographer who already has a working knowledge of the software.

PhotoCentral—Hayward Area Recreation and Park District

For photographers at all levels *Across Bay from SF — 1099 E Street, Hayward, CA 94541* **Voice:** 510-881-6721 **Fax:** 510-881-6763 **E-mail:** Photocentrl@aol.com **Founded:** 1983 **Open:** Year-round **Cost:** $60 for 5-week classes; $140 for weekend workshops **Degree or Certification:** Certificates for different aspects of photography

PHOTOCENTRAL, an outgrowth of the Hayward Area Recreation and Park Department, bills itself as a community-based facility where photographers can work, study and share ideas. Teachers Geir and Kate Jordahl offer instruction in everything from basic camera, to black & white darkroom, to several travel workshops to destinations in the West. Students can earn a certificate upon completion of a series of specified courses.

Darkroom space is available for rent. Prices are very reasonable.

Point Reyes Field Seminars

For photographers, visual artists and naturalists *Pacific coast 1½ hr. N of Golden Gate Bridge — Point Reyes National Seashore Assoc., Point Reyes Station, CA 94956* **Voice:** 415-663-1200 **Founded:** 1976 **Open:** May–Oct. **Cost:** $50 for 1 day; $210 for weekend

POINT REYES National Seashore is a carefully protected ecosystem along the ocean north of San Francisco. All of the field seminars touch on preservation of and appreciation for this delicate natural resource. Five to 8 photo seminars each year are built around photographing the meadows, forests and shoreline as well as the lovely light that makes Point Reyes such a special place.

The seminars vary from 1-day outings to a full weekend (for which dorm lodging is included in the fee). Teachers are local professionals and nationally known outdoor photographers.

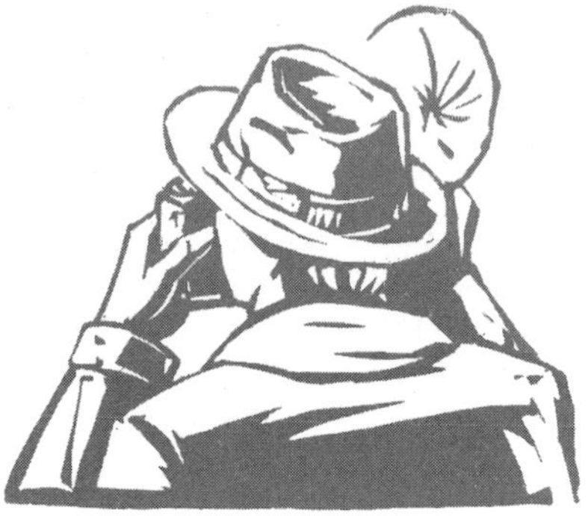

Proam Photo Workshops

For b&w, portrait/glamour and landscape photographers *Small town 7 mi. S of San Luis Obispo — P.O. Box 3157, Shell Beach, CA 93449* **Voice:** 805-773-5254; 805-473-4225 **Fax:** 805-773-8572 **Contact:** Joe Dickerson, Dir. **Founded:** 1974 **Open:** Varies **Cost:** $175 for system workshop; $250 for portrait/glamour workshop; $200 for field workshops **Group Size:** 10–12

JOE DICKERSON'S studio and oversize darkroom in Shell Beach, on the coast halfway between Los Angeles and San Francisco, is the base for a series of 3 different types of photography workshops. Weekend black & white workshops teach the concept and practice of the Zone system for precise control of contrast. Studio portraiture and glamour workshops teach lighting and the art and technique of photographing people.

Dickerson, who has been teaching for over 20 years, also takes photographers to such destinations as Yosemite or Mono Lake to work on landscape photography in color as well as black & white.

Ray McSavaney Photographic Workshops

For serious photographers *California and the West — 1984 North Main St., Studio 402, Los Angeles, CA 90031* **Voice:** 213-225-1730 **Contact:** Ray McSavaney **Founded:** 1990 **Open:** Mar.–Oct. **Cost:** $350–$625 for 5- to 7-day workshops; $225 for weekend **Group Size:** 8 per instructor

THE SOFT-SPOKEN Ray McSavaney attempts to do more than just teach photography in his workshops. He strives to support serious image makers in their creative evolution.

Teaching alone or in concert with other accomplished instructors, McSavaney takes participants to some of the quiet places in the West, to situations where form and light lend themselves to interpretive photography. The instructors provide technical and aesthetic assistance, and encourage participants to explore and experiment with their relationship to their work.

Many photographers work in 4 x 5 black & white in these workshops, though other formats and films may be used. McSavaney teaches only about 6 weeklong workshops per year, which fill up quickly. He also offers a weekend workshop on the urban landscape of Los Angeles.

Redwood Exposure

For nature photographers *Redwood forest, 280 mi. N of San Francisco — P.O. Box 525, Arcata, CA 95518* **Voice:** 707-839-0216; 800-995-8688 **Fax:** 707-839-3208 **E-mail:** redwood@northcoast.com **Web Site:** www. northcoast.com/~redwood **Contact:** Rose Bond **Founded:** 1993 **Open:** Year-round **Cost:** $1,200 for 5 days (meals and lodging incl.) **Group Size:** 2–6

EMBRACED BY silence, surrounded by nature, Jim and Rose Bond's expeditions through the redwoods and along the coastline of Northern California afford nature photographers the chance to explore their internal worlds while photographing the external one. The Bonds are natural scientists by training, and intimately familiar with the ecosystem of the region. They can help photographers through the difficulty of shooting under a forest canopy, and provide guidance in composition, the use of filters and the technique of shooting birds and other wildlife.

Each program is custom-planned to provide a pleasurable experience, as well as photographic opportunities; the programs can run from 1 to 7 days. The most popular choice is a 5-day workshop, which includes 3 days of instruction and 2 footloose days. The main season is from April through October. Winter season programs (November–March) require groups of 6 or more.

Ron Sanford

For nature and wildlife photographers *Several places in California, plus Alaska and sometimes overseas — P.O. Box 248, 599 Oregon St., Gridley, CA 95948* **Voice:** 916-846-4687 **Fax:** 916-846-0656 **Contact:** Ron Sanford **Open:** Varies **Cost:** $118 for local weekend workshops; $2,295 for 1 week in Alaska (meals and lodging incl.) **Group Size:** 8 in Alaska; larger groups locally

WILDLIFE AND wilderness photographer Ron Sanford leads groups of photographers at all levels to a variety of destinations in California, as well as to Alaska and occasionally overseas.

Sanford is an accomplished photographer with an enviable list of publication credits (*Outdoor Photographer, Travel & Leisure*) in the U.S. and abroad. Participants can take advantage of his years of experience as both a photographer and a marketer of images. His workshops stress developing your personal vision and include plenty of shooting time, all in a casual atmosphere.

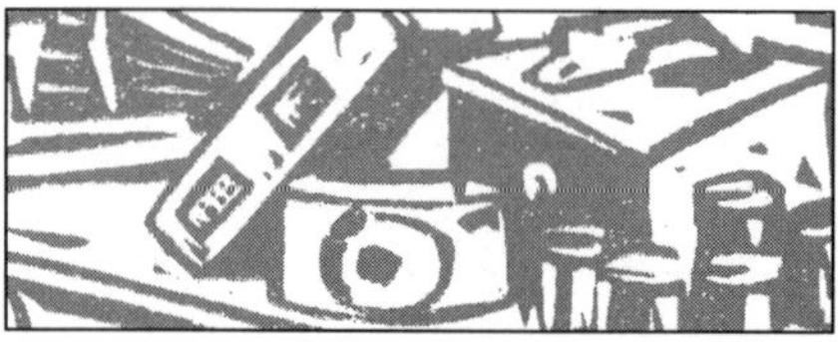

Samy's Digital Imaging

For photographers and digital artists *Hollywood area — 200 S. La Brea Blvd., Los Angeles, CA 90036* **Voice:** 213-857-9915 **Fax:** 213-857-9916 **E-mail:** samyscam@earthlink.net **Web Site:** www.net101.com/samyscamera **Contact:** Carolyn Mishne, Class Coord. **Cost:** $125 for 3-hr. classes; $350 for Essentials class **Group Size:** 6 **Handicapped Access**

THIS FULL-SERVICE photography store/digital service bureau offers early-stage courses in Adobe Photoshop and other graphics programs. Photoshop 101 through 505 are 3-hour classes that concentrate on particular aspects of using the software. The Photoshop Essentials course, spread over 3 class sessions, covers all the basics of how you might use the program most efficiently in real-life situations.

Sierra Photographic Workshops

For outdoor photographers *Scenic locations around U.S. — P.O. Box 124096, Sacramento, CA 95821* **Voice:** 916-974-7200; 800-925-2596 **E-mail:** lkemper@aol.com **Contact:** Lewis Kemper **Founded:** 1981 **Open:** 6 weeks throughout year **Cost:** $995–$1,195 for weeklong workshops (lodging incl.); higher for wildlife workshop and Alaska cruise; $85 for 1-day digital seminar **Group Size:** 8 per instructor

LEWIS KEMPER AND William Neill are established photographers with fine reputations. In their half-dozen annual workshops, teaching individually or together, they provide personalized instruction in the art and technique of outdoor photography. The workshops take place in some of the most dramatic settings in the American landscape (Yosemite, Tetons, Smoky Mountains); specific locations may vary

Digital Imaging Software: The Choices

Adobe Photoshop is far and away the most popular digital imaging software. It is the first choice of the majority of photographers and graphic artists who alter, manipulate and combine images on a computer. It is also the standard software with which images are transferred to printers and publishers, and the dominant vehicle for posting images on the World Wide Web.

When using Photoshop you first choose which portion of a computerized image you want to manipulate. You then use a series of digital tools to change color or texture, or to reshape, move or combine images. Whether you are working on large sections of a picture or focusing on individual pixels, in Photoshop you work directly on the image before you, as if you were repainting sections of a canvas. The digital tools that select areas of the image for treatment and perform the actual operations are straightforward and relatively easy to use.

Photoshop, which is available for both the Macintosh and the PC, works somewhat better on the Mac because its internal architecture corresponds more closely to the way an Apple computer functions. Most training courses in Photoshop are taught on the Macintosh platform.

The other widely used digital imaging software is Live Picture, which operates on a different model than Photoshop and can be more difficult to learn. In Live Picture the user writes a script, or set of instructions, for working on portions of the image rather than manipulating them directly. The script is then turned over to the software for execution.

Live Picture is especially good at collages and masking, and at working with large image files. It has the unique ability to perform detailed work on a small, low-resolution image file and then instruct the program to duplicate the operation on a very large (up to hundreds of megabytes) high-resolution file. This can save a tremendous amount of time compared to Photoshop, where the same operation would require direct alteration of a huge number of pixels. Photographers and designers working on complex projects sometimes use Photoshop and Live Picture together on a single image.

The only other professional-grade digital imaging software is Picture Publisher, from Micrografx. It is a PC-only program that works pretty much the way Photoshop does. Photographics Unlimited, in New York City, is the only major training facility that offers instruction in Picture Publisher.

The professional versions of Photoshop and Live Picture cost $500 or more, while Picture Publisher and other less sophisticated programs cost somewhat less. Adobe's Photo Deluxe, a stripped-down version of Photoshop, is useful primarily for retouching and costs under $75.

from year to year. Their special wildlife workshop is at a preserve in Montana.

A 1-day digital seminar introduces digital technology for the outdoor photographer.

Summit Photography Workshops

For nature and wildlife photographers *California, Southwest, Alaska — P.O. Box 889, Groveland, CA 95321* **Voice:** 209-962-4321 **Fax:** 209-962-4323 **Contact:** Barbara Brundege **Founded:** 1990 **Open:** May–Nov. **Cost:** $95 for 1-day workshop, $139–$199 for weekend. Tours: $795–$1,395; $4,295 for Alaska; lodging and most meals incl.

BARBARA BRUNDEGE, a former Rochester Institute of Technology photography teacher, leads about 15 workshops, lasting from 1 day to 1 week, to unspoiled places in California and the Southwest. Yosemite, Mono Lake and Zion National Park are some of her favorite locations. One of her workshops is limited to women photographers. Her annual late-summer 2-week foray to Alaska visits the seashore, forests and mountains, with an opportunity to photograph bears and humpback whales.

The Darkroom

For photographers at all levels *708 57th St., Sacramento, CA 95819* **Voice:** 916-454-4906; 800-676-9691 **Contact:** Gene Kennedy **Founded:** 1986 **Cost:** $75 for 1-day workshops; $105–$180 for 4- to 6-week evening classes; $180–$220 for weekend sessions **Group Size:** 15 **Handicapped Access**

WHAT BEGAN AS a state-of-the-art rental darkroom facility 10 years ago now offers beginning to advanced classes in black & white and color printing. There is also a course in studio lighting and view camera technique. The workshops vary in length: 1-day sessions, weekend workshops and 4 to 6 weeks of evening classes. Students supply their own film and paper.

Facilities for rent include digital imaging workstations, for which personalized instruction is available.

UC Santa Cruz Extension

For photographers at all levels *UCSC campuses in several N California cities; also Yosemite and other scenic locations — 740 Front St., Suite 155, Santa Cruz, CA 95060* **Voice:** 800-660-8639; 408-427-6600 **Fax:** 408-427-6690 **E-mail:** adminj1@cats.ucsc.edu **Web Site:** www. ucsc.edu/unex **Contact:** Lori Aitken, Program Rep. **Founded:** 1972 **Open:** June–Aug. **Cost:** $100–$400 for 1- to 5-day workshops (some incl. lodging and meals) **Group Size:** 12–20 **Handicapped Access**

THE UNIVERSITY OF California offers a series of photography courses as part of its extension program each summer. Many of the dozen or so courses take place in scenic locations around Northern California and are directed to nature and landscape photography and the artistry of vision required for this approach to the medium. Others introduce new processes, such as Polaroid transfers, or address practical skills, such as how to light people for portraiture and black & white darkroom work. Instructors are experienced teachers and photographers.

United Digital Artists/West

For photographers, digital artists and multimedia artists *Brisbane, S of San Francisco — P.O. Box 548, FDR Station, New York, NY 10150* **Voice:** 212-777-7200; 800-227-4935 **Fax:** 212-777-7222 **E-mail:** UDIGART@applelink.apple.com **Web Site:** www.uda.com **Contact:** Maryalice Quinn, Program Dir. **Founded:** 1994 **Cost:** $645 for 2-day classes; $1,850 for Certification in Imaging **Group Size:** 14 **Handicapped Access**

The West Coast branch of this New York–based digital techniques training service operates at the facilities of Star Graphic Arts in Brisbane, just south of San Francisco. The courses and certificate programs parallel those offered in New York (see that chapter). The New York office handles enrollment for both venues.

Villa Montalvo Artist Residency Program

For photographers and artists in selected other disciplines *Foothills of Santa Cruz Mountains, 1 hr. S of San Francisco — 15400 Montalvo Rd., Saratoga, CA 95071* **Voice:** 408-741-3421 **Fax:** 408-741-5592 **E-mail:** villamnt@artswire.org **Contact:** Judy Moran, Residency Dir. **Founded:** 1942 **Open:** Year-round **Admission:** Application ($20), 5 slides, resume, project description **Deadlines:** Sept. 1 for spring-summer; Mar. 1 for winter-fall **Cost:** Transportation and meals **Financial Aid:** Fellowship **Group Size:** 5

A Mediterranean-style villa in the hills above Silicon Valley is the centerpiece of the 175-acre Villa Montalvo, the oldest artists' colony in the western U.S. Senator James Phelan built the estate, to which he would invite the likes of Jack London and Ethel Barrymore to work on individual artistic projects.

Today Villa Montalvo invites early-career and established professional artists for 1- to 3-month residencies. Artists have separate apartments, and studios where necessary. Those who come in the spring and summer can take advantage of a lively arts and performance calendar that fills the lavish grounds with activity during the warm part of the year. Fall and winter, by contrast, are quiet times, more suited to artists who need peace and solitude to complete their work. Montalvo offers several small fellowships, which are awarded entirely on merit and cannot be applied for separately.

VISCOMM West

For photographers and multimedia designers *Moscone Convention Center, in South of Market district, San Francisco — 1420 MacArthur Dr., Suite 104, Carrollton, TX, 75007* **Voice:** 203-852-0500; 800-243-3238 **Fax:** 203-838-3710 **E-mail:** viscomm@tradeshow.com **Contact:** Andrea Cassello, Marketing Mgr., ext. 288 **Founded:** 1985 **Open:** 3 days in Apr. **Admission:** Professional photographers. Under 18 must be accompanied by qualified adult. **Deadlines:** 1 mo. ahead for early registration **Cost:** $25 entry (free with seminars); $90 for most seminars; $645 for hands-on digital workshops **Group Size:** 8,000 total; workshops up to 200 **Handicapped Access**

The VISCOMM show brings an exhibit hall full of photographic products and services and a full slate of seminars to the Moscone Center in San Francisco every April. Thousands of professional photographers attend the 3-day event to investigate traditional and electronic equipment and to advance their art, craft and business savvy.

Manufacturers of cameras, lighting and all sorts of accessories promote their products and invite photographers to handle and ask about the latest equipment. Experts in electronic photography technology explain and demonstrate the state-of-the-art in hardware and software. This is an information show, not the place to buy or sell equipment.

Some 75 seminars and workshops run all during the show, with photographers and industry experts presenting insight and advice on aesthetic, business and technical matters. VISCOMM seminars specialize in being on the cutting edge of what is happening in the industry. The show offers a rare opportunity to address a whole host of photographic concerns in one densely packed event. Hands-on digital workshops on Photoshop, Live Picture, multimedia and the Internet are presented in conjunction with United Digital Artists (see listing above).

Over and above the value of the seminars and exhibits, attending a show like this helps build a sense of community among often-isolated individual photographers. VISCOMM also includes a multimedia and design conference, plus exhibits for the photo lab industry.

Students get free admission and discounts on seminars. Discounts are also available for early enrollees and those attending multiple seminars.

(See *New York* for the East Coast VISCOMM.)

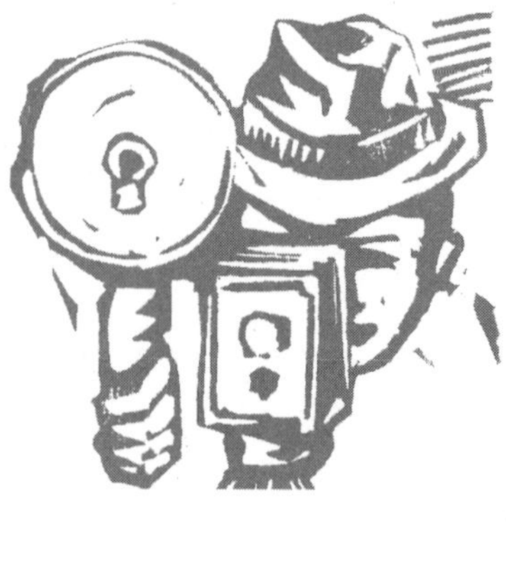

West Coast School of Professional Photography

For wedding and portrait photographers *Santa Barbara, San Diego, occasionally Napa — 121 W. Jones St., Santa Maria, CA 93454* **Voice:** 800-439-5839 **Fax:** 805-928-9757 **Contact:** Richard Giachetto **Founded:** 1957 **Open:** 1 week in Apr., 1 week in June, sometimes others **Cost:** $295 for 3-day, $450 for 5-day workshops **Financial Aid:** Scholarship **Group Size:** 90–180; classes 30

THE WEST COAST School is the senior member of the Winona-affiliated schools of the Professional Photographers of America (see *Georgia*), with a track record of serving professional photographers for over 40 years. It runs from two to four 3-day and 5-day courses in several California locations each year, and always manages to bring in the most attractive teachers and lecturers. Seminar topics include a blend of portrait and wedding instruction, plus some courses on the business of running a photography studio.

Wilderness Photographic Workshops

For nature photographers *Scenic locations in West — P.O. Box 1653, Ross, CA 94957* **Voice:** 415-927-4597 **E-mail:** wpworkshop@aol.com **Contact:** Brenda Tharp **Open:** Varies **Cost:** $375 for 4-day, $995 for weeklong workshops (lodging incl.)

BRENDA THARP, whose photos appear on notecards and calendars and in magazines, leads about a dozen nature photography workshops each year to some of the loveliest locations in the U.S. In the deserts of Arizona, the redwoods of Northern California, the Sierras and the Tetons, photographers can spend 4 days to a week or more with this experienced nature photographer and teacher exploring the shapes, colors and spectacular light of the West. The "Women in the Wilderness" workshop in September in Colorado concerns women's unique voice in photography.

Wilderness Travel

For outdoor and nature photographers *801 Allston Way, Berkeley, CA 94710* **Voice:** 510-548-0420; 800-368-2794 **Fax:** 510-548-0347 **E-mail:** info@wildernesstravel.com **Contact:** Carmen Gomez Love **Founded:** 1979 **Open:** Year-round **Cost:** $3,200–$4,600 (lodging and most meals incl.) **Group Size:** 15–18

THIS LARGE TOUR organization has arranged for special photography tours to places like East Africa and South America with a distinguished cadre of photographic experts, such as Frans Lanting and Galen Rowell. Each trip includes a concentrated photography session—a discussion of issues related to making pictures and a chance to critique images that have been processed on the tour. The rest of the time is spent on tour, with one of the photographer/leaders acting as guide.

Yosemite Field Seminars

For outdoor and nature photographers *Yosemite National Park — P.O. Box 230, El Portal, CA 95318* **Voice:** 209-379-2321 **Fax:** 209-379-2486 **E-mail:** YOSE_yosemite_association@nps.gov **Founded:** 1974 **Open:** Feb.–Nov. **Cost:** $120–$175 for 2- to 4-day weekend workshops **Group Size:** 10–15

THE MAGNIFICENT natural beauty of Yosemite is the subject of this series of about a dozen photography workshops that run in all 4 seasons in the National Park. Each workshop attends to a specific subject—a region of the park, the quality of light or the particular season—to afford photographers a variety of intimate ways to experience Yosemite.

Instructors are California-based photographers who share an intimate knowledge of the natural characteristics of the Sierras. Some workshops are geared to less experienced, some to more advanced, photographers.

Zzyzx

For photographers and digital artists *Hollywood — 949 N. Highland Ave, Los Angeles, CA 90038* **Voice:** 213-856-5260 **Fax:** 213-856-5270 **E-mail:** elizabeth@zzyzxworld.com **Web Site:** www.zzyzxworld.com/ **Contact:** Elizabeth Kotter **Founded:** 1993 **Open:** Year-round **Cost:** $350 for beginner and intermediate courses; $100 per hour for advanced instruction **Group Size:** 4

A DIVISION OF A&I Color, a major professional color lab, Zzyzx teaches Adobe Photoshop courses at the beginner, intermediate and advanced levels. Beginner and intermediate evening classes run for 4 weeks, or you can choose 2 consecutive Saturday mornings or afternoons. Advanced instruction is usually hands-on guidance for a photographer working on a particular project. Classes include scanning original slides and some output to print.

Colorado

Anchell Photography Workshops

For photographers of landscapes and the human figure *Figure studies: Big Sur, CA, and Taos, NM; Landscape workshops: around U.S. — 234 Sweetgrass Overlook, Crestone, CO 81131* **Voice:** 719-256-4157 **Fax:** 719-256-4157 **Contact:** Steve Anchell or Donna Conrad **Founded:** 1979 **Open:** Spring and fall **Admission:** Application form **Cost:** $525 for figure studies (model fees and some meals incl.); $895 for landscape workshops (lodging and most meals incl.) **Group Size:** 12 for figure; 16 for landscape

STEVE ANCHELL AND his wife and assistant, Donna Conrad, lead 2 distinct categories of workshops. The Nude in the Environment series consists of 2 weekends of outdoor figure studies, one in Big Sur in May, the other in northern New Mexico in the fall. Anchell provides some guidance, but not extensive instruction, in how to work with the 4 professional models during four 3-hour sessions outdoors. The models all sign releases that allow participants to use the images for editorial and fine art, but not commercial, purposes.

The landscape workshops, in such places as New Mexico, New England or the canyons of Utah, include plenty of photographic instruction. In addition, Anchell and Conrad encourage participants to expand their photographic seeing beyond the limits of the workshop and to integrate artistry in all aspects of life. Film processing during the week helps make these workshops excellent teaching tools for photographers at all levels.

Anderson Ranch Arts Center

For photographers and artists in selected other disciplines *A reconfigured old ranch nestled in the Rockies — P.O. Box 5598, Snowmass Village, CO 81615* **Voice:** 970-923-3181 **Fax:** 970-923-3871 **Web Site:** www.apogeephoto.com/anderson_ranch.html **Contact:** Bill Thomas, Photo Dir. **Founded:** 1966 **Open:** Workshops: June–Sept.; Artist-in-residence program: Oct.–Apr. **Admission:** Artists-in-residence: application, slides of work, references, resume **Deadlines:** Artists-in-residence: Mar. 15 **Cost:** $395–$700 for workshops, $850–$950 for digital (equipment fee incl.); room and board $320+ per week **Financial Aid:** Scholarship; Work/Study **Group Size:** 40–100 participants per week; classes 10–14; 12 artists-in-residence

WHERE SHEEP ONCE grazed beneath the craggy peaks of the Rocky Mountains, the Anderson Ranch has become an important interdisciplinary arts center. Every summer, woodworkers, potters, painters and photographers flock to Snowmass Village, a few miles from Aspen, to study and pursue their respective métiers.

The emphasis here is on artistry and personal exploration, with a healthy dose of craftsmanship. About 20 week-long workshops, plus a growing slate of digital imaging courses, attract seasoned photographers and novices alike. "We put a higher priority on commitment to learning than skill level," says executive director Jim Baker.

Several photo courses focus on alternative processes. Facilities are modern, with no more than 2 people per black & white darkroom. Color classes take advantage of professional-grade processing available in nearby Aspen.

One unique feature of Anderson Ranch is that participants from one discipline may sit in on courses in all the others. Artists from all fields dine together in the Ranch's cafe, and those who choose dormitory housing are intentionally paired up with roommates working in other media. Teachers and other visiting artists share their work with one and all most evenings. Baker says the cross-pollination of ideas and creative thrust provide inspiration well beyond the benefits of the individual workshops.

In addition to Snowmass-based courses, several field workshops take a dozen intermediate to advanced photographers for 1 to 3 weeks to selected locations in the Southwest, where they explore the land and their own photographic souls. Special courses for children as young as 6 are offered throughout the summer session. The Ranch staff encourages families to partake of the different workshops at the same time.

From October to April, Anderson Ranch functions as a retreat for a dozen artists-in-residence, including 2 photographers, who take advantage of 7 full months of freedom in a supportive atmosphere to create according to their own inner calling. Full use of all facilities, plus 5 breakfasts and dinners a week, are provided at no cost. Artists-in-residence volunteer 20 hours of work to the Ranch each month.

Emerging-artists scholarships and 2 or 3 photo program assistantships are available each year; apply by early March.

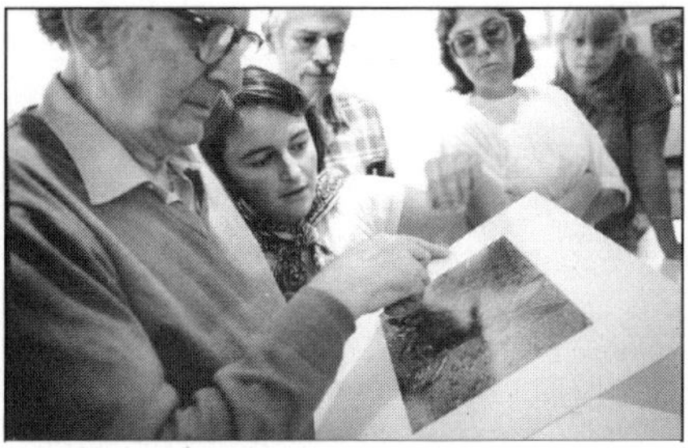
ANDERSON RANCH ARTS CENTER

Critique with Frederick Sommer at Anderson Ranch, Snowmass Village.

Anderson Ranch was a working sheep ranch until 1966. Today even the new buildings match the pioneer-style architecture of the original ones. A car is unnecessary because the workweek is intense, leaving little time for exploring. There is a shuttle service to Aspen. Participants should be prepared for a day or two's shortness of breath when ascending from sea level to the ranch's 8,200-foot altitude.

Branson Reynolds Photographic Workshops

For photographers of nature, landscape and the human figure *Southwest — P.O. Box 3471, Durango, CO 81302* **Voice:** 970-247-5274 **Web Site:** www.simwell.com/reynolds/ **Contact:** Branson Reynolds **Founded:** 1992 **Open:** Apr.–Oct. **Admission:** Application form **Cost:** $695 for most 5-day workshops; $465 for 3-day figure in landscape; $1,350 to photograph Native Americans; $1,250 for llama trek **Group Size:** 6

The Four Corners region of the Southwest and the Rocky Mountains are Branson Reynolds's specialty and the areas into which he leads photographers to explore and take photos. His 15 trips per year center on the natural beauty of canyons and mountains, or on Native Americans, some of whom will sign model releases. Several of the trips use llamas as pack animals or are on horseback (food and lodging are included in all fees). He also conducts several figure and landscape workshops in the Durango area.

Conifer Photographic Workshops

For advanced photographers
25 mi. SW of Denver and in Rockies — 12794 S. Hwy 285, Conifer, CO 80433 **Voice:** 303-838-4848; 303-860-7502 **E-mail:** mfulks@apogeephoto.com **Web Site:** http://www.apogeephoto.com/conifer.html **Contact:** Michael Fulks or Scott Kilborn **Founded:** 1983 **Open:** Summer and early fall **Admission:** Application form **Cost:** $300–$350 for weekend workshops (some meals incl.); $225 for fall caravan ($325 for a couple) **Group Size:** 12–16

FINE ART PHOTOGRAPHERS travel to the high country of Colorado each summer for Michael Fulks and Scott Kilborn's workshops in figure studies and infrared landscape photography. Landscape workshops offer photographers a chance to explore the subtleties and surprises of black & white infrared film. Figure study workshops, some of which are conducted exclusively in infrared, work with a nude model outdoors against a pristine Rocky Mountain landscape. All infrared workshops include special instructions in how to use and handle this specialized product. Film is processed each Saturday night for critiquing the next morning. Photography continues until the workshop ends Sunday evening.

A weeklong RV caravan to photograph the brilliant color of fall aspen trees takes place in late September. A nude photo workshop for women photographers only is offered some years.

Dramatic Light Nature Photography

For nature photographers
Mostly West and Canada; also Africa — 2292 Shiprock Rd., Grand Junction, CO 81503
Voice: 970-244-8855; 800-207-4686 **Contact:** Joseph Lange **Founded:** 1996 **Open:** Year-round **Admission:** Application form **Cost:** $1,095 for most weeklong workshops (lodging incl.); up to $1,995 per week for Africa **Group Size:** Up to 5 per instructor

AWARD-WINNING nature photographer Joe Lange has 25 years experience stalking the beautiful light and dramatic scenery of the American West. His workshops offer photographers a chance to spend a full week exploring and photographing at many of our National Parks and Monuments, plus select destinations in Canada and Africa.

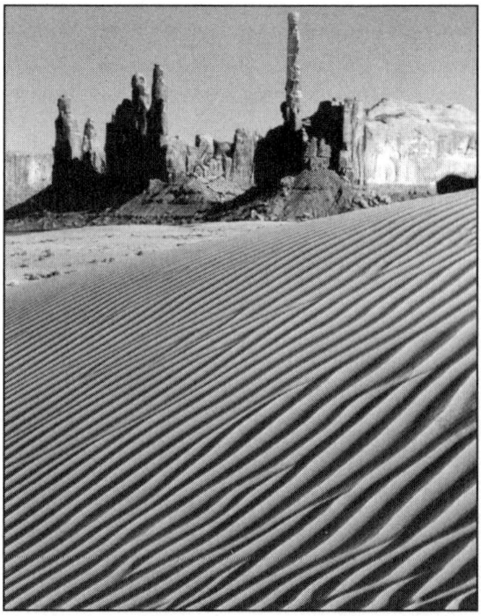

JOSEPH K. LANGE

Monument Valley totem pole and sand dunes, an image from Dramatic Light Nature Photography.

Each group is limited to no more than 10, with 2 instructors to provide maximum personal guidance. During bad weather, Lange and his wife, Bonnie, are prepared with indoor instruction programs in composition and technique. Participants are urged to bring samples of previous work for discussion.

First Light Photography Tours

For nature photographers

Florida, Colorado, Montana, New Mexico, Alaska — P.O. Box 11066, Englewood, CO 80151 **Voice:** 303-762-8191 **E-mail:** zshort@aol.com **Contact:** Andy Long **Founded:** 1994 **Open:** Varies **Admission:** Application form **Cost:** $550–$1,050 for 4- to 7-day workshops (lodging and meals incl.); $125 per day for individual photo-guide in CO **Group Size:** 6

PHOTOGRAPHER Andy Long leads nature and wildlife photographers throughout the Rocky Mountain area, as well as to Alaska and the Florida coast. Most trips specialize in photographing animals, such as bison in Montana, sandhill cranes in New Mexico, coyotes in Yellowstone and eagles in Alaska. Others concentrate on landscapes and wildflowers. Long is an expert in the fine points of photographic technique and can provide as much or as little instruction as a participant wishes.

Latigo Ranch Photography Workshops

For nature photographers *Rocky Mountains — P.O. Box 237, Kremmling, CO 80459* **Voice:** 970-724-9008; 800-227-9655 **Fax:** 970-724-9009 **Contact:** Kathie Yost **Founded:** 1985 **Open:** July, Sept. **Admission:** Application form **Cost:** $1,465 for 1 week (meals and lodging incl.) **Group Size:** 6 per instructor **Handicapped Access**

WILDFLOWERS IN July and a cattle roundup amid fall colors are the 2 weeklong photo workshops offered annually at this deluxe guest ranch high in the Colorado Rockies. Photographers shoot in the

Workshop Information on the World Wide Web

In keeping with the current explosion in information technology, a service on the Internet now lists photographic workshops and training programs.

The Colorado-based Apogee Photo Directory solicits advertising from the organizers of some of the workshops included in this book, as well as producers of photography-related publications and videos. Its listings are concise and informative. It also features its own on-line-only general-interest photography magazine.

If you have access to the Internet, you may want to visit this site to see what's available and to keep up with the most recent schedules and information on workshops. The address on the World Wide Web is: http://www.apogeephoto.com.

beautiful morning and evening light, blending color and form under the guidance of experienced instructors.

While not shooting or discussing pictures, participants can enjoy horseback riding, swimming and other activities in Latigo Ranch's magnificent mountain setting. A well-planned children's program makes this ideal for a family vacation.

Natural Habitat Adventures

For nature and wildlife photographers *Africa and the Americas — 2945 Center Green Ct., Boulder, CO 80301* **Voice:** 303-449-3711; 800-543-8917 **Fax:** 303-449-3712 **Founded:** 1984 **Open:** Year-round **Admission:** Application form **Cost:** $1,900–$6,300, depending on location and duration **Group Size:** 10–15

THIS ECOTOURISM company operates tours all over the world, a number of which are specifically designed for photographing wildlife. Well-known photographer/tour leaders have been contracted to lead groups to watch the wildebeest migration in Kenya, the arrival of the baby harp seals in Canada, and wildlife in their natural habitat in Costa Rica and eastern and southern Africa.

The Photo-tour program differs from Natural Habitat's many other tours in that participants travel with more room to accommodate equipment, and take the time to allow photographers to wait for sensitive situations to develop. Small groups assure each participant ample access to tour leaders.

Photography at the Summit & Sports Photography Workshop

For documentary and nature/wildlife photographers; for sports photographers *Summit: Jackson Hole, WY. Sports: varies — 3200 Cherry Creek S. Dr., Suite 650, Denver, CO 80209* **Voice:** 303-744-2538; 800-745-3211 **Fax:** 303-744-2556 **E-mail:** 102005,550@compuserve.com **Contact:** Rich Clarkson **Founded:** 1986 **Open:** Summit: Sept. Sports: July of non-Summer Olympic years **Admission:** Application form **Cost:** $695 for Summit (either workshop); $700 for Sports **Group Size:** 70 sports; 30 each Summit workshop

IMAGINE SPENDING a week in the Tetons of Wyoming, studying documentary or nature photography with some of America's most accomplished photographers. Or a week with veteran sports photographers and editors covering Olympic athletes as they prepare for competition. These two programs, put on by former *Sports Illustrated* photographer and *National Geographic* photography director Rich Clarkson, offer serious photographers an extraordinary chance to heighten their skills and advance their careers.

The Summit workshops break into two parts: documentary/editorial and nature/wildlife. The documentary workshop covers the creation of picture stories, from the genesis of an idea through photographing and editing. The nature workshop affords a chance to study with some of the best in the business in one of the visually richest natural areas in

Professional Advancement Conference

Rich Clarkson, Sean Callahan (founding editor of *American Photo*) and others conduct a weekend conference on building careers in association with the Summit workshops in Jackson Hole (above). Topics include book publishing, exhibitions and creative options including the use of electronics. The conference is free to Summit workshop attendees and costs $175 for others.

the country. Each participant works intimately with one of the faculty members and has access to all the others.

The Sports Photography workshop has traditionally taken place wherever the summer Olympic festival is being held around the country. Participants get to meet and discuss technique with *Sports Illustrated* photographers and other top sports journalists while photographing the best young athletes in 37 sports. Film is processed daily to yield up-to-the-minute feedback.

The up-and-coming professional photographer with a burning desire to be the best could hardly find a better workshop in which to advance a career than one of these. (Participants must arrange for their own lodging and meals.)

Robert Winslow Photo Tours

For wildlife photographers *The West, Africa, Canada, South America — P.O. Box 334, Durango, CO 81302* **Voice:** 970-259-4143 **Fax:** 970-259-7748 **Contact:** Robert Winslow **Founded:** 1988 **Open:** Varies **Admission:** Application form **Cost:** $1,385–$3,000 to photograph captive animals (lodging incl.), surcharges for some animals; $3,000–$9,000 for tours **Group Size:** 6–12

ROBERT WINSLOW'S tours specialize in photographing captive animals in controlled situations made to look as if they were in the wild. Subjects include wolves, bears, exotic cats and birds of prey. These shoots generally run 4 or 5 days.

An expert on animal behavior, Winslow usually leads 1 trip to Africa each year, and sometimes to other exotic destinations. Some tours book through Voyagers International (see *New York*). Groups are generally quite small, and the tours last up to 2½ weeks.

Rocky Mountain Seminars

For nature and landscape photographers *On the Continental Divide, 65 mi. NW of Denver — Rocky Mountain National Park, Estes Park, CO 80517* **Voice:** 970-586-1258 **Fax:** 970-586-1310 **E-mail:** shupa@linden.fortnet.org **Contact:** Kris Marske, Seminar Coord. **Open:** Mar.–Oct. **Admission:** Application form **Cost:** $75–$125 for 2- or 3-day weekend workshops

THE ROCKY MOUNTAIN Nature Association in Estes Park sponsors about half a dozen photography seminars each year. The seminars run on weekends, with topics covering the flora, fauna and mountain landscape of Rocky Mountain National Park. Instructors are leading Colorado-based nature photographers and workshop leaders.

Camping in the park is encouraged (and free). Other lodging is available through the local Chamber of Commerce.

Connecticut

New England School of Photographic Arts

For photographers at all levels *15 mi. N of Danbury — P.O. Box 1509, 22 Bennitt St., New Milford, CT 06776* **Voice:** 860-355-5367 **Fax:** 860-355-5367 **Contact:** Barbara Soares, Exec. Dir. **Founded:** 1987 **Admission:** Application form **Cost:** $145–$185 for 4- to 6-week classes; $35–$65 for 1-day or evening classes; $500 for 1-week travel workshop; discounts for members. **Group Size:** 10

THE WOODED HILLS and valleys of western Connecticut are home to this nonprofit community organization that teaches basic and advanced techniques to photographers from around the region.

NESPA features a gallery and a regular schedule of basic photography and darkroom classes taught by staff instructors. Master teachers are brought in 6 or 8 times per year to present seminars or provide hands-on instruction to no more than 10 students at a time. Courses in Ilfochrome direct positive color printing and nontraditional processes are especially popular. NESPA provides an intimate environment in which to pursue a casual or passionate involvement with photography.

Occasional travel workshops go to scenic places in the U.S.

District of Columbia

PhotoProExpo

For professional photographers *Washington Convention Center, DC — 14 Strawberry Hill Ave., Norwalk, CT 06855* **Voice:** 203-899-7990; 800-499-9195 **Fax:** 203-899-7995 **Contact:** Brian Vargas, Pres. **Founded:** 1991 **Open:** 3 days in Apr. or May **Admission:** Application form **Deadlines:** 1 mo. ahead for discounts **Cost:** Free admission to exhibit hall; $65 for most seminars ($10 discount for early registration) **Group Size:** 10,000

THIS LARGE ANNUAL conference features about 50 seminars on photographic strategies and techniques and an exhibit hall full of equipment and services for the working photographer.

Many of the seminars are oriented to the wedding and portrait photographer, while others address such topics as advertising, photojournalism and stock. A number of them teach lighting skills. The digital seminars illustrate the use of Adobe Photoshop but do not allow for hands-on experience.

The exhibit hall is an active marketplace where prospective buyers can find an enormous selection of cameras, lights, accessories, film and professional services, all in one place. Photographers have the chance to ask the questions, consider the choices and then purchase equipment directly from retailers on the exhibit hall floor.

Intended for the trade only, PhotoProExpo is a feast of opportunities for the early-career photographer as well as the seasoned pro.

Florida

Atlantic Center for the Arts

For photographers and artists in selected other disciplines *20 mi. S of Daytona — 1414 Art Center Ave., New Smyrna Beach, FL 32168* **Voice:** 904-427-6975 **Fax:** 904-427-5669 **E-mail:** acansb@aol.com **Contact:** Program Dept. **Founded:** 1982 **Open:** Year-round **Admission:** Associates chosen by individual Master Artists **Deadlines:** 3 to 4 mo. prior to residency **Cost:** $300, plus $500 housing **Financial Aid:** Scholarship **Group Size:** 25–40 total **Handicapped Access**

ATLANTIC CENTER'S program is unique among art residencies. Six times each year, ACA invites 3 or 4 Master Artists—distinguished professionals with international reputations in a variety of fields, including photography—to work in residence for 3 weeks. Each Master Artist then accepts 8 to 10 Associates—mid-career artists who have applied specifically to work with that person—to join in.

ACA distributes its list of upcoming Master Artists broadly so that would-be Associates around the country will know who is coming and be able to apply. The fee includes housing but not meals or transportation. Scholarship assistance is available, based on ability to pay.

The Atlantic Center is a modern facility with well-equipped studios, a library, an amphitheater and other buildings all connected by a wooden boardwalk that weaves through the trees in a quiet area on the Florida coast.

Bike Week Workshops

For photojournalists *Daytona Beach — SE Museum of Photography, P.O. Box 2811, Daytona Beach, FL 32120* **Voice:** 904-254-4475 **Fax:** 904-254-4487 **E-mail:** nordsta@dbcc.cc.fl.us **Contact:** Alison Nordstrom **Founded:** 1979 **Open:** 1 week in Mar. **Admission:** Application form **Deadlines:** Feb. 15 **Cost:** $300 **Group Size:** 20

HUNDREDS OF BIKERS roar into Daytona Beach every March for the annual gathering of Harley-Davidson riders. And every year the Southeast Museum of Photography enlists one of the top photojournalists in the country to conduct a weeklong workshop on photographing this most pictorial subject.

This is a photojournalism workshop, with daily assignments and frequent film processing and critiques. Bikers present a dramatic environment in which photographers can test their human relations and photographic skills. Subjects move in a vivid splash of color and shiny metal. Personalities are not what most photographers find around home. Add the technical requirements of exposure and composition while working in close, and this workshop promises challenges beyond what one finds in more traditional photo workshops.

Birds as Art

For bird specialists *Workshops in FL, NY, NJ, NM, OH, and in Ontario and Manitoba, Canada — 1455 Whitewood Dr., Deltona, FL 33725* **Voice:** 407-860-2013 **Contact:** Arthur Morris, Dir. **Founded:** 1992 **Open:** Varies **Admission:** Application form **Cost:** $300 for 3 days; $1,899 for week in Churchill, Manitoba (lodging incl.) **Group Size:** 3–8

ARTHUR MORRIS'S Instructional Photo-Tours focus exclusively on birds in a variety of ornithologically rich places from Florida to Queens, New York, to northern Canada. Known for his own aesthetically elegant bird pictures, Morris understands bird behavior and knows where and at what time of year to find certain species. He is a former schoolteacher who prides himself on his ability to explain how to best use camera equipment to produce artistic bird photos. Groups are very small and include Morris's pet cat.

COMPrehend Computer Education Centers

For photographers and graphic artists *3200 N. 29th Ave., Hollywood, FL 33020* **Voice:** 954-920-3899 **Fax:** 954-923-0126 **E-mail:** comped1@aol.com **Contact:** Teresa Williamson **Founded:** 1990 **Open:** Year-round **Admission:** Application form **Cost:** $498 for level 1 Photoshop; $269 for level 2 **Group Size:** 8

THIS DIVERSIFIED computer-training facility offers a 2-day introductory course and a 1-day intermediate course in Adobe Photoshop. Hands-on training is conducted on advanced Mac and PC workstations every few weeks. COMPrehend also offers courses in other graphics and business software applications.

Crealde School of Visual Art

For photographers and artists in selected other disciplines *Just N of Orlando — 600 St. Andrews Blvd., Winter Park, FL 32792* **Voice:** 407-671-1886 **Contact:** Rick Lang, Photo Dir. **Founded:** 1976 **Open:** Year-round **Admission:** Application form **Cost:** $115–$130 for 8-week classes; workshop and field trip costs vary; discounts for members **Group Size:** 15

PHOTOGRAPHERS and other artists in the Orlando area look to the non-profit Crealde School for a variety of basic to advanced art classes. Most classes meet 1 evening per week for 4 to 8 weeks, and a few travel workshops and field trips are scheduled each year. Nationally known artists visit occasionally for 1-day seminars and workshops. Crealde School also offers special courses for children.

Everglades Photo Safari

For nature and wildlife photographers *Various parts of Everglades — 8390 S.W. 132nd St., Miami, FL 33156* **Voice:** 305-255-3111 **Contact:** Vic Ramos **Founded:** 1986 **Open:** Nov.–Apr. **Admission:** Application form **Deadlines:** None, but recommended to book at least 1 mo. in advance **Cost:** $300 per day for 2 people, $100 add'l per extra person **Group Size:** 4

VIC RAMOS KNOWS about as much about the Everglades as anybody. In his custom-designed 18-foot boat, he takes photographers and others to explore shores and inlets in search of exotic birds, crocodiles and alligators, and the occasional pod of dolphins.

Each 1-day excursion is planned according to weather conditions, tides and what the client wants to see. Ramos is a commercial photographer in Miami who has spent years fishing and shooting pictures in the Everglades. He can instruct photographers in wildlife technique or simply guide them around the flora and fauna of this remarkable region.

Florida School of Professional Photography

For wedding and portrait photographers *Daytona Beach — 2312 Farwell Dr., Tampa, FL 33603* **Voice:** 800-330-0532 **Fax:** 813-875-9174 **Contact:** Teresa Saylor, Reg. **Founded:** 1993 **Open:** 1 week in May **Admission:** Application form **Cost:** $395 for weeklong workshop and banquet ($325 for members of Florida Professional Photographers) **Group Size:** 120; classes 25

AFFILIATED WITH the Winona International School of Professional Photography (see *Georgia*), the Florida school concentrates on the wedding/portrait studio photographer. Five or 6 classes are offered each year during 1 week in mid-May in Daytona Beach. Subjects include photographic technique and the business of running a studio. Instructors are advanced PPA photographers.

Macro/Nature Photography

For nature photographers interested in close-up work *Gulf Coast, 30 mi. S of Sarasota — P.O. Box 1649, Englewood, FL 34295* **Voice:** 941-475-0757 **Fax:** 941-473-4247 **Contact:** Bob Sisson **Founded:** 1989 **Admission:** Portfolio (10 slides) **Cost:** $200 per day **Group Size:** 1

BOB SISSON OFFERS one-on-one instruction to photographers of nature and scientific subjects, with a particular emphasis on close-up work. There is no preordained curriculum, as Sisson helps his students with the subjects and techniques they desire.

Bob Sisson has shot for 87 different *National Geographic* stories since he went on staff there in 1942. His experience with and knowledge of macrophotography is vast. He has been teaching other photographers for over 30 years.

Monte Zucker Portrait/Wedding Classes

For wedding and portrait photographers *Sites around the U.S. — 4468 Ascot Circle N., Sarasota, FL 34235* **Voice:** 941-355-4392 **Fax:** 941-355-4392 **E-mail:** mzphotog@aol.com **Founded:** 1968 **Open:** Varies **Admission:** Application form **Cost:** $500 for 4-day workshop **Group Size:** 25 **Handicapped Access**

Monte Zucker is one of the best-known portrait and wedding photographers in the country, with years of teaching experience on his own and on the PPA/ Winona school circuit (see *Georgia*). His 4-day seminar, given in locations around the country, is a crash course in lighting, posing and working with clients. Zucker's upbeat presentation teaches not only photographic technique but also how to build up a studio business and increase profits. As part of the class, he introduces digital technology as it applies to the wedding business.

Nature Images Workshops

For nature and wildlife photographers *U.S., Canada, Costa Rica — P.O. Box 2037, W. Palm Beach, FL 33402* **Voice:** 561-622-0795 **Fax:** 561-622-6438 **Web Site:** www.apogeephoto.com/natureimages.html **Contact:** Helen Longest-Slaughter, Dir. **Founded:** 1987 **Open:** Varies **Admission:** Application form **Cost:** $100–$250 for weekend workshops; $700–$1,200 for weeklong workshops (lodging and some meals incl.) **Group Size:** 5–8

Helen Longest-Slaughter is a passionate environmentalist. As president and photo editor of the magazine *Nature Photography*, she instructs photographers in photographic thinking, planning and technique, all with an ethical concern for land and wildlife. Her weekend and weeklong workshops visit places in North and Central America, from the Northwest Territories of Canada to the Florida Everglades to Costa Rica. Her 1-day seminars, taught around the country, teach the basics of natural-light photography and artistry.

New Vision Workshops

For architectural and panoramic photographers *Boca Raton and other cities in Florida — 6463 La Costa Dr., Boca Raton, FL 33433* **Voice:** 407-361-9551 **Fax:** 407-361-9551 **Contact:** Manny Abraben **Founded:** 1996 **Open:** Varies **Admission:** Application form **Cost:** $295 for 3-day course (film and processing incl.) **Group Size:** 25

What does a retired architect who has always loved photography do? Manny Abraben wrote a book, *Point of View,* and is now teaching workshops in the art of architectural photography.

The 3-day course is a hands-on session in photographing the built environment for professional and advanced amateur photographers. Participants may use any format camera, including the unique panoramic Roundshot cameras that will be provided. The program explores perspective, building types, natural and artificial light and related subjects.

Abraben also teaches a course in photographing architecture specifically for working architects.

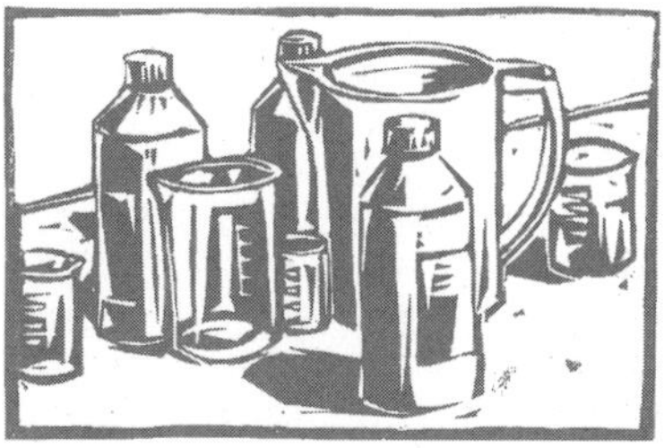

Palm Beach Photographic Centre

For photographers at all levels *Atlantic coast of S. Florida — 55 N.E. Second Ave., Delray Beach, FL 33444* **Voice:** 407-276-9797 **Fax:** 407-276-1932 **E-mail:** palmbphoto@aol.com **Web Site:** www.pbphoto.workshop.org **Contact:** Fatima NeJame, Co-Dir. **Founded:** 1986 **Open:** Jan.–Apr.; digital and travel workshops year-round **Admission:** Application ($25) **Cost:** $700 for most weeklong workshops (lab fee incl.); $200–$250 for 2- or 3-day digital **Financial Aid:** Scholarship; Work/Study **Group Size:** 30–60; classes 15 **Handicapped Access**

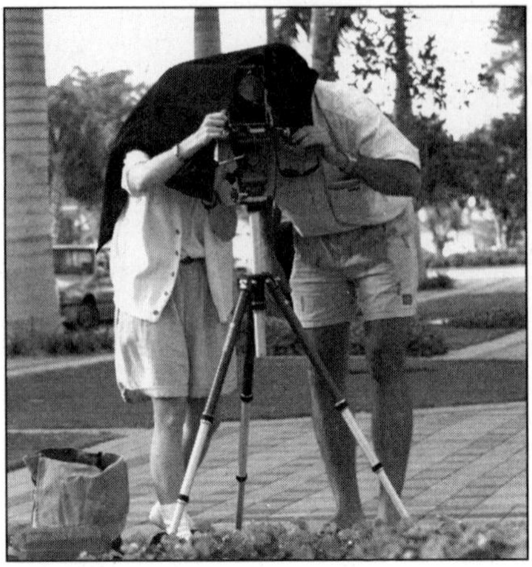
PALM BEACH PHOTOGRAPHIC CENTRE

Tête à tête at Palm Beach Photographic Centre.

THE GOLD COAST of Florida becomes a mecca for photographers every year from January to April, as photographers at all levels flee the northern winter to attend some 50 weeklong and weekend workshops.

Fatima and Art NeJame have created the nonprofit Palm Beach workshops to include a little of everything. There are courses on beauty and glamour photography, nature and landscape, portraiture, architectural and medical photography, color and black & white printing and such special techniques as hand-coloring. Several of the offerings are specifically geared to the beginning professional. Teachers are drawn from the ranks of the best-known photographers in the country, including Larry Dale Gordon, John Sexton and Lynn Goldsmith.

A slate of 2- and 3-day digital imaging workshops runs year-round, with beginning and advanced courses in Adobe Photoshop, Live Picture, and multimedia and graphic design software. Every student in any course may attend a demonstration of digital imaging. A series of evening lectures by visiting artists complements the workshop schedule.

Photographers who long to travel can take advantage of Palm Beach Centre's travel programs to East Africa, Peru, Israel, Ireland and other exotic destinations. Programs run from 1 to 2 weeks, and prices vary.

Half-price scholarships are available only to full-time students and educators.

Talent Convenes at FOTOFUSION

Palm Beach Photographic Centre's FOTOFUSION is a great convocation of photographers that takes over Delray Beach for 5 days each midwinter. Some of America's most accomplished photographers, and a couple of thousand others, gather for pointed seminars, photo exhibits and general elbow-rubbing. Evening presentations by the likes of James Nachtwey and Gordon Parks draw almost a thousand people to the tennis stadium.

In keeping with the NeJames' spirit of inclusiveness, FOTOFUSION seminars cover an astonishing array of topics. Photographers can find plenty to pique their interest. Perhaps even more valuable is the creative boost you gain from participating in such a whirlwind of talent and passion in your chosen field. The fee for FOTOFUSION is under $500 for all 5 days. Hotel reservations should be booked well ahead of time.

Work/study is a possibility for the whole winter season or for the whole summer of digital courses.

The newly (1995) refurbished home of the Palm Beach workshops houses a lovely museum/art gallery and a professional-grade photo store, 2 large gang darkrooms, and 2 digital classrooms with 16 modern workstations. The windowless cinder-block class meeting rooms are adequate for basic teaching—and provide ample motivation to get outside into the clear South Florida air to shoot. There is a small cafeteria, but participants must attend to their own meals.

Delray Beach is an older Florida coastal town, about halfway between West Palm Beach and Boca Raton. Over the past few years, local officials have done an outstanding job of sprucing up its tired main street, now filled with pleasant shops and eateries. Workshop attendees stay in the local Holiday Inn or the 1920s-vintage Colony Hotel, with its white wicker–filled lobby (lodging is not included in the fee). A car is recommended, though not absolutely necessary.

Touch of Success Seminars

For outdoor photographers and nonfiction writer/photographers *P.O. Box 194, Lowell, FL 32663* **Voice:** 904-867-0463; 502-769-1823 **Web Site:** www.apogeephoto.com/touch_of_success.html **Contact:** Bill Thomas **Founded:** 1978 **Open:** Varies **Admission:** Application form **Cost:** $295 for weekend workshops; $850–$1,000 for weeklong outdoor workshops; lodging and some meals incl. **Group Size:** 12

BILL THOMAS IS a semi-retired but active "nature-photojournalist" with an impressive list of magazine photo credits and over 2 dozen books to his name, among them *How to Make $50,000 a Year as a Nature Photojournalist*. His Touch of Success Seminars are designed to convey the wisdom of his experience to outdoor photographers.

Thomas's travel workshops go to impressive (but not the most famous) scenic locales around the country, including the Okefenokee Swamp and Mt. St. Helens. Weekend workshops are near his Ocala, Florida, home or his farm in rural Kentucky.

The rugged yet folksy Thomas mixes exploration and a bit of adventure with the chance to study at the elbow of a man who has made a long and successful career of photographing nature. His writing workshops are oriented to the photographer who wants to be able to sell complete articles to publications.

WaterHouse Photo Tours

For underwater photographers *Caribbean, Pacific Ocean, Red Sea, etc. — P.O. Box 2487, Key Largo, FL 33037* **Voice:** 305-451-2228; 800-272-9122 **Fax:** 305-451-5147 **E-mail:** lexag@aol.com **Contact:** Maria DiPasqua **Founded:** 1986 **Open:** Year-round **Admission:** Application form **Cost:** WaterHouse tours: $2,000–$2,500 for 5- to 8-day tours (lodging and meals incl.); Nikon programs: $800–$1,500 resort/dive fee per week (may include meals), plus $250 (basic) or $500 (advanced) instructor fee **Group Size:** 12

WATERHOUSE RUNS its own underwater photo tours and administers programs of the Nikon School of Underwater Photography.

The WaterHouse tours are boat-based dive and photography trips to witness all manner of undersea life, from sponges and coral to humpback whales. Guide Stephen Frink is a widely published underwater photographer who will assist participants as needed, though the trips are not primarily instructional in nature.

The weeklong Nikon school sessions combine exotic vacations and thorough instruction for the beginning to advanced underwater photographer. Nikonos underwater cameras are available for rental, or participants can bring their own equipment. All divers must show valid certification cards.

Underwater "Shootout"

Four annual Nikonos Shootouts combine a party atmosphere with a prestigious underwater photo contest. A hundred or more photographers gather in the Caribbean or in Monterey, California, to compete for thousands of dollars in photo equipment and other prizes. The Shootouts provide a rare chance for underwater photographers to meet a large number of colleagues at one time, to view work and to discuss the intricacies of this photographic specialty. Contact Water-House (above) for details.

Georgia

Georgia School of Professional Photography

For wedding and portrait photographers *North Georgia Technical Institute, Clarkesville, 50 mi. NE of Atlanta — P.O. Box 1373, Cartersville, GA 30120* **Voice:** 770-386-2702 **Fax:** 770-386-4003 **Contact:** Louis Tonsmeire **Founded:** 1972 **Open:** 1 week in Apr. **Admission:** Application form **Cost:** $395 for weeklong class **Financial Aid:** Scholarship **Group Size:** 80–125 **Handicapped Access**

This Winona-affiliated school (see below) offers classes in wedding and portrait techniques and in related skills for the local studio photographer. Its digital classes cover both creative photo manipulation and retouching. Digital students supply their own computer hardware, which allows classes to be priced the same as traditional photographic training courses.

Hambidge Center

For photographers and artists in selected other disciplines *In Blue Ridge Mountains, 120 mi. N of Atlanta — P.O. Box 339, Rabun Gap, GA 30568* **Voice:** 706-746-5718 **Fax:** 706-746-9933 **E-mail:** jbarber@artswire.org **Contact:** Judith Barber, Exec. Dir. **Founded:** 1934 **Open:** Mar.–Dec. (main season May–Oct.) **Admission:** Application ($20), 10 slides, resume, references, project statement optional **Deadlines:** Jan. 31 for main season; Aug. 31 for other times **Cost:** $125 per week **Group Size:** 8–10 during summer; fewer other times

Mary Crovatt Hambidge believed that human creativity finds its best source in the creativity of nature. The center she founded provides 600 acres, crisscrossed with nature trails, in a deep cove in the Blue Ridge Mountains where artists in many disciplines can feed themselves on nature and devote their attention, uninterrupted, to their work.

Residencies at the Hambidge Center last 2 to 6 weeks, and from May to October include dinners 5 nights a week at the main Rock House building (all other meals are the responsibility of the individual artists). Seven private cabins afford living space from March to December, along with a few additional rooms in Rock House during the summer months. The atmosphere is respectful and supportive at evening gatherings, but otherwise quiet. Hambidge's darkroom is primitive by modern standards, suitable for only basic black & white work.

New Horizons Computer Learning Center

For photographers and digital artists *1706 Northeast Expwy., Atlanta, GA 30329* **Voice:** 404-235-3500, ext. 152 **Fax:** 404-235-3518 **Contact:** Linda Smith **Open:** Year-round **Admission:** Application form **Cost:** $295 for 1-day class, $495 for 2 days

NEW HORIZONS is a major computer-training organization, offering hundreds of courses in dozens of software programs on both Mac and PC platforms. The introductory and intermediate Adobe Photoshop courses are both 1-day events, while beginning Photoshop takes up 2 days. Other graphics and multimedia classes are also available.

New Horizons has a series of "club" plans through which you can take any or all of a series of loosely related classes during a 6- or 12-month period. The costs range from $699 to $1,999 for a 6-month plan, $899 to $2,199 for a full-year plan. These club plans are a great deal for anyone who wants to take more than 3 or 4 separate classes, and they allow unlimited repeating.

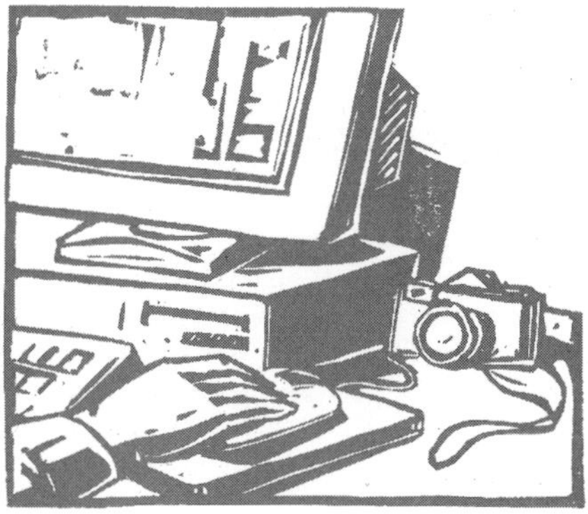

Portfolio Center

For students of commercial photography and other commercial arts *Buckead area of Atlanta — 125 Bennett St., Atlanta, GA 30309* **Voice:** 404-351-5055; 800-255-3169 **Fax:** 404-355-8838 **E-mail:** portfolioc@aol.com **Contact:** Parlee Teague, Admissions **Founded:** 1980 **Open:** 4 quarters yearly **Admission:** Application ($75 fee), 10–20 samples of work **Deadlines:** Mid-Feb. for spring quarter; mid-Aug. for fall quarter **Cost:** $2,750 per quarter; materials approximately $1,500 per quarter **Financial Aid:** Scholarship; Work/Study **Group Size:** 300 students, 30 photographers **Degree or Certification:** Certificate **Job Placement:** Yes **Handicapped Access**

TWO YEARS OF intensive training at the Portfolio Center prepares photographers to enter the world of commercial photography. The entire focus of the program is on building a portfolio good enough to get work from designers and art directors in major markets.

Photography students work closely with students in graphic design and art direction to create mock advertising projects, using formats from 35mm to 4 x 5. Courses cover camera technique, lighting, propping, lab and the use of Adobe Photoshop to alter images digitally. Each student specializes in fashion, product or still life and has a private studio in which to work.

PPA Imaging Conference and Expo

For PPA members and other photographers *Varies — P.O. Box 102056, Atlanta, GA 30368* **Voice:** 800-786-6277 **Fax:** 404-614-6400 **Contact:** Kathy Friestad **Founded:** 1891 **Open:** 5 days in July **Admission:** Application form **Cost:** $160 registration fee for PPA members, $350 for nonmembers (includes entry to most seminars); $35–$50 for special workshops and awards banquet; $25 for trade show only **Group Size:** 5,000 **Handicapped Access**

THE PROFESSIONAL Photographers of America annual convention is a 5-day event that takes place in a different city each year. The busy schedule includes over a hundred 1- to 3-hour seminars and workshops, most of which are free to conference registrants. The majority of them concern wedding and portrait photography, but there are also a sizable number of electronic imaging seminars and a growing number of commercially oriented offerings.

The Expo part of the convention is a trade show at which many suppliers of equipment and accessories have booths. There are also keynote speakers, a large print exhibit and an awards banquet.

The greatest benefit of attending this kind of conference may be the creative boost and feeling of camaraderie one receives from meeting so many colleagues and sharing personal and professional experiences. (For more on the PPA, see "Joining Up.")

Savannah College of Art & Design

For student photographers, visual and computer artists, architects and artists in many media *Downtown Savannah — 201 W. Charlton St., Savannah, GA 31402* **Voice:** 912-238-2487; 800-869-7223 **Fax:** 912-2428 **E-mail:** admissions@scad.edu **Web Site:** www.scad.edu **Contact:** Steven Mosch, Chair **Founded:** 1978 **Open:** Year-round **Admission:** Application ($50), portfolio, other requirements **Cost:** $12,000 per year **Financial Aid:** Scholarship; Fellowship; Work/Study **Group Size:** 150 total; classes 16 **Degree or Certification:** BFA, MFA, MA **Job Placement:** Yes **Handicapped Access**

THIS LEADING ART college provides an interdisciplinary approach to photography education. Students receive a solid background in the art and craft of photography (including digital), as well as training in other art forms. The program nurtures the expressive voice so that students will have the self-knowledge and confidence to choose the proper career path.

The photography department is housed in its own large building in the lovely Southern city of Savannah. Off-campus programs permit students to earn credit while studying in Canada, France, Italy and New York.

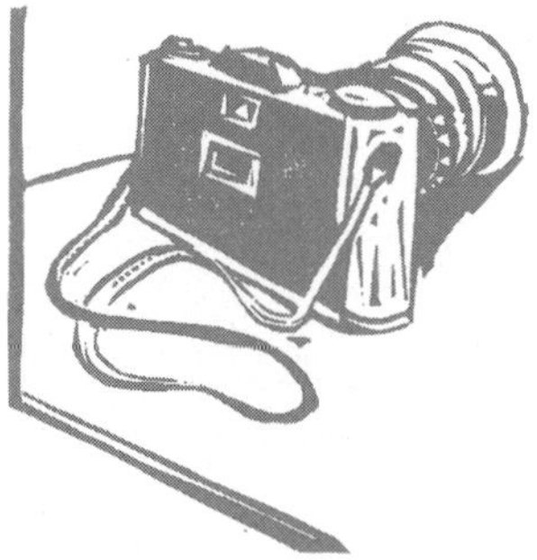

Winona International School of Professional Photography

For wedding and portrait photographers *Downtown Atlanta — 57 Forsyth St. N.W., Atlanta, GA 30303* **Voice:** 404-522-3030; 800-742-7468 **Fax:** 404-614-6401 **E-mail:** 76231.2451@compuserve.com **Contact:** Erin Metcalf, Adm. **Founded:** 1921 **Admission:** Application form **Cost:** $500–$900 for photo courses, $1,100–$1,500 for digital; PPA members receive discounts of $200–$400 **Financial Aid:** Scholarship **Group Size:** 16; 14 for digital

WINONA International School of Professional Photography is the educational arm of the Professional Photographers of America, offering fundamental and advanced training for the wedding/portrait photographer in a series of 3-, 4-, and 5-day workshops. Sessions cover photographic and lighting techniques for wedding/portrait as well as a few commercially oriented classes for the photographer aiming for advertising and corporate clients. Several classes provide guidance about the business aspects of operating a photography studio.

The teachers here are established photographers who have attained advanced certification through the PPA.

GREGORY AIDE

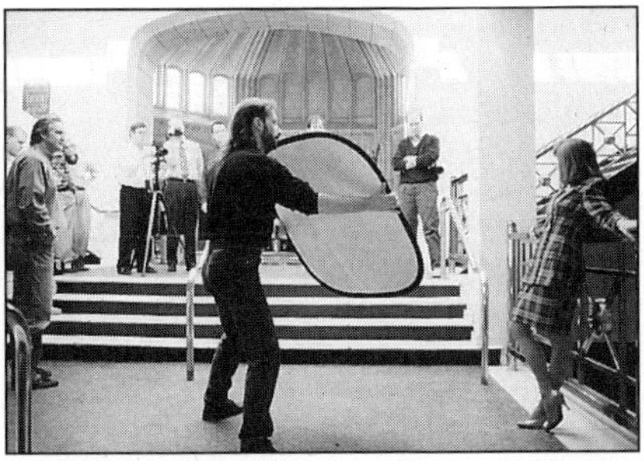

Lighting adjustments at Winona International School of Professional Photography, Atlanta.

The workshops take place in a special teaching studio at PPA headquarters in downtown Atlanta and on location in studios of advanced photographers elsewhere across the country. In addition to traditional photography courses, Winona offers digital photography training (primarily Adobe Photoshop).

Note: The Winona School is affiliated with a group of 17 regional photographer-operated schools providing similar courses in locations from coast to coast. These affiliates bring in experienced PPA instructors for advanced training in wedding/portrait photography. Most courses run only 1 week per year. Each is listed here under its own state.

Hawaii

Kalani Honua Eco-Resort Artist-in-Residence Program

For photographers and artists in selected other disciplines *On SE coast of big island of Hawaii — RR 2, Box 4500, Pahoa, HI 96778* **Voice:** 808-965-7828; 800-800-6886 **E-mail:** kh@ILHawaii.net **Web Site:** www.randm.com/kh.html **Contact:** Richard Koob, Dir. **Founded:** 1980 **Open:** Year-round **Admission:** Application, samples of work, resume **Cost:** $30–$50 per day, plus $25 for 3 meals **Financial Aid:** Stipend

KALANI HONUA is Hawaiian for "the harmony of heaven and earth." The Kalani Honua resort, set on 20 acres of tropical forest and dramatic coastline, is an ecologically oriented hideaway that blends healthy living with the pleasures and beauty of Hawaii's largest conservation area.

The artist-in-residence program provides a stipend covering half the normal accommodation fee for up to 3 months. Performers, writers and visual and folk artists, including photographers, have the use of shared studio spaces and outdoor facilities to work on ongoing projects or to blaze new creative trails. Three healthful meals per day are available, as is private studio space (at an additional fee).

Kalani Honua offers many programs and opportunities for visitors to embrace Hawaiian culture through workshops and recreational activities in year-round tropical weather. Stipends are most readily available during the May–July and September–December seasons. The residency program is a way for this resort to fulfill its educational mission and enhance its appeal by providing an incentive for artists to choose Hawaii as a place to work on their projects. The majority of applications are accepted.

Idaho

Natural Photography

For nature and wildlife photographers *Yellowstone National Park region — 418 Knottingham Dr., Twin Falls, ID 83301* **Voice:** 800-574-2839 **Fax:** 208-733-2839 **Contact:** Douglas Bobb, Dir. **Open:** June–Oct. **Admission:** Application form **Cost:** $1,200 (lodging, meals and local transportation incl.) **Group Size:** 5

NATURALIST AND outdoorsman Douglas Bobb leads small groups of photographers into Yellowstone to photograph plant and animal species and the general splendor of the region. Weekly Monday–Friday trips concentrate on the special features of each season, such as wildflowers and animal families in the spring, or colorful trees in the fall. Participants live in cozy cabins just outside the park boundary and enjoy 3 home-cooked meals daily. Trips in midsummer involve more hiking than in other seasons, in order to get away from the crowds at the most popular locations.

Illinois

Ambient Light Workshops

For fine art, nature and architectural photographers *1-day workshops in Chicago area; weeklong workshops in western states — 5 Tartan Ridge Rd., Hinsdale, IL 60521* **Voice:** 708-325-5464 **Contact:** John Mariana, Dir. **Founded:** 1990 **Open:** Varies **Admission:** Application form **Cost:** $875–$1,500 for weeklong workshops (lodging and transportation incl.); $55–$85 for 1-day programs **Group Size:** 10 on tours; 14 for local workshops with 2 instructors

JOHN MARIANA IS a fine art photographer who teaches a series of photography workshops on natural and architectural forms in the Chicago area and also leads tours to Yosemite, Monument Valley and other destinations in the American West. His workshops, given in all film formats, afford each participant plenty of one-on-one time with instructors. His stated goal is that students finish each workshop with photos they would not have been able to achieve on their own beforehand.

Art Ketchum Workshops

For fashion, figure and boudoir photographers *Chicago and other cities — 2818 W. Barry Ave., Chicago, IL 60618* **Voice:** 312-478-9217; 312-842-1406 **E-mail:** ketch13@aol.com **Contact:** Art Ketchum **Founded:** 1994 **Open:** Varies **Admission:** Application form **Cost:** $249 for weekend workshop; $85 for 1-day seminar **Group Size:** 15

ART KETCHUM'S instruction covers lighting and photographing people in the studio for fashion, glamour, portraiture and boudoir photography. His hands-on workshops give participants the chance to photograph live models using advanced techniques and an array of props.

Ketchum, author of *Profitable Model Photography* and a successful commercial photographer for the past 20 years, helps students in every aspect of glamour photography, from working with models to building a portfolio. These workshops are as valuable for the wedding and portrait studio owner as they are for the commercial or fashion photographer.

ART KETCHUM STUDIOS

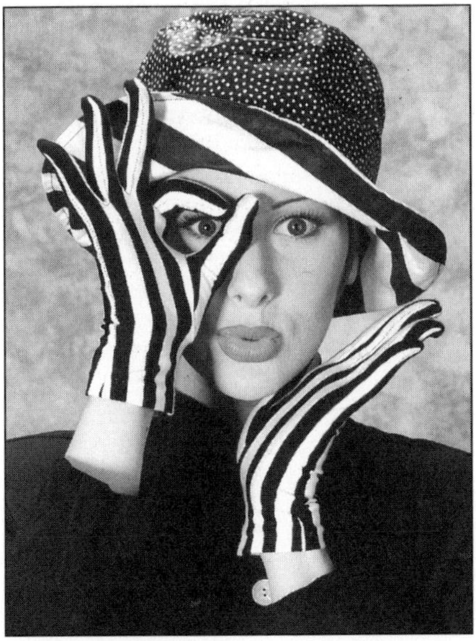

The flair for fashion at Art Ketchum Studios, Chicago.

Center for Photonics Studies

For anyone interested in holography *Lake Forest College, 30 mi. N of Chicago — Lake Forest College, 555 N. Sheridan Rd., Lake Forest, IL 60045* **Voice:** 847-735-5160 **Fax:** 847-735-6291 **E-mail:** crist@lfc.edu **Contact:** Virginia Crist **Founded:** 1972 **Open:** July **Admission:** Application form **Cost:** $900 for Holography Workshop 1; $300 for 1-day tutorial; campus housing $18 per night **Group Size:** 18 **Degree or Certification:** 2 semester-hours credit toward degree **Handicapped Access**

HOLOGRAPHY Workshop 1 introduces the world of holograms—3-dimensional images achieved with lasers—to the uninitiated. Prof. Tung Jeong provides technical and historical information in lectures and demonstrations. By the end of the 5-day workshop, students gather in groups to create their own holograms. A series of 1-day tutorials in more advanced holography techniques takes place during the following week.

Campus housing is available.

Dynamic Graphics Educational Foundation

For photographers and digital artists *6000 North Forest Park Dr., Peoria, IL 61614* **Voice:** 309-688-8800; 800-255-8800 **Fax:** 309-688-5873 **E-mail:** 76377.1475@compuserve.com **Contact:** Brenn Anderson **Founded:** 1977 **Open:** Year-round **Admission:** Application form **Cost:** $895 for 3-day course (lunch incl.); $50 discount for early registration **Group Size:** 11 **Handicapped Access**

THE EDUCATION division of the Dynamic Graphics, Inc., offers a host of graphics, design and production courses at its modern training center in Peoria. The 3-day hands-on course in Adobe Photoshop, offered once each month, teaches the sophisticated use of this versatile program on Macintosh computers. DGEF programs are oriented primarily toward graphics professionals rather than photographers. Those seeking introductory courses in Photoshop should call to check if these courses will satisfy their needs.

Gamma Technical Institute

For photographers and digital artists *River West, Chicago — 314 W. Superior St., Chicago, IL 60610* **Voice:** 312-337-0022 **Fax:** 312-337-3753 **Contact:** Lee Miller or Tom Petrakis **Founded:** 1995 **Admission:** Application form **Cost:** $100–$150 for 3-hr. sessions **Group Size:** 5 **Handicapped Access**

ONE OF THE LARGEST photo labs in the Chicago area, Gamma offers digital training on Macintosh computers in Adobe Photoshop, Live Picture, the Internet and other graphics programs. The 3-hour classes are designed to introduce Gamma's photography customers to the cutting edge of digital technology.

Although Gamma offers 3 separate levels of Photoshop courses, the classes are simply too short to provide the time necessary to gain confidence and practical experience with this intricate software. Gamma's classes are still new as of this writing. Photographers may want to check to see if more in-depth classes have been added.

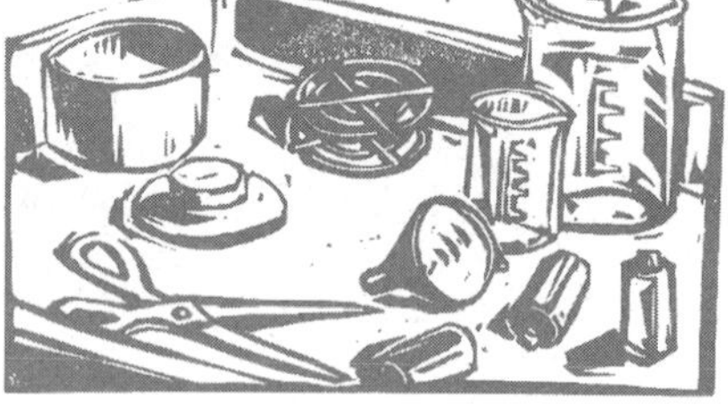

Illinois Workshops

For portrait and wedding photographers *Pere Marquette State Park, Grafton, IL — 229 E. State St., P.O. Box 318, Jacksonville, IL 62650* **Voice:** 217-245-5418 **Fax:** 217-243-6729 **Contact:** Bret Wade **Founded:** 1994 **Open:** 1 week in mid-June **Admission:** Application form **Cost:** $465 for weeklong course (meals incl.) **Financial Aid:** Scholarship **Group Size:** 30–40; classes 10–15

A WINONA-AFFILIATED school (see *Georgia*), the Illinois Workshops offers PPA photographers and others a week of study with 1 of 5 experts in portraiture, weddings or the business of running and promoting a studio. The workshops are held in a rustic 1930s-era lodge overlooking the Mississippi River in Pere Marquette State Park in southern Illinois. Faculty and workshop topics vary from year to year.

MAC University

For photographers, graphic designers and visual artists *1000 N. Halsted St., Chicago, IL 60622* **Voice:** 312-943-9000 **Fax:** 312-943-8342 **E-mail:** macuniv@aol.com **Contact:** Admissions **Founded:** 1992 **Admission:** Application form **Cost:** $260 for 6-hr. class; $1,495 for Bootcamp **Group Size:** 8–10 **Handicapped Access**

CREARE SUPRA OMNIA ("to create above all") is the motto of this computer-training facility, which teaches graphics-oriented programs in addition to Adobe Photoshop. The levels I and II Photoshop classes are 6-hour courses of study in the use of the software package.

For those who want to learn Photoshop in depth, the Bootcamp program consists of 2 sessions of hands-on training per week for 6 weeks—36 hours of training in all. Graduates may audit the class free for a year.

Classes are offered days and evenings, and a technical support crew stands ready to assist all graduates. MAC U. carries the college model to the point of having quizzes, even in the basic course.

Mt. Carroll Center for Applied Photographic Arts

For wedding and portrait photographers and others *2½ hr. W of Chicago — 301 N. Division, Polo, IL 61064* **Voice:** 815-946-2370 **Fax:** 815-946-2520 **Contact:** Doug Bergren, Dir. **Founded:** 1995 **Open:** May–Aug. **Admission:** Application form **Cost:** $475 for most weeklong workshops; $295 for 3-day classes; $675 for 2-week introductory class; fees include lodging and 2 meals per day **Financial Aid:** Scholarship **Group Size:** 6–10

THIS WINONA-AFFILIATED school (see *Georgia*) for PPA members and other wedding and portrait photographers is unique in several ways. It offers only 2 or 3 classes at a time—running from 3 days to 2 weeks—over the course of 3 months in a quiet, out-of-the-way setting. Classes are hands-on and limited to very small groups. Mt. Carroll amplifies the standard menu of wedding, portraiture and studio management instruction with classes in landscape and architectural photography and in several print coloring techniques.

Darkroom facilities allow for a class in fine printing. The 2-week introductory course for early-career photographers is an intensive study in setting up and operating a general photography studio. Mt. Carroll fills a void in the PPA/Winona network by stressing artistic training in addition to the skills needed to sustain a business.

Ragdale Foundation

For photographers, visual artists and artists in selected other disciplines *30 mi. N of Chicago on Lake Michigan — 1260 N. Green Bay Rd., Lake Forest, IL 60045* **Voice:** 847-234-1063 **Fax:** 847-234-1075 **E-mail:** ragdale@artswire.org **Contact:** Peg Laemle, Admissions Coord. **Founded:** 1976 **Open:** Jan.–Apr. and June–mid-Dec. **Admission:** Application ($20), resume, project description, 6–10 slides **Deadlines:** Jan. 15 for June–Dec.; June 1 for Jan.–Apr. **Cost:** $15 per day **Group Size:** 12

RAGDALE HAS BEEN a haven for artists since it was first built by architect Howard Van Doren Shaw a hundred years ago. Today it is the premier midwestern artists' colony, and one of the largest in the nation.

Ragdale has always favored writers and composers, though photographers and other visual artists are welcome. Each resident has a comfortable room and the use of a studio. There is no darkroom. Dinner is the only shared meal—residents prepare breakfast and lunch themselves from ample supplies in the kitchen. Informal evening readings and open studios allow residents, from the Chicago area and around the world, to get to know each other and discuss their work.

The Ragdale House and Barnhouse are set in a beautifully landscaped estate adjacent to a nature preserve near Lake Michigan. Lake Forest is a mile away, and there is an hourly train to Chicago.

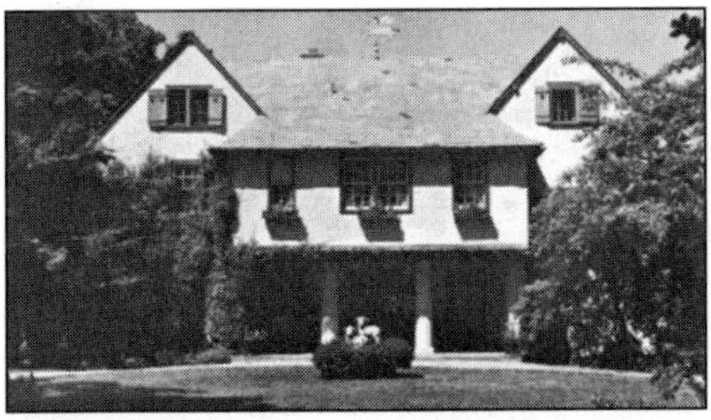

PAUL WHITING

Ragdale Foundation, Lake Forest

School of the Art Institute of Chicago

For student photographers and other artists *Downtown Chicago — 37 S. Wabash Ave., Chicago, IL 60603* **Voice:** 312-443-3783 **E-mail:** bdegenevieve@artic.edu **Web Site:** www.artic.edu/saic **Contact:** Barbara DeGenevieve, Chair **Founded:** 1866 **Open:** 4 terms yearly **Admission:** Application ($45), portfolio, personal statement **Deadlines:** Mar. 15 for fall; Nov. 15 for spring **Financial Aid:** Scholarship; Fellowship; Work/Study **Group Size:** 16 graduate students **Degree or Certification:** BFA, MFA **Handicapped Access**

ONE OF THE VERY best arts education schools in the country, the Art Institute School program blends an interdisciplinary approach into comprehensive artists' training. Photographers learn technical skills and develop their conceptual understanding of the medium simultaneously. Traditional and digital techniques are taught from the very beginning. Superb facilities permit just about any variation on photography or innovative use of technique and media that a student may want to try. All faculty members teach classes at all levels, so that each student can benefit from every teacher. The program is creatively rigorous: personal and artistic growth is expected at every level.

Chicago is one of America's great cities, with an unparalleled architectural heritage and a large and active photographic community. The Art Institute of Chicago, adjacent to the school, houses one of the world's premier photography collections.

Southern Illinois University at Carbondale

For undergraduate and graduate student photographers *Southernmost IL, 100 mi. SE of St. Louis — Dept. of Cinema & Photography, Carbondale, IL 62901* **Voice:** 618-453-2365 **Web Site:** www.siu.edu/departments/cmcma **Contact:** Georgia Wessel, Academic Advisor **Admission:** University application procedures; MA and MFA applicants submit samples **Deadlines:** MFA: Mar. 1 for fall semester; Nov. 1 for spring **Financial Aid:** Scholarship; Fellowship; Stipend; Work/Study **Group Size:** 270 undergraduate, 25 graduate students total **Degree or Certification:** BA, MA, MFA **Handicapped Access**

THE CARBONDALE campus of Southern Illinois University is home to one of the country's major university photography programs. Combined in 1 department with cinema education, the program offers undergraduate specialization in either fine arts or professional photography (commercial and editorial) and a graduate MFA. SIUC boasts excellent facilities and equipment for work in traditional methods and a new media center for digital work. The permanent faculty is diversified enough to provide a thorough education in both the theory and the practice of photography.

The Carbondale campus is set at the edge of the beautiful Shawnee National Forest in southernmost Illinois.

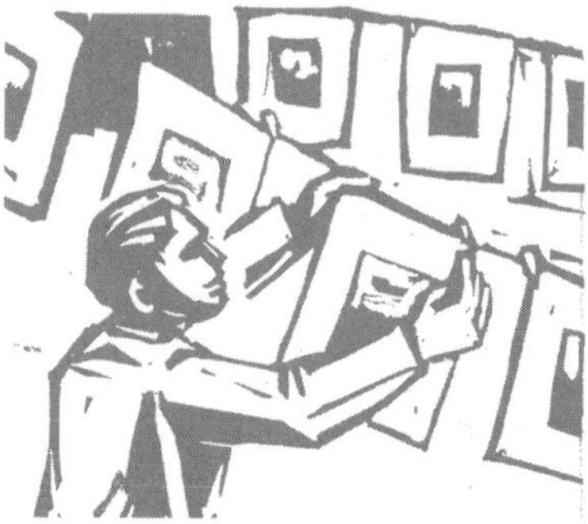

Studios Midwest

For photographers and other visual artists *185 mi. SW of Chicago — P.O. Box 291, Galesburg, IL 61401* **Voice:** 309-344-1177 **Contact:** Mona Tourlentes, Pres. **Founded:** 1986 **Open:** June–Aug. **Admission:** Application, samples of work, references **Deadlines:** Fall **Cost:** Meals and transportation **Group Size:** 4–6 per summer

GALESBURG, ILLINOIS, in America's heartland, opens its arms to 4 to 6 visual artists, including photographers, for 8-week residencies each summer. This is a chance for established as well as emerging artists to devote a summer to a project. Although residents have few requirements other than exhibiting their work, many choose to participate in the arts life of this appreciative and supportive midwestern community. Applicants are selected by a panel of local academic and professional artists.

Indiana

Mary Anderson Center for the Arts

For photographers and artists in selected other disciplines *Southernmost IN, 15 min. from Louisville, KY — 101 St. Francis Dr., Mount St. Francis, IN 47146* **Voice:** 812-923-8602 **Fax:** 812-923-8602 **Contact:** Sarah Yates, Exec. Dir. **Founded:** 1989 **Open:** Year-round **Admission:** Application and sample of work **Deadlines:** Dec. 15 for Brinly-Hardy Fellowship application **Financial Aid:** Fellowship **Group Size:** Up to 6 at a time **Handicapped Access**

A PASSION FOR supporting the arts is alive in southern Indiana, where the Mary Anderson Center invites artists for periods of a few days to 3 months to work on a specific project or idea. A private room and all meals are provided at the Center's headquarters at Loftus House, across from the Mount St. Francis Friary and just 15 minutes from Louisville, Kentucky. Residents work in relative isolation and quiet. There is no darkroom on the premises.

For photographers, the Brinly-Hardy Company, a farm machinery manufacturer, sponsors a 1-week fellowship at the Mary Anderson Center that entails artistic photography of new and antique farm implements at its nearby factory.

Iowa

Mid-America Institute of Professional Photography

For wedding and portrait photographers *University of Northern Iowa, Cedar Falls — 220 E. Second St., Ottumwa, IA 52501* **Voice:** 515-683-7824 **Contact:** Janet Lee, Reg. **Founded:** 1980 **Open:** 1 week in early June **Admission:** Application form **Cost:** $575 (dorm lodging and meals incl.); $100 discount for early registration **Financial Aid:** Scholarship **Group Size:** 200 total; classes 17–25 **Handicapped Access**

THIS WINONA-AFFILIATE school (see *Georgia*) conducts about a dozen 4-day classes each June for local studio photographers who shoot primarily portraits and weddings. Courses cover beginning to advanced photographic techniques, plus creativity and the business of managing a studio.

Kansas

Kansas Professional Photographers School

For wedding and portrait photographers *Bethel College, Newton, KS — 4105 SW 29th St., Topeka, KS 66614* **Voice:** 913-271-5355 **Contact:** Mark Weber **Founded:** 1985 **Open:** 1 week in early June **Cost:** $275 for half-week, $475 for week (lunches incl.); discounts for early registration; dorm rooms $25 per night **Group Size:** 75–100 total; classes 10–20

ANOTHER OF THE Winona affiliates (see *Georgia*), the Kansas program offers 8 classes on varying subjects of interest for the wedding and portrait photographer. The week of study is divided into 2 segments, which allows participants to enroll in 2 half-week programs or 1 program for the whole week. Classes cover portraiture, weddings and business concepts for the local studio photographer.

Kentucky

Great American Photography Weekend

For outdoor and nature photographers *Various natural locations in U.S. and Canada; also Africa, Galapagos, Caribbean — 160 Whirlaway Trail, Corbin, KY 40701* **Voice:** 606-523-1653 **Fax:** 606-523-9112 **Web Site:** www.apogeephoto.com/gapweek1 **Contact:** Diane Fortney, Office Mgr. **Founded:** 1993 **Open:** Year-round **Admission:** Application form **Cost:** $155; $195 extra for 2-day extension; $395 for Extended Event Weekends; $495–$599 for smaller group sessions **Group Size:** Up to 200; 75 for Extended Weekends; 20–25 for smaller group sessions

LARGE GROUPS, such celebrity photographers as John Shaw and Frans Lanting and plenty of corporate sponsorship distinguish GAPW from most photo workshops. Nature and out-

BILL FORTNEY

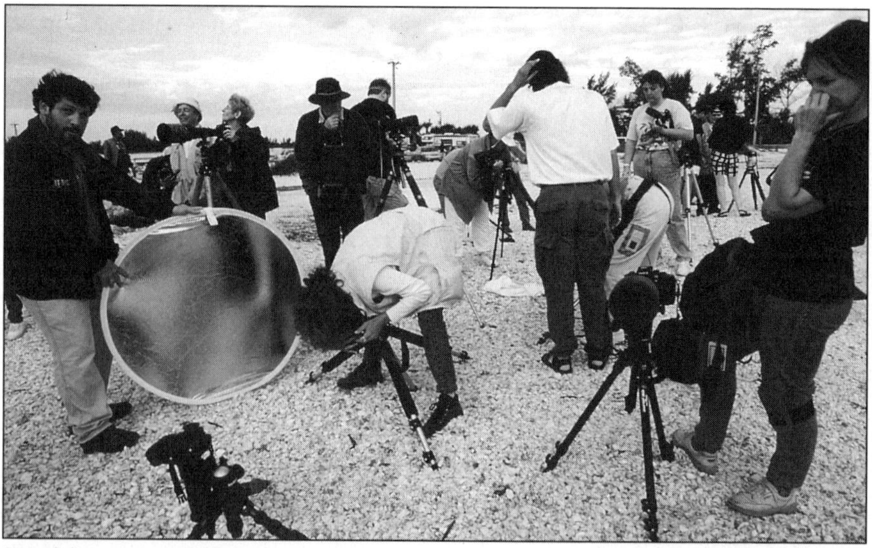

Practicing setup and lighting at Great American Photography Weekend, Corbin, KY.

door photographers gather in beautiful locations in a dozen states plus Canada for weekends of discovery and photography. Typical locations include the National Parks and Monuments of the Southwest, the Smokies, Sanibel and Captiva islands in Florida and the Grand Tetons. The standard GAPW program includes extensive lectures and audiovisual presentations, 1 day of shooting (which includes a free roll of film) and a photo contest. Participants may extend some of the weekends by 2 days for more shooting time.

Other programs include Extended Event Weekends, with 75 participants and 6 instructors ($395), and weekend workshops and 4-day mini-tours for small groups of 20 to 25 ($495 to $599). Some of these smaller workshops are specifically oriented to more advanced photographers, while the mini-tours spend more time shooting with less lecture and instruction. Overseas tours to the likes of Africa and the Galapagos are being planned.

One of the benefits of large group outings is the opportunity to meet and exchange ideas with other photographers from around the country. The lure of a famous instructor, however, could be misleading. With so many photographers gathered for such a short time, it may be nearly impossible to get direct personal guidance from the workshop leader. Fortunately other experienced photographers, some of whom work for sponsoring organizations, are there to support the event and offer help.

GAPW provides a list of hotels where participants can make living arrangements.

Mountain Workshop

For photojournalists *Small town in Kentucky — Garrett Center 215, Western Kentucky University, Bowling Green, KY 42101*
Voice: 502-745-6292 **Fax:** 502-745-6207 **E-mail:** mike.morse@wku.edu **Contact:** Mike Morse, Dir. **Founded:** 1977 **Open:** 4 days in early Oct. **Admission:** Application form **Cost:** $325 **Group Size:** 50

TELLING STORIES with pictures is what photojournalism is all about. In the Mountain Workshop, photographers immerse themselves in a small-town community in the Cumberland River valley for 4 days and emerge with a complete picture story about people, places and a way of life.

This workshop is a high-pressure environment, "a boot camp kind of experience," says director and Western Kentucky University photojournalism professor Mike Morse. Photographers get up early to shoot, bring film in regularly for processing, then go out and shoot some more. The workshop replicates what it is like to work on a daily newspaper, where the ability to talk to and work with people is as important as photographic technique in producing strong individual pictures and convincing stories. The 7-person faculty, all leading photographers and editors, press participants to the limit in daily supervision and long and detailed late-night critiquing sessions.

This workshop has changed quite a few lives, says Morse. It is an extraordinary opportunity for the advanced photojournalism student or early-career pro to experience firsthand the day-to-day life of a working photojournalist.

Maine

Acadia National Park Artist-in-Residence Program

For photographers and artists in selected other disciplines *On the coast, 165 mi. NE of Portland — P.O. Box 177, Bar Harbor, ME 04609* **Voice:** 207-288-5459 **Web Site:** www.acadia.net/anp **Contact:** Coordinator **Open:** Spring and fall **Admission:** Resume, project description, samples of recent work, references **Deadlines:** Jan. 10 **Cost:** Meals and transportation **Group Size:** 1 at a time

IN RECOGNITION OF the important part artists have played in recording and making available to others the beauty of the American landscape, Acadia National Park sponsors an artists-in-residence program for photographers and artists in selected other media. Each artist is provided housing for 2 weeks during the shoulder seasons, in either May or September-October. In return, each is expected to donate a piece of work that is representative of the time spent.

Acadia is the epitome of coastal Maine, a glorious mix of salt air and waves crashing against rocks, with inland lakes and forest trails to inspire any creative soul. Residents live in cottages and are responsible for their own meals and transportation. The short season permits only 4 or 5 residencies in all media per year.

Carina House: A Monhegan Residency

For visual artists who reside in Maine *Monhegan Island, 9 mi. off the central coast — Farnsworth Art Museum, P.O. Box 466, Rockland, ME 04841* **Voice:** 207-596-6457 **Open:** Summer **Admission:** Resume, description of background and expectations for residency, slides of recent work, references **Deadlines:** Mid-Mar. **Financial Aid:** Stipend **Group Size:** 1 at a time

THIS PROGRAM IS designed to enhance the careers of Maine artists by offering the use of Carina House, an artist's summer cottage, and a $500 stipend to 2 individuals for separate 5 weeks' stay on tiny, picturesque Monhegan Island. The Farnsworth Art Museum, which sponsors the residency, wishes to provide living and working space especially to those local artists who could not afford to visit and work on Monhegan on their own. This residency is a solitary creative period, with no overnight visitors or sale of work permitted during the 5 weeks.

Monhegan, reachable only by ferry, has been popular with artists since the 19th century. It is home as well to a tremendous variety of bird life and wildflowers.

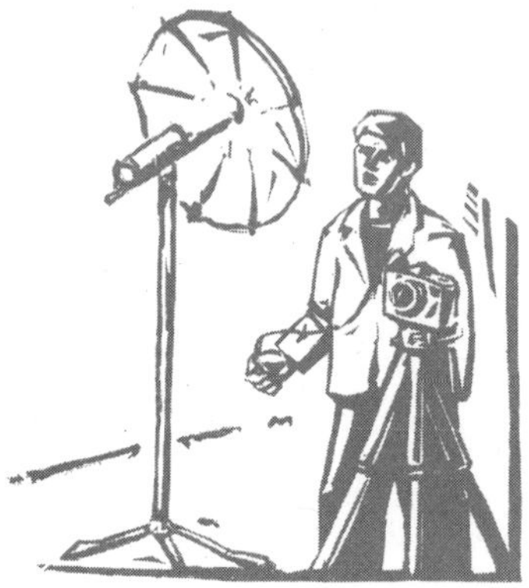

Maine Photographic Workshops

For photographers, filmmakers and digital artists *Coastal town near Camden — Box 200, Rockport, ME 04856* **Voice:** 207-236-8581 **Fax:** 207-236-2558 **E-mail:** MEWorkshop@ aol. com **Web Site:** www.MEWorkshops.com **Contact:** Christy Smith **Founded:** 1973 **Open:** Most of year; summer is main season **Admission:** Application ($35); portfolio for master classes except for ASMP, PPA, NPPA and APA members **Cost:** $400–$800 **Financial Aid:** Scholarship; Work/Study **Group Size:** 100–250; 15 per class **Degree or Certification:** AA, MFA

THE LARGEST OF the summer workshops, MPW offers programs for new photographers and working professionals alike. Participants choose from over a hundred 1-week courses, from basic photographic instruction to master classes taught by some of America's leading professionals. Participants can fine-tune their skills and develop their personal vision and style in art photography, photojournalism, corporate, portraiture or almost anything else.

Many MPW teachers have been leading classes for years and are excellent communicators. Most make themselves available for evening chats or after-class dinners, which can be as valuable as the formal daytime sessions. Some of the better-known teachers at MPW are Bill Allard, Mary Ellen Mark, Arnold Newman and John Sexton.

The facilities at MPW are spread around the tiny seacoast town of Rockport, all within a 10-minute walk of MPW's offices at Union Hall in the town center. A car is not absolutely necessary unless you want to shoot away from Rockport or go exploring.

In addition to the 1-week workshops, MPW offers 2-week basic photography courses, a 6-month fall/spring residency program in practical craft and aesthetic development and 2 new degree programs leading to a 2-year As-

Choosing a Master Class

Some of the most accomplished photographers in the world teach classes and workshops. You can find these courses listed as Master Classes in the catalogues of some of the larger teaching organizations, including the Maine, Palm Beach, and Santa Fe workshops. Master classes offer an extraordinary opportunity to learn from the best. How do you know which one to choose?

A good approach is to go through the list of courses offered and check off all the ones that appeal to you. Whose work have you admired for years? Which images in the catalogue affect you most strongly or do you wish you had taken? Whose style of seeing and making pictures is closest to what you want your own style to be?

Narrow down the list to the few you like best. If you have a good photography bookstore or library nearby, it may be worth your while to look up some of the photographers' other work. Then call the workshop organization and ask about your preferred photographers' teaching abilities. It is important that a teacher know how to transmit knowledge, and not every great visual artist is skilled at communicating ideas in words. Someone at the workshop organization should be able to discuss the teaching strengths and weaknesses of photographers who teach there. You may also be able to ask for references. When in doubt, follow your gut.

Some master classes require a portfolio or membership in a professional organization for admittance. Others are open to anyone. If you know you want to participate in a workshop with a well-known photographer, make your commitment early. Most courses are limited to only 15 or 16 students, and the good ones fill up months ahead.

sociate of Arts degree or an MFA. MPW has special courses for high-school-age photographers as well. A series of travel photography workshops venture off to Mexico, France, Italy or Alaska with the likes of Joyce Tenneson or David Alan Harvey.

Digital is the fastest-growing category of courses at MPW. Several levels of Adobe Photoshop courses are offered, plus multimedia and production for photographers, designers and filmmakers. A whole slate of film and video workshops and a few acting courses complement the still-photography offerings.

Rockport and the surrounding areas around Camden are a delightful place to spend a week, even if you are working hard on your photography. Though the place is swarming with tourists and "blue-dots," as the locals used to call workshop participants, you can always find an idyllic country road leading to a field of Belted Galloway cattle or a rocky bit of Penobscot Bay shoreline.

MPW will arrange accommodations at several levels of comfort and cost, and provides communal dining at a reasonable fee. Its staff will work with participants to arrange a payment plan. The 1-week courses are intense. Participants should not count on spending much time with family or friends during workshop time.

Photo Week Workshops

For landscape photographers *Mt. Desert Island, adjacent to Acadia National Park — P.O. Box 513, Northeast Harbor, ME 04662* **Voice:** 207-276-4062 **Fax:** 207-244-5167 **Contact:** Jack Ledbetter, Dir. **Open:** 2 weeks in summer **Admission:** Application form **Cost:** $485 **Group Size:** 10

LANDSCAPE photography among the hills, forests, and rocky Maine coastline is the subject of Jack Ledbetter's 2 weeklong workshops each summer. Working in color in 35mm or larger formats, photographers spend the week photographing in and around beautiful Acadia National Park, or out on the islands just offshore. Film is processed during the week to allow for rapid feedback and critiquing. Ledbetter is always nearby to provide hands-on instruction to participants. His book of photos, *Maine: The Coast and Islands,* was published by Rizzoli.

Participants are responsible for their own accommodations and meals. Local motels tend to fill quickly, especially in August.

Skowhegan

For photographers and other visual and performing artists *Lake district of central Maine — 200 Park Ave. S., #1116, New York, NY 10003* **Voice:** 212-529-0505 **Fax:** 212-473-1342 **Founded:** 1946 **Open:** June–Aug. **Admission:** Application ($35), 12 slides **Deadlines:** Early Feb. **Cost:** $5,100 (room and board incl.) **Financial Aid:** Fellowship **Group Size:** 65 **Degree or Certification:** Degree credit recognized by many schools

THE 9-WEEK Skowhegan residency program is a stimulating multidisciplinary art experience that has had a major impact on the lives of many artists. In the forested lake district of central Maine, a diverse group of talented early-career and student artists live and work together in an intensive mix of creative effort and thoughtful critical appraisal.

Each summer's faculty consists of about a dozen prominent artists, who are either in residence or serving as visiting artists. (Nan Goldin was a visiting artist in 1996.) Faculty members make regular studio visits to critique participants' work individually. There is also a weekly open critique session in which all participants may share and discuss their work with their peers.

Residents at Skowhegan, mostly in their early 20's to early 40's, live 2 or 3 to a room and have the use of 24-hour studio space and the 300-acre lakefront campus. A darkroom is available for photographers.

Skowhegan was founded by artists for artists. Many of its residents go on to become practicing professionals in a variety of arts media. Residents must commit to the entire 9 weeks of the program. Financial aid is based on need.

Yankee Schooner Cruises

For photographers and painters

On a schooner out of Camden — 5 Sharp's Wharf, P.O. Box 696, Camden, ME 04843 **Voice:** 207-342-5740; 800-255-4449 **Fax:** 207-236-3269 **E-mail:** roseway@midcoast.com **Web Site:** www.midcoast.com/~roseway **Contact:** Neal Parent **Founded:** 1982 **Open:** 1 week in July **Admission:** Application form **Cost:** $700, plus $175 instructor fee **Group Size:** 14 cabins

THE SCHOONER *Roseway* takes 1 week of its summer schedule to cater to photographers and painters on a cruise around Penobscot Bay. Much of the time is spent ashore on coastal islands under the tutelage of photographer and storyteller Neal Parent and watercolorist Carol Sebold. Parent attempts to demystify equipment, and urges photographers to relax and shoot what appeals to them. The use of Polaroid instant slide film allows students to see the results of their labors even while cruising.

Maryland

Latent Image Workshop

For experienced photographer/artists

Just outside Washington, DC — 5613 Johnson Ave., West Bethesda, MD 20817 **Voice:** 301-897-0083 **Contact:** Lowell Anson Kenyon **Founded:** 1974 **Open:** Varies **Admission:** By application

ONLY THE MOST serious of photographers should even consider becoming affiliated with Lowell Anson Kenyon. Kenyon, a longtime teacher and former Smithsonian photographer, is passionately involved in the medium and expects his students to participate on that level. His teaching takes the form of ongoing study over an extended period of time, without preset schedule or standardized fee.

Workshop content involves discussion of issues related to photography, visits to exhibitions and weekend field trips. Kenyon stresses thinking, thinking, thinking about all aspects of photography for his few dozen students, many of whom become long-standing friends. Latent Image is oriented to art photography, primarily in black & white, in small and large formats.

Many students are professionals in other fields whose fervor for photography draws them to study with Kenyon. The long-term commitment of working with Kenyon makes this form of study suitable only to people living in the D.C. area.

Osprey Photo Workshops & Tours

For nature and wildlife photographers *Natural areas in eastern U.S., South America, Africa — 2719 Berwick Ave., Baltimore, MD 21234* **Voice:** 410-426-5071 **Contact:** Irene Hinke Sacilotto **Founded:** 1981 **Open:** Varies **Admission:** Application form **Cost:** $270–$635 for weekend to week-long domestic workshops (lodging incl.); overseas workshops vary **Group Size:** 6

IRENE HINKE SACILOTTO has been photographing wildlife and the natural world for over 20 years. Besides exotic foreign destinations in places like the Falkland Islands and Kenya, she leads workshops in natural areas in the eastern U.S. near her Maryland home. Her workshops specialize in taking very small groups into natural settings for an intimate experience of a place and its denizens.

IRENE HINKE SACILOTTO

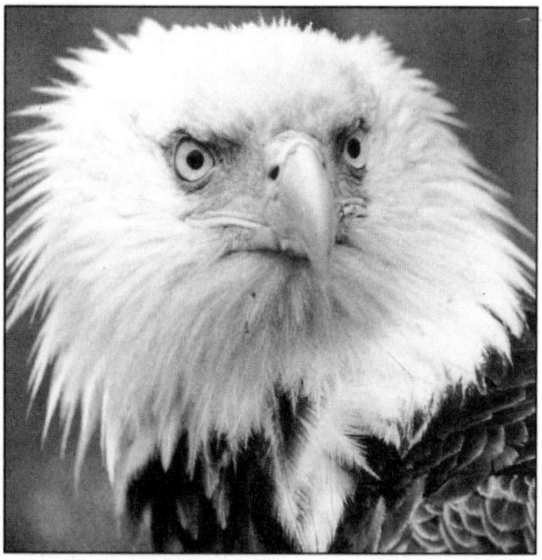

Osprey Photo Workshops & Tours, Baltimore.

Massachusetts

Boston Photo Collaborative

For beginning to advanced photographers *Jamaica Plain section of Boston, SW of downtown — 67 Brookside Ave., Jamaica Plain, MA 02130* **Voice:** 617-524-7729 **Fax:** 617-524-4357 **E-mail:** bosphotoco@aol.com **Contact:** Eliza Brown **Founded:** 1991 **Open:** Year-round **Admission:** Application form **Cost:** $65–$175 for classes and for 1- and 2-day workshops **Group Size:** 8–10

A NONPROFIT organization that makes a special effort to teach photography to city youth and seniors, the Boston Photo Collaborative offers workshops in beginning and advanced photographic techniques and several darkroom processes. Most workshops run for 1 or 2 days on weekends and are taught by Boston-area professional photographers. Subjects include environmental portraiture, location lighting, basic darkroom and platinum printing.

Digital classes are offered in conjunction with Digital Works (see below) downtown.

Cape Cod Photo Workshops

For photographers at all levels *The upper Cape (the "forearm") — P.O. Box 1619, N. Eastham, MA 02651; 135 Oak Leaf Rd.* **Voice:** 508-255-6808 **Fax:** 508-255-6864 **Contact:** Linda McCausland, Program Dir. **Founded:** 1996 **Open:** June–Sept. **Admission:** Application ($25) **Cost:** $235–$395 for 2- to 5-day workshops (lab fee incl.) **Group Size:** 8

THE HISTORIC TOWNS of Wellfleet, Orleans and Chatham provide the setting for this neat summertime series of about thirty-five 1- to 5-day photo workshops. Courses cover a general mix of subjects: black & white and color darkroom, view camera, personal vision and figure and landscape studies. There is even a course on taking pictures while roaming the Cape by bicycle.

Instructors are seasoned working photographers and technicians, mostly from the Boston-area professional community. Meals and lodging are extra. Because summer is the busy tourist season on the Cape, participants should reserve rooms well ahead of time.

Contemporary Artists Center

For photographers and other visual artists *NW corner of MA — 189 Beaver St., North Adams, MA 01247* **Voice:** 413-663-9555 **Contact:** Eric Rudd, Dir. **Founded:** 1990 **Open:** June–Aug. **Admission:** Application with resume or art experience, samples of work **Cost:** Residency: $550 for 1st week, $350 for 2nd, $250 thereafter; room & board $250 per week. Workshops: $550 per week **Financial Aid:** Scholarship; Fellowship **Group Size:** Maximum 25 at a time

IN THE SPACIOUS converted Beaver Mill building in North Adams, a town in northwestern Massachusetts near the Vermont border, visual artists of all kinds can come for 1 to 7 weeks of summer work and contemplation. The Contemporary Artists Center was

Assisting: Education in the Real World

Assisting an established photographer is the single best way to learn what it is really like to be a working professional photographer. Many well-known professionals, such as Eric Meola, Greg Heisler and Anthony Edgeworth, started out working for somebody else.

Assisting may begin with lugging lights and making coffee. Eventually an assistant can become an important part of a busy photographer's creative team and even help manage the business. Assistants build sets and set up lighting. They take detailed light meter readings and make sure cameras are working properly. During a shoot they keep an eye out for errant reflections, specks of dirt or double shadows. They work at the photographer's elbow, attending to details so the photographer can concentrate on making the perfect picture. Photo assistants answer phones, deliver film to the lab and generally make a photo studio or business run more smoothly. They are as much a part of the commercial photography process as operating room nurses are indispensable for surgery.

Photographer's assistants learn by doing, and by watching how an experienced pro works. By the time they are ready to move on and launch their own careers, they have the real-life business experience no school can teach.

founded by artists for artists. It offers the time and space to paint, sculpt or make prints in a variety of media. Besides having time to concentrate on their work, residents enjoy the benefits of sharing ideas with peers and meeting with some of the guest experts—curators, gallery owners and critics—who visit CAC during the summer.

Residencies begin each Sunday. Artists may stay for as many or as few weeks as they wish, though the pricing structure is designed to encourage longer stays. Housing is in the mill building or nearby townhouses, and home-cooked lunches and dinners are included. The large 24-hour studios are open, with separated but not locked spaces, and there is a basic black & white darkroom.

In addition to the residencies, CAC runs a series of weeklong workshops, mostly in the non-photographic visual arts. North Adams is less than an hour from other cultural centers of the Berkshires and is home of the fledgling Massachusetts Museum of Contemporary Art.

CAC admits serious working artists who have made the commitment to art being a central force in their lives. Some grant money is available by application (March 30 deadline), as is additional financial assistance directly from CAC based on need.

Digital Works

For digital imaging professionals *1 block from Boston Common — 355 Boylston St., Boston, MA 02116* **Voice:** 617-267-4900 **Fax:** 617-266-6946 **E-mail:** GJarvis@bostonphoto.com **Web Site:** www.bostonphoto.com/bpi **Contact:** Guy Jarvis **Founded:** 1995 **Admission:** Application form **Cost:** $325 per day **Group Size:** 6

DIGITAL WORKS is one of a new breed of educational facilities, an adjunct to a traditional photo lab/digital service bureau. DW teaches only computer-oriented classes geared to the working "imaging professional." Subjects include Adobe Photoshop, Live Picture, Kodak Photo CD, and classes in scanning, prepress and retouching.

Scheduled classes take place over only 4 to 8 classroom hours. This time frame may be too short to go beyond the rudiments of digital imaging. Longer custom classes can be arranged. DW offers students extra value for participating in classes, such as free or discounted prints or reduced prices on computer rental.

Fine Arts Work Center in Provincetown

For up-and-coming photographers and artists in selected other disciplines *Tip of Cape Cod — 24 Pearl St., Provincetown, MA 02657* **Voice:** 508-487-9960 **Fax:** 508-487-8873 **Contact:** Michael Wilkerson, Exec. Dir. **Founded:** 1968 **Open:** Oct. 1–May 1 **Admission:** Application ($35), samples of work **Deadlines:** Feb. 1 **Cost:** Transportation only **Financial Aid:** Fellowship; Stipend **Group Size:** 20

PHOTOGRAPHERS, writers and visual artists in the emerging stages of their careers are the beneficiaries of these 7-month fellowships on Cape Cod. Each artist, selected by a jury of professionals, receives an apartment with separate studio, the use of a basic darkroom, and a monthly stipend of $375 plus a materials fee. The goal of the Work Center, as articulated by its founding artists and patrons, is to support creative freedom among a group of peers as the best catalyst for artistic growth. This is a competitive program, with a 25-year reputation for excellence and only 10 spaces available for visual artists in all media.

Provincetown has a long history as an arts colony. Situated at the end of the hook that is Cape Cod, surrounded by ocean and the sand dunes of the Cape Cod National Seashore, it sports a busy summer beach and vacation life. The winters, however, are quiet, allowing young artists at the Work Center to breathe life into their creative vision among equally dedicated contemporaries.

Fitchburg State College Photoshop Workshop

For photographers interested in digital imaging *50 mi. NW of Boston — Division of Graduate & Continuing Education, 160 Pearl St., Fitchburg, MA 01420* **Voice:** 508-665-3181 **Fax:** 508-665-3658 **E-mail:** dgce@fsc.edu **Contact:** Joanne Walsh **Founded:** 1996 **Open:** Spring–summer **Cost:** $500 **Group Size:** 15 **Handicapped Access**

FITCHBURG STATE College offers this program, new as of this writing, to photographers who want a solid introduction to the digital imaging world. Peter Laytin, an experienced photography teacher, leads students through the ins and outs of Adobe Photoshop over 3 full days, Friday to Sunday. Students should have basic Macintosh skills.

Sponsorship by the college makes this program more affordable than similar training offered elsewhere. Add in the cost of accommodations, however, if you're too far away for a daily commute.

Hallmark Institute of Photography

For career-oriented photography students *Pioneer Valley, 35 mi. N of Springfield — P.O. Box 308, Turner's Falls, MA 01376* **Voice:** 413-863-2478 **Fax:** 413-863-4118 **E-mail:** hallmark@tiac.net **Web Site:** www.hallmark-institute.com **Contact:** Tammy Murphy, Dir. of Admissions **Founded:** 1975 **Open:** Sept.–June **Admission:** Application ($25), references **Cost:** $10,450, plus $2,500 materials **Financial Aid:** Scholarship; Work/Study **Group Size:** 80–100; classes 10–14 **Degree or Certification:** Certificate **Job Placement:** Yes **Handicapped Access**

AT THE FOOT of the Berkshires in rural north central Massachusetts, the Hallmark Institute conducts a 10-month program that gives aspiring photographers the training, skills and knowledge to enter the profession.

The intensive course, taught by working professionals, touches on many aspects of photography including photojournalism, retouching and digital (thorough instruction in Adobe Photoshop). Its primary focus, however, is on portraiture and commercial work because these are the fields most likely to lead to gainful employment. Instruction in the business of running a studio, in addition to photography classes, is designed to enable students to start up and sustain their own businesses right away.

Hallmark Institute operates out of its own custom-designed building in Turner's Falls, a woodsy New England town near the Vermont border and the Connecticut River, and not far from Amherst and Northampton (the 5-college area). Students are responsible for providing their own accommodations and meals.

Interactive Factory Workshops

For photographers and digital artists *Boston waterfront — 386 Congress St., Boston, MA 02210* **Voice:** 617-426-0609 **E-mail:** workshops@ifactory.com **Web Site:** www.ifactory.com **Contact:** Jean Wallace **Founded:** 1994 **Admission:** Application form **Cost:** $350 for 1 day; $600 for 2 days; 20% discount for college students and ASMP members

INTERACTIVE FACTORY, located near the Tea Party ship on the Boston waterfront, is a digitally based design house and computer-training center oriented toward the graphic arts, including photography. It offers a 1-day introductory class in Adobe Photoshop and 2-day intermediate and advanced courses. Other courses cover multimedia, digital design and video, and Internet topics including Web site design.

Medicine Wheel Artists' Retreat

For photographers and artists in selected other disciplines *Rural setting in central New England — P.O. Box 1088, Groton, MA 01450* **Voice:** 508-448-3717 **Fax:** 508-448-3717 **E-mail:** medwheel@tiac.net **Contact:** Cheri Amarna **Founded:** 1989 **Open:** Late summer **Admission:** Application, 4–10 slides, project description **Cost:** $175 per week (meals incl.) **Financial Aid:** Scholarship; Work/Study **Group Size:** 20 per week

QUIET TIME FEEDS the artist's muse. Medicine Wheel provides a quiet retreat for artists in all fields, from early-career part-time professionals to the well established, during late August and September.

The site of this free-form retreat varies from year to year, from a rustic summer camp to a tranquil abbey. Whatever the location, 3 prepared meals a day for up to 3 weeks afford artists time to work virtually uninterrupted on personal projects. Not all of the possible sites are equipped with darkrooms, but commercial film processing can be found not too far away. The founders of Medicine Wheel believe all artists need a certain amount of retreat time to dedicate to the search that is at the heart of artistic creation.

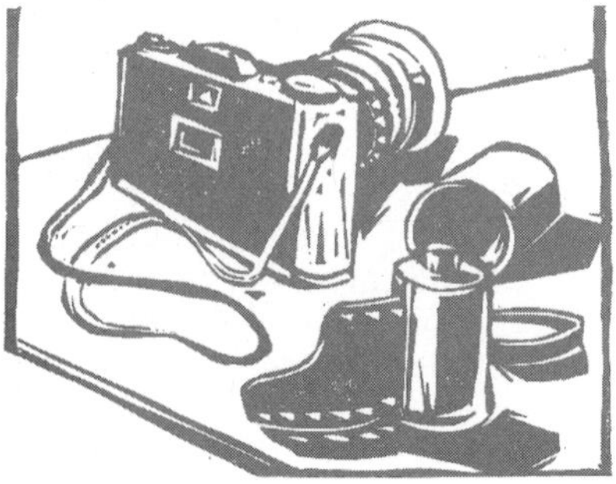

Nantucket Island School of Design & the Arts

For photographers and artists in all media *30 mi. off Cape Cod — 23 Wauwinet Rd., P.O. Box 958, Nantucket, MA 02554* **Voice:** 508-228-9248 **Fax:** 508-228-2451 **Contact:** Kathy Kelm, Dir. **Founded:** 1973 **Open:** Residencies: Mar. 1–June 30, Sept. 1–mid Dec.; Courses: summer. **Admission:** Residencies: application, resume, letter of intent, 5–10 slides, references; Summer Institute: application, resume, statement of interest. **Cost:** Residencies: $250–$350 per week; $600–$800 per month; plus utilities and studio rental. College courses: $330 per month or $545 for summer, plus lab fees. Institutes: $500 (lab fee incl.). **Financial Aid:** Work/Study; Scholarship **Degree or Certification:** Degree credit through Massachusetts College of Art

THE TOWN OF Nantucket is a classic bit of New England history, with cobblestone streets and the elegant architecture of a 19th-century whaling capital. Rejuvenated as a summer resort, this small (14-mile-long) island draws visitors from around the world to enjoy its timeless village ambiance and ocean breezes. Artists especially have flocked here for decades. So it is no wonder that the Nantucket Island School of Design & the Arts has created a residency program and educational facility to support artists of all types and to encourage creative expression in many media.

The residencies, which take place in 6-week to 2-month segments in the spring and fall, offer the solitude of Nantucket in the off-season. Photographers live in NISDA's Harbor Cottages (at $600–$800 per month without meals)

and have the use of darkrooms and a 24-hour studio in which to work, plus the island's beaches, moors and picture-perfect communities for inspiration.

Summer offerings during the bustling tourist season in July and August include weekly evening classes, as well as full-week "Institute" courses in arts and culture. There is also a selection of college credit courses, taught in two 4-week segments, that immerse students in a multidisciplinary approach to artistic endeavor. Much of the teaching takes place outdoors to benefit from the rich natural and man-made living museum that is Nantucket.

New England Institute of Professional Photography

For wedding and portrait photographers *Falmouth, on Cape Cod — 659 Sandy Lane, Warwick, RI 02886* **Voice:** 401-738-3778 **Fax:** 401-732-0852 **Contact:** Sal Genuario, Dir. **Founded:** 1961 **Open:** 1 week in Mar. **Deadlines:** mid-Feb. **Cost:** $700–$820 (lodging, meals and PPANE membership incl.); $70 discount for current members **Group Size:** 340 maximum; 20–30 per class

ONE OF THE PPA-affiliated regional schools (see *Georgia*), the New England Institute takes over the Sea Crest resort on Cape Cod for 1 intensive week of photography instruction in the early spring. Master PPA instructors teach intermediate and advanced wedding, portrait and related studio photography skills. One course focuses on marketing and the business of running a small studio. Others teach traditional and digital print enhancement, and the specialized use of digital imaging, primarily for retouching.

New England School of Photography

For student photographers *Kenmore Square — 537 Commonwealth Ave., Boston, MA 02215* **Voice:** 617-437-1868; 800-676-3767 **Fax:** 617-437-0261 **Contact:** Martha Hassell **Founded:** 1968 **Admission:** Application **Cost:** $8,400 plus about $3,500 expenses per year. Applied Photography Program: $3,400, plus about $1,500 expenses **Financial Aid:** Scholarship **Group Size:** 120 total; classes 16 maximum **Degree or Certification:** Certificate **Job Placement:** Yes

THE 2-YEAR NESOP Professional Photography Program is designed for students who want a career in still photography. It begins with basic black & white craft in 35mm and 4 x 5 formats. Creative development follows as technical proficiency grows, leading students to major in 1 of 7 photographic categories (such as photojournalism,

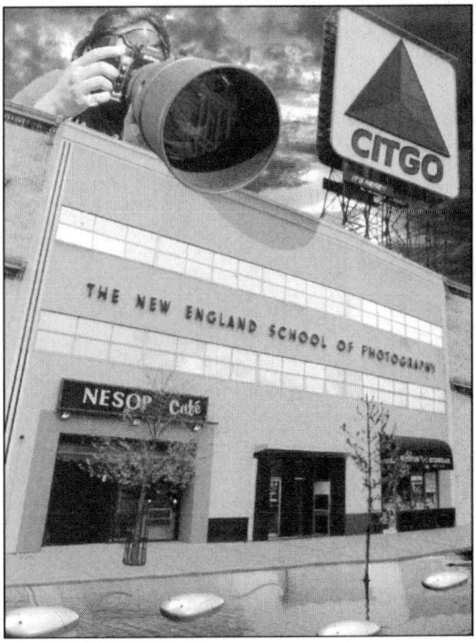

CRAIG ROTH

Digital composite image, New England School of Photography, Boston.

wedding and portraiture or commercial) during the second year.

The emphasis here is on professionalism. The faculty are all working photographers and photography consultants. Courses in sound business practices—from portfolio construction to pricing, to creating a business plan—are required of all students.

NESOP occupies 2 floors in Kenmore Square, adjacent to Boston University (baseball's Fenway Park is nearby). Besides classrooms, there are 3 studios, 26 individual color darkrooms, professional black & white and color film processors, a computer lab and an exhibit gallery. Students are responsible for their own accommodations and meals (budget carefully: Boston is not cheap).

The school also offers 1-night-a-week evening classes in a variety of photographic subjects. The Applied Photography Program is a 24-week professional training course taught evenings and Saturdays for those who cannot attend a full-time program. The 12-week digital imaging evening class costs about $600.

Photographic Resource Center

For serious photographers in various specialties *At Boston University, Kenmore Square — 601 Commonwealth Ave., Boston, MA 02215* **Voice:** 617-353-0700 **Fax:** 617-353-1662 **E-mail:** prc@bu.edu **Web Site:** web.bu.edu/trc **Contact:** Lizzie Fischbein, Admin. Dir. **Founded:** 1977 **Open:** Sept.–May **Admission:** Application form **Cost:** Up to $90 for 1 day; $200 for weekend; digital courses higher **Group Size:** 12

PHOTOGRAPHIC RESOURCE Center is a nonprofit membership organization that serves the photographic community of the Boston area. Its primary focus is on the art of photography, which is broadly interpreted to include landscape, photojournalism, portraiture and digital applications. The workshop agenda introduces different photographers and subjects from year to year, providing an ever-changing parade of photographic points of view and styles. Distinguished photographers, such as Constantine Manos, Duane Michaels and Olivia Parker, lead 1-day or weekend courses on their own personal approach to the medium. An irregular slate of digital courses at a downtown Boston facility teaches artistic as well as purely functional uses of computer imaging.

The PRC is keenly aware of its obligations to its membership and tends to offer service courses on such subjects as how to build a portfolio or publish a photographic book. It encourages members to submit images for display in its gallery, which also brings in exhibits by nationally known photographic artists. Loosely affiliated with Boston University and housed in the basement of a BU auditorium, it has no darkroom facilities.

Photography Workshops International

For serious black & white photographers *Darkroom workshops in Springfield; location workshops on Block Island and in the Southwest — 114 Bellevue Ave., Springfield, MA 01108* **Voice:** 413-739-3480; 800-563-9156 **Fax:** 413-739-0033 **Contact:** Jack Holowitz and Steve Sherman, Dirs. **Founded:** 1984 **Open:** Varies **Admission:** Application **Cost:** $350 for 2-day, $450 for 3-day darkroom workshops; $695 for location workshops **Group Size:** Up to 20 on location; limit of 8 in darkroom

THE ZONE SYSTEM of black & white photography is the central theme of photographers Jack Holowitz and Steve Sherman's 5 or 6 annual workshops. Participants spend either a couple of days on figure studies and printing technique in Holowitz's Springfield studio, or a week on Block Island or in the Southwest working on perception and fine art technique.

About half the participants in location workshops use large-format cameras, though any kind of equipment is welcome. Those attending darkroom workshops should have prior darkroom experience.

Michigan

Alden B. Dow Creativity Fellowships

For photographers and other creative individuals in the arts, sciences and humanities *Central MI — Northwood University, 3225 Cook Rd., Midland, MI 48640* **Voice:** 517-837-4478 **Fax:** 517-837-4468 **Founded:** 1979 **Open:** 8 weeks in summer **Admission:** Application ($10), project description, resume, references, samples of work **Deadlines:** Dec. 31 **Cost:** None **Financial Aid:** Fellowship; Stipend **Size-Attendees:** 4

THE ALDEN B. DOW Fellowships offer creative people in the arts, sciences, education and business a summer's worth of time to nurture innovative projects. Four fellows are chosen each year to spend 8 weeks of independent study on an idea that has the potential for impact in its field. Fellows must present the results of their efforts to a selected audience at the completion of their residency. Past residents have spent their time on such diverse projects as filmmaking technology, a writing program for prisoners and performance art. There are no specific requirements concerning the age or academic qualifications of applicants.

Fellows live in their own furnished apartments on the campus of Northwood University and receive a $750 stipend plus lunches and a per diem for other meals. Travel expense to Midland from locations within the U.S. is covered as well.

Alden B. Dow (1904–1983) was a distinguished architect (a student of Frank Lloyd Wright) and heir to the Dow Chemical fortune. A native of Michigan and eventually its architect laureate, his passion for the creative process helped in the conception and creation of Northwood University. This program supports innovation and endeavor in the spirit of Dow.

Gerlach Nature Photography

For nature photographers *Seminars around U.S.; nature workshops on Michigan's Upper Peninsula — P.O. Box 259, 3749 E. Cold Springs Rd., Chatham, MI 49816* **Voice:** 906-439-5991 **Fax:** 906-439-5144 **Contact:** Bill Jasko, Adm. **Founded:** 1985 **Open:** Seminars: Mar.–May. Tours: varies **Admission:** Application form **Cost:** 1-day seminars $70; workshops $425 **Size-Attendees:** 18 for nature workshop; 125 for seminar

JOHN AND BARBARA Gerlach are active nature photographers with publication credits from many national nature and wildlife magazines. Together they teach nature photography in seminars and workshops. Their 1-day seminars, which they present in cities around the country in the spring, offer a tightly organized agenda of lecture and demonstration on equipment, exposure, light and composition.

Weeklong workshops at Pictured Rocks National Lakeshore in Michigan are held during the most colorful times of year, in summer and autumn. These workshops are heavy on instruction, with the Gerlachs sharing their intimate knowledge of the terrain and local plant and animal species. Lodging information is provided.

The Gerlachs also lead several international photo tours, including locations in Africa and South America, under the aegis of Voyagers International (see *New York*).

Great Lakes Institute of Photography

For wedding and portrait photographers *At Northwood University in Midland, MI — 19276 Eureka Rd., Southgate, MI 48195* **Voice:** 313-283-8433 **Fax:** 313-283-0950 **E-mail:** ppofmich@aol.com **Contact:** Ron Tocco **Founded:** 1996 **Open:** June **Cost:** $595 (meals and dorm room incl.); digital class $1,045; $100 discount for early registration **Size-Attendees:** 200; classes 15–30

THIS WINONA-AFFILIATE school (see *Georgia*), in its first season as of this writing, offers 8 classes for the wedding and portrait photographer of all levels. Besides classes in photographic technique, there is a class in retouching and an introductory session in Adobe Photoshop.

Howard Bond Workshops

For photographers working in black & white *Michigan; Colorado for field workshops — 1095 Harold Circle, Ann Arbor, MI 48103* **Voice:** 313-665-6597 **Web Site:** www.apogeephoto.com/howard_bond.html **Contact:** Howard Bond **Founded:** 1976 **Open:** Varies **Admission:** Application form **Cost:** $145 for 2 days; $195 for 3 days; $45 for 1-day workshops

BLACK & WHITE photography using a view camera or other formats is Howard Bond's specialty. He teaches the Zone system and the intricacies of working with the view camera in a 1-day workshop. His 3-day outdoor workshop in the Great Sand Dunes National Monument in Colorado is a field study in photographic technique. Bond also offers darkroom workshops where participants (limited to 11 people) spend 2 days refining the process of making fine black & white prints.

Bond has been photographing for over 50 years and teaching photography for over 20. His work is in the collections of many museums.

Meteor Technology Education

For photographers interested in digital imaging *North suburban Detroit — 1099 Chicago Rd., Troy, MI 48083* **Voice:** 810-597-1702; 888-638-3671 **Fax:** 810-583-6287 **E-mail:** suzanne_bolter@meteor.com **Web Site:** www.meteor.com **Contact:** Suzanne Bolter **Founded:** 1994 **Open:** Year-round **Admission:** Application form **Cost:** $300 per 6-hr. class **Size-Attendees:** 8 **Handicapped Access**

PHOTOGRAPHERS AND graphic designers in the Detroit area can learn Adobe Photoshop and a series of design-oriented software at Meteor in Troy, a short distance north of the city. Photoshop classes are offered at the beginning, intermediate and advanced levels. Each level runs 6 hours and can be taken in a single day or broken up into 2 evening sessions. Customized classes and special instruction are also available.

Midwest Photographic Workshops

For photographers at all levels *Suburban Detroit; darkroom classes in Detroit's East English Village — 28830 W. 8 Mile Road, Farmington Hills, MI 48336* **Voice:** 810-471-7299 **Fax:** 810-542-3441 **Contact:** Alan Lowy and C. J. Elfont, Dirs. **Founded:** 1980 **Open:** Year-round **Cost:** $65–$125 for 1-day workshops; $135–$175 for weekend; $195 for 5-week darkroom class; travel workshops up to $1,295 per week

WORKING PHOTOGRAPHERS Alan Lowy, C. J. Elfont and Bryce Denison offer instruction to photographers at all levels in the Detroit area. The majority of their 60-plus workshops take place over a single day or a weekend, with weekend and longer field trips to surrounding areas.

Courses cover figure studies, weddings and fashion, nature, plus commercial and darkroom techniques. A few of their field trips, up to a week in length, venture out to sites in southern Canada, the Smoky Mountains of Tennessee and the West. Most classes are small (a limit of 8 in the studio workshops), and prices are reasonable.

Photo Explorer Tours

For nature and travel photographers *China, Turkey, Antarctica and elsewhere — 22111 Cleveland, #211, Dearborn, MI 48124* **Voice:** 313-561-1842; 800-315-4462 **Fax:** 313-561-1842 **E-mail:** decoxphoto@aol.com **Contact:** Dennis Cox **Founded:** 1981 **Admission:** Application form **Cost:** $1,850 (all land expenses incl.) for 2 weeks in China; other tours vary **Size-Attendees:** 10–16

CHINA USED TO BE the exclusive focus of Dennis Cox's Photo Explorer Tours, and his vast knowledge of that country still makes him an outstanding choice for photographers who wish to visit and photograph there. These are not tourist-with-a-camera trips, but carefully planned itineraries designed to maximize each photographer's opportunity to see and shoot in the world's most populous country. Besides visiting the best sites with Cox and Chinese photographer Liu Liqun, the tours are flexible enough to allow individuals to separate from the group for a while to pursue individual interests.

In upcoming years, Cox is planning tours to Antarctica, Turkey, Myanmar (Burma) and New Zealand. All will be organized with the same concern for finding the right places and the right conditions for getting the best possible pictures.

Rod Planck Presents

For nature photographers
Michigan's Upper Peninsula; 1-day seminar at locations around the U.S — P.O. Box 106, Metamora, MI 48455 **Voice:** 810-678-2141 **Contact:** Marlene Planck **Founded:** 1994 **Open:** Selected weeks in May–Oct. **Admission:** Application form **Cost:** Workshops: $500 plus $39–$45 per day for lodging; 1-day seminars: $59 **Size-Attendees:** 12

NATURE PHOTOGRAPHY is Rod Planck's passion, experience, and the subject of his seminars and workshops. The weeklong workshops—in Hiawatha National Forest and Pictured Rocks National Lakeshore on the Upper Peninsula of Michigan—are designed for photographers at any level who want to enhance their skills. Planck, who has a reputation as a terrific teacher, personally instructs students in the art and technique of nature photography. Special attention is paid to the use of cameras and lenses, how to use the different qualities of light and composing pictures of landscapes, flowers and birds.

The 1-day seminar is a tightly organized presentation that covers equipment basics, light and exposure, composition and creativity and tips for nature photographers. Planck's 20-plus years of photographing the natural world have yielded publication credits in *Audubon, Sierra,* and other magazines, as well as calendars and educational materials.

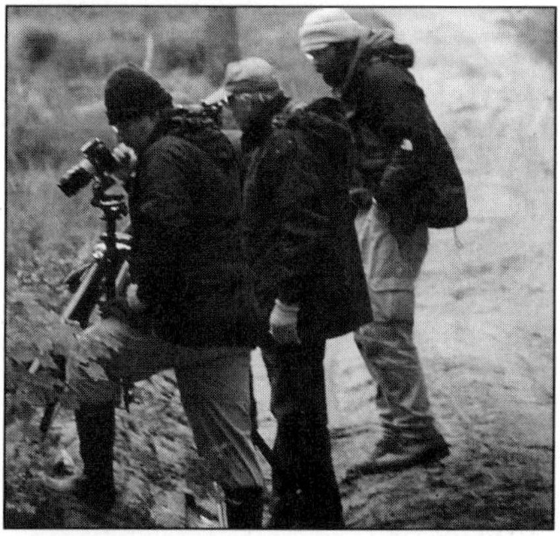

ALLAN STAVE

Setting the shot with Rod Planck, nature photographer, Metamora, MI.

Summer Weekend of Photography

For beginning to advanced photographers *At Hope College in Holland, MI — 380 Montezuma Rd., Benton Harbor, MI 49022* **Voice:** 616-925-8238 **Contact:** Sylvia Schlender **Founded:** 1974 **Open:** 1 weekend in midsummer **Cost:** Under $100; $10–25 for some seminars and field trips; $100 for meals and dorm lodging **Size-Attendees:** Up to 700

THE SOUTHWESTERN Michigan Council of Camera Clubs sponsors this amiable gathering at Hope College, near the shores of Lake Michigan. Some 25 seminars, workshops and field trips offer advice and instruction to photographers from the untrained enthusiast to the aspiring pro. Local professionals and the occasional well-known national figure teach and present their own work. (George Lepp taught in 1996.)

Minnesota

Electronic Imaging Center

For photographers and digital artists *15 S. 9th St., Suite 100, Minneapolis, MN 55402* **Voice:** 612-673-8980 **Fax:** 612-673-8988 **Contact:** David Erickson **Admission:** Application form **Cost:** $295 for Photoshop start-up; $595 for Photoshop in-depth

THE EICENTER, as it's known, offers courses in Adobe Photoshop and other imaging and graphics software. It holds frequent seminars to introduce the rudiments of the programs, a basic Photoshop class (4 mornings over 2 weeks), and an advanced class (2 full days). Instructor Doug Meisner has been working with imaging on the computer for longer than just about anyone.

St. Cloud State University Summer Photo Imaging Workshop

For photographic educators and advisors *70 mi. NW of Minneapolis — 720 Fourth Ave. S., St. Cloud, MN 56301* **Voice:** 612-255-2107 **Fax:** 612-654-5122 **Contact:** Wayne Braith and John Gammel **Founded:** 1974 **Open:** Two 10-day sessions during summer **Admission:** Application form **Cost:** $300 **Financial Aid:** Stipend **Size-Attendees:** 20–24 **Handicapped Access**

PHOTOGRAPHY TEACHERS, advisors and counselors, and those who would like to be photographic educators, can stay up-to-date on recent developments in black & white and color materials through this specialized course. A combination of lectures and lab work gives each participant an overview of what is happening in the industry, with plenty of chance to experiment with photographic materials.

Among photo workshops, this is the only one directed specifically at those who teach and guide photographers, rather than at photographers themselves.

On-campus housing and meals are available. Some materials are provided by sponsors, such as 3M, Agfa and Ilford, and a $200 stipend check is sent to each student after completion of the course.

Superior/Gunflint Photography Workshops

For editorial and fine art photographers interested in wilderness photography *Wilderness areas in northern MN — P.O. Box 19286, Minneapolis, MN 55419* **Voice:** 612-824-2999 **Fax:** 612-825-3075 **Contact:** Layne Kennedy **Founded:** 1990 **Open:** 1 week in winter, 1 week in summer **Admission:** Application form **Cost:** $785 (lodging and meals incl.) **Size-Attendees:** 8

EACH WINTER AND summer, magazine photographer Layne Kennedy takes photographers on an adventure to the wilderness of northern Minnesota. Participants learn to drive a dogsled across the frozen landscape or to sea-kayak in Lake Superior while Kennedy provides guidance on how to approach and shoot a picture story, and how to market it to publications. Participants should be healthy but do not need to be especially rugged or fit.

Kennedy's work has been featured in *Smithsonian, Outside* and *Backpacker* magazines. Film is processed the next-to-last day of the workshop for critiquing.

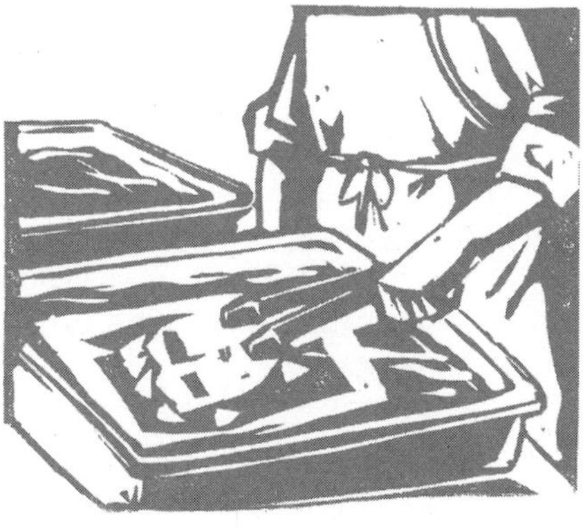

Missouri

Missouri Photo Workshop

For photojournalists *A different Missouri town each year — University of Missouri School of Journalism, 27 Neff Annex, Columbia, MO 65201* **Voice:** 314-882-4442 **Fax:** 314-884-4999 **E-mail:** jourlab@muccmail.missouri.edu **Founded:** 1949 **Open:** 1 week in early fall **Admission:** By portfolio: 20 prints or slides and letter of reference **Deadlines:** Early Aug. **Cost:** $400 **Financial Aid:** Scholarship **Size-Attendees:** 48 **Handicapped Access**

SERIOUS PHOTOJOURNALISTS and a faculty of America's leading news photographers and editors gather each fall to document the life of a small Missouri town and learn about photojournalism. It is a total-immersion week: observing, researching, shooting, editing and laying out picture stories that tell the tale of the people of the community and how they live. The faculty changes from year to year; it has included Tom Kennedy, director of photography for *National Geographic,* and staff photographers from papers such as the *San Francisco Examiner, Minneapolis Tribune,* and *Boston Globe.*

The Missouri Photo Workshop was born a half century ago, inspired by the Farm Services Administration photos of the '30s. Those gritty, content-rich photos by the likes of Walker Evans seemed the model of all that photojournalism should be. Today the workshop strives to enhance photojournalistic skills and knowledge for those photographers who retain a passion for telling stories in pictures.

Washington University Summer Art Study in Florence

For photography students

Florence, Italy — Campus Box 1031, One Brookings Dr., St Louis, MO 63130 **Voice:** 314-935-8406 **Fax:** 314-935-8412 **E-mail:** sjstremb@art.wustl.edu **Contact:** Stan Strembicki **Founded:** 1879 **Open:** June **Admission:** Application form **Cost:** $1,325 for Florence program **Financial Aid:** Fellowship **Size-Attendees:** 12 in Florence **Degree or Certification:** BFA, MFA

WASHINGTON University's 3½-week summer program in Florence affords up to 12 students the opportunity to photograph the natural and urban landscape of northern Italy. The emphasis here is on black & white shooting. Students are encouraged to use the darkroom only as much as is necessary to make work prints for class discussion. Optional trips to other parts of Tuscany and a close working relationship with the faculty make this a great chance to improve your photography while visiting this glorious region.

The university's School of Art offers undergraduate degrees and an MFA for those photographers who want to work out their own creative relationship with photography. The major is structured loosely enough to allow individual pursuit within the framework of a well-equipped photography department at a major university.

Montana

Allaman's Montana Photographic Adventures

For serious outdoor and wildlife photographers *80 mi. S. of Missoula — 185 Red Dog Trail, Darby, MT 59829* **Voice:** 406-821-3763 **Contact:** Ken or Melody Allaman **Founded:** 1975 **Open:** Year-round **Admission:** Application form **Cost:** $775–$895 (meals and cabins or camping facilities incl.) **Size-Attendees:** 4

ALLAMAN'S WORKSHOPS are for passionate photographers who want to immerse themselves in Montana's landscape and wildlife. They consist of 5 days of dedicated photography of individual animal species in the wild, plus the wilderness and historic sites of the northern Rocky Mountain area.

Some trips specialize in elk or in newborn bighorn sheep. Others explore ghost towns or the snow-covered winter landscape. Ken Allaman, an outfitter and guide for over 20 years, understands wildlife habits, and includes biology and outdoorsmanship lessons in the workshops. Groups are intimate to minimize impact on the land and ensure plenty of personal attention.

Glacier Institute

For nature and travel photographers *100 mi. N of Missoula — P.O. Box 7457, Kalispell, MT 59904* **Voice:** 406-755-1211 **Contact:** Shawn Lowney, Dev. Dir. **Founded:** 1984 **Open:** Summer and fall **Admission:** Application form **Cost:** $150–$225

The Glacier Institute is a nonprofit educational organization that focuses on the diverse natural and cultural resources of the northern Rockies region. Its field seminars foster an appreciation of plants, birds, wild animal species, and man's aesthetic and spiritual connection to nature. Two weekend photography workshops—1 in the summer and 1 in the fall—feature the natural beauty and wildlife of Glacier National Park. These workshops are suitable for photographers at all levels who want to spend a couple of days photographing in this unspoiled place.

Montana Artists Refuge

For photographers and artists in selected other disciplines *25 mi N of Butte — P.O. Box 8, Basin, MT 59631* **Voice:** 406-225-3525 **Open:** Year-round **Admission:** Statement of intent, resume, 10 slides **Cost:** $200–$400 per month (plus heat in winter) **Size-Attendees:** 3–6

The old gold camp of Basin, near the Continental Divide, has a population of only about 250, including a core of dedicated artists who have created the Montana Artists Refuge. Art residents have the use of several apartments and studios, mostly in a former bank building. It is a casual atmosphere, open to all, where photographers and other self-directed creators can spend their time exploring and interacting or working in complete solitude. While there is no darkroom or local film processing, the length of the residency—from 3 months to a year—would permit a photographer to invest a substantial period of time into creating a body of work. A small fund exists to help residents with the rent.

Rocky Mountain School of Photography

For amateur and career-minded photographers *P.O. Box 7697, Missoula, MT 59807* **Voice:** 406-543-0171; 800-394-7677 **Fax:** 406-721-9133 **E-mail:** rmsp@marsweb.com **Web Site:** http://www.apogeephoto.com/rsmp.html **Contact:** Sunni Bradshaw, Program Dir. **Founded:** 1987 **Open:** Workshops: Feb.–Nov.; summer intensive program: June–Aug. **Admission:** Application ($40) for career programs **Cost:** $500–$750 for most domestic workshops; $1,895–$4,995 for travel workshops (lodging and possibly meals incl.); $3,750 for summer intensive; $1,195–$2,195 for career programs **Financial Aid:** Scholarship; Work/Study **Size-Attendees:** 8–12 for workshops

Photographer, teacher and arts entrepreneur Neil Chaput de Saintonge must have a pretty good life. As director of the Rocky Mountain School of Photography, he spends his summers teaching a subject he loves to eager students from all over the country. At other times, he leads workshops to photograph the scenery and culture in destinations from Martha's Vineyard to New Zealand. During off-hours he gets to enjoy the lively university town of Missoula and the natural beauty of the nearby National Parks, mountains and forests of the northern Rockies.

The Rocky Mountain School offers 2 distinct kinds of curricula: career training programs during the summer, and workshops—over 2 dozen of them—throughout the year. The biggest single program is the 11-week summer intensive, a complete immersion into the world of photography. Career-minded and amateur photographers take classes in camera technique, lighting, black & white darkroom, image marketing, and an introduction to digital imaging. Classroom time in Missoula is mixed with field study in the great outdoors. This program is designed for young people who may want to explore a career in photography and for anyone interested in thorough photographic training but unable to devote more than a summer to study.

The 3 specialized career training programs, which last from 10 days to 3 weeks, offer the choice of nature photography, portraits and weddings, or photojournalism. These are advanced courses: a telephone interview and written exam are required for admission. The faculty of all the summer sessions is made up of RMSP staff, plus visiting photographers and teachers.

The workshops fall into 5 categories: "Montana workshops," taught in Missoula or the not-too-distant Glacier National Park, stress photographic technique, such as the use of the view camera and the Zone system. "Wildlife workshops" focus on captive-bred animal species at the Wild Eyes animal preserve (see below) nearby. "National workshops" take participants farther afield for 6 to 10 days of discovery and photography in New England, New Orleans, Alaska or Hawaii. "International workshops" go to Russia, South America or elsewhere for 2 weeks or more, while "spiritual photography workshops" combine meditation and spiritual self-discovery with guidance on creative self-expression through photography.

RMSP is passionate about providing good service to its students. Instructors are chosen for their teaching skills as well as photographic expertise and include such well-known experts as Dave Middleton and Galen Rowell, as well as the school's permanent staff. The entire organization is diligent about its ecologically friendly orientation and high professional and ethical standards.

NEIL CHAPUT DE SAINTONGE

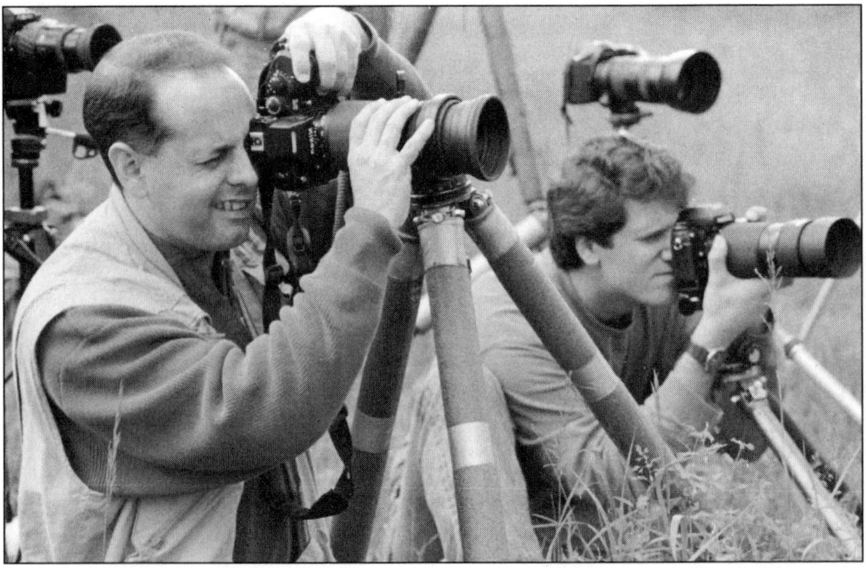

Forest of tripods, and students, Rocky Mountain School of Photography, Missoula.

Wild Eyes Photo Adventure

For wildlife photographers (still and moving picture) *125 mi. N of Missoula — 894 Lake Dr., Columbia Falls, MT 59912* **Voice:** 406-387-5391 **Fax:** 406-387-5391 **Web Site:** www.apogeephoto.com/wildeyes.html **Contact:** Robin Allen **Founded:** 1989 **Open:** Year-round **Cost:** $795 for 3-day workshop, $1,250 for 5-day (lodging in cabins and meals incl.); private sessions $300–$500 per day **Size-Attendees:** 6

WOLVES, BEARS, cougars, bobcats and many other elusive species of land animals and birds of prey are the attraction at Wild Eyes. Captive animals are trucked to nearby preserve land in Montana and set up for portraits and action pictures for the benefit of still photographers and Hollywood movie studios alike.

Hosts Brent and Robin Allen offer photographers fifteen to twenty 3- to 5-day prearranged workshops throughout the year. Longer and shorter custom sessions can also be arranged. An experienced wildlife photographer is available to offer advice to workshop groups unless otherwise requested.

The different seasons provide a constantly varying background against which to shoot the animals (with a camera, of course). Animals may be photographed individually, in groups, or with their young when possible. Long lenses, 200mm and above, and lots of film are recommended. The Allens even have a Siberian tiger.

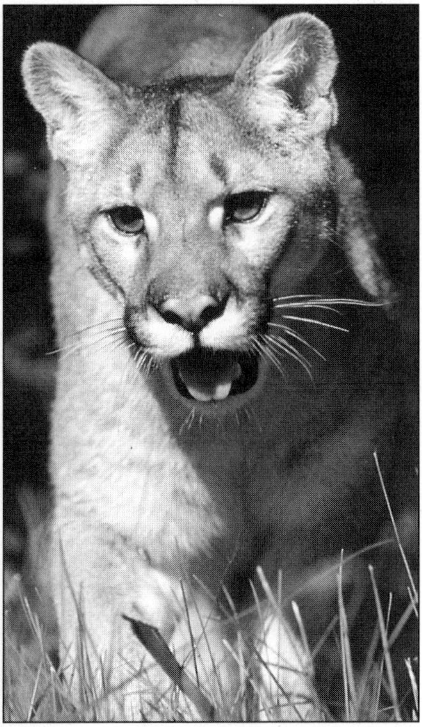

Close encounters, Wild Eyes Photo Adventures, Columbia Falls, MT.

Wilderness Photography Expeditions

For nature photographers *Yellowstone National Park — 402 S. 5th St., Livingston, MT 59047* **Voice:** 406-222-2302; 800-521-7230 **Fax:** 406-222-2480 **Contact:** Bonnie Murphy **Founded:** 1986 **Open:** Jan.–Feb., June, Sept. **Admission:** Application form **Cost:** $1,695 for 6 days/5 nights (lodging and meals incl.) **Size-Attendees:** 8

TOM AND BONNIE Murphy love to share their love affair with Yellowstone. About 8 times each year, in winter, spring, and fall, they lead groups of photographers and others into the park to visit the splendid scenery, natural phenomena and wildlife. Tom Murphy, an expert photographer whose images have appeared in *Time, Newsweek,* and *Audubon* magazines, guides participants in how to approach and record the many wonders Yellowstone has to offer.

Nebraska

Bemis Center for Contemporary Arts

For photographers and other visual artists *In the Old Market district on the fringe of downtown Omaha — 724 S. Twelfth, Omaha, NE 68102* **Voice:** 402-341-7130 **Fax:** 402-341-9791 **E-mail:** bemis@artswire.org **Contact:** Cheri VanAuker, Adm. Ass't. **Founded:** 1981 **Open:** Year-round **Admission:** Application ($25), resume, slides of recent work **Deadlines:** Sept. 30 **Cost:** None **Financial Aid:** Stipend **Size-Attendees:** 5–6 **Handicapped Access**

A COUPLE OF renovated old warehouses house several large studios and ample living space for resident artists at this community-sponsored arts organization. The program tends to mix artists working in different media, so that a photographer may spend the 2- to 3-month residency working near painters and sculptors. Each artist lives and works in a private studio loft, equipped with a kitchen. Access to a darkroom is available for photographers.

The Bemis Center prides itself on its ability to support its resident artists completely with room, board and a $500 to $1,000 monthly stipend. If the artist becomes involved in community teaching, an additional stipend may be available. While residents may work on a project of their own choice, it is expected that 1 work, suitable for inclusion in Bemis's permanent collection, will be donated upon completion of the residency. Artists are also expected to present a slide show and discussion of their work at some point during their stay, and may have an exhibit of their work in the gallery or outdoor exhibition space.

Selection is made by a jury of 4 artists and 1 curator once a year, in the fall, for residencies beginning the following March. The Bemis Center has strong local ties and initiates programs to bring the arts to children and adults throughout the Omaha community.

New Hampshire

International Model Testing Workshops

For beginning and experienced glamour photographers *Caribbean, Florida, California; some in Norway, Australia — 465 Timbertop Rd., P.O. Box 272, New Ipswich, NH 03071* **Voice:** 603-878-1737 **Fax:** 603-878-1737 **E-mail:** bobchernis@top.monad.net **Web Site:** www.apogeephoto.com/icms.htm **Contact:** Bob Chernis, Dir. **Founded:** 1993 **Open:** Several times per year **Admission:** Application form **Cost:** $395

HOW DOES ONE GET into the fashion and glamour end of photography? Bob Chernis has created an innovative program that brings together photographers and models who need more experience and exposure to advance their careers. In destinations from Florida to Australia, photographers and models work together, often one-on-one, on images that will benefit them both.

These 3- to 4-day workshops are geared primarily to early-career photographers and those working professionals who need to expand their repertoire of skills, though amateurs may also attend. Portrait photographers seeking a new avenue of endeavor and commercial photographers who lack the skills in directing and lighting subjects have benefited the most. Models, some of whom already have successful careers, participate because they recognize the importance of networking and want to meet new photographers who may present them in new ways.

MacDowell Colony

For photographers and artists in selected other disciplines *40 mi. W of Manchester — 100 High Street, Peterborough, NH 03458* **Voice:** 603-924-3886 **Fax:** 603-924-9142 **E-mail:** macdowell@artswire.org **Contact:** Pat Dodge, Adm. Dir. **Founded:** 1907 **Open:** Year-round **Admission:** Application ($20), samples of recent work, references **Deadlines:** Sept. 15 for Jan.–Apr.; Jan. 15 for May–Aug.; Apr. 15 for Sept.–Dec. **Cost:** Artists are asked to pay what they can **Size-Attendees:** 31 summer; 22 other seasons **Handicapped Access**

AARON COPLAND, Studs Terkel, Jules Feiffer and Leonard Bernstein have all been colonists at MacDowell, one of the country's most prestigious artists' colonies. The quiet former farm in the New Hampshire woods provides studios, room and board on a pay-as-you-can basis to established artists for up to 8 weeks of intense creative endeavor. MacDowell tends to accept better-known artists, though talented early-career artists are invited to apply as well.

"Colonists" have their own studios—there are 2 darkroom-equipped photo studios—and reside nearby. Breakfast and dinner are communal; lunch is brought to your door to permit an uninterrupted day's work. The studios are simply furnished and rarely even within sight of each other. MacDowell's 40-odd buildings, spread over its 400-acre campus, are an eclectic showcase of architectural styles. It has been on the National Register of Historic Places since 1966.

Though traditionally associated with composers and writers, MacDowell encourages photographers to apply for as many as 12 to 15 photography openings per year. The admissions panel consists of distinguished professionals in the field, and selection is based purely on talent.

New Jersey

Country Photography Workshops of New Jersey

For photographers at all levels *Highlands 60 mi. W of Newark — 20 Musconetcong River Rd., Hampton, NJ 08827* **Voice:** 908-537-7511 **Contact:** Brian Lav, Dir. **Founded:** 1991 **Open:** July–Aug. **Admission:** Application ($15) **Cost:** $200–$380 (meal plan available) **Financial Aid:** Scholarship; Work/Study **Size-Attendees:** 16 total; classes 8

TEACHER/DIRECTOR Brian Lav calls on his own years as a fine black & white printer and on accomplished New York City photographers to provide instruction at his summer workshops for students at all levels. Some of the classes concentrate on black & white, with shooting sessions, lectures and darkroom practice included. Others teach artistic subjects, such as personal vision, working with light, creative portraiture and documentary image making. The workshops vary from 2- to 5-day sessions.

A brand-new 1,800-square-foot facility, "the Barn," has just been built to accommodate the workshops in air-conditioned comfort.

Nature One Photography & Wildlife Adventure

For nature and wildlife photographers *U.S. & Canadian West, New England, Florida, Europe — P.O. Box 531, Haddonfield, NJ 08033* **Voice:** 609-427-9223; 800-659-9718 **Fax:** 609-427-9139 **Contact:** John Finley, Dir. **Founded:** 1987 **Open:** Varies **Admission:** Application form **Cost:** $695–$2,000 for domestic workshops (most include lodging); up to $6,000 for ballooning in Europe

JOHN FINLEY GEARS his photography programs to amateur photographers who want to visit and focus their cameras on landscapes in North America and Europe, or on wildlife such as bears, wolves, whales and eagles. Some trips go to beautiful natural settings: Vermont in the fall or the Canyonlands of the Southwest. Others visit overseas destinations, to cruise the canals of Europe or float in a hot-air balloon over France and Switzerland. Wildlife model workshops take place at a preserve in Montana where captive animals allow for up-close pictures of otherwise hard-to-find species.

Finley personally leads many of the workshops. Other instructors, such as Leonard Lee Rue III, his son Len Rue Jr., and Branson Reynolds, are professional nature photographers with years of teaching experience.

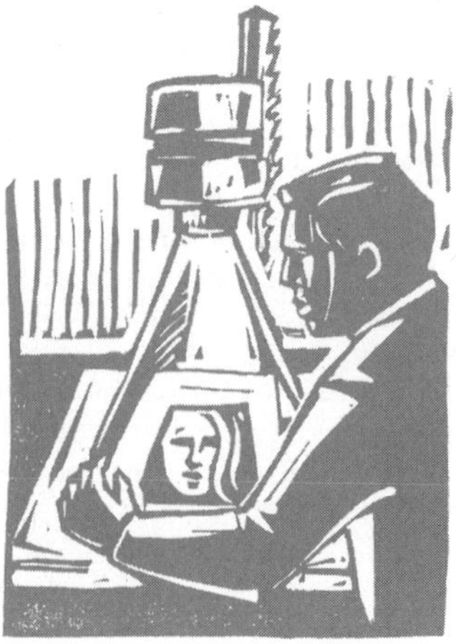

Peters Valley Craft Center

For photographers and artists and craftspeople in selected other disciplines *Northernmost NJ — 19 Kuhn Rd., Layton, NJ 07851* **Voice:** 201-948-5200 **Fax:** 201-948-0011 **E-mail:** photopz@aol.com **Founded:** 1971 **Open:** June–Aug. **Admission:** Application ($15) **Deadlines:** June–Aug. **Cost:** $190 (3 days)–$290 (5 days), plus materials and lab ($25–$160); room and board $60 per day ($255 for 5 days) **Financial Aid:** Work/Study **Size-Attendees:** 40–80 total; classes 8–12

A DOZEN PHOTOGRAPHY workshops focus on the art and craft of photography at this interdisciplinary center in the Delaware Water Gap National Recreation Area in rural northwest New Jersey. Beginners' classes teach camera technique and composition. Artistic workshops on specialized topics for more advanced photographers are taught by the likes of George Krause and Harvey Stein. Darkroom courses feature instruction in color, black & white and platinum printing.

The center has a limited number of simple accommodations available to participants on a first-come, first-served basis for $50 to 60 per night (including meals in the community kitchen). Other accommodations are also available.

Peters Valley's summer assistantship program in photography and other disciplines provides young people the chance to help out with the program in exchange for learning. Anyone interested should send a sample of slides and a professional recommendation by April 1. Accomplished photographers who seek a long-term position may apply to be the artist-in-residence / program coordinator for photography. The 1 photographer chosen—the position can last from 1 to 4 years—receives a studio and living space at a nominal rate. Write for further information.

Peters Valley is a nonprofit membership organization dedicated to the tradition of fine handwork as a part of our American heritage.

New Mexico

Camera & Darkroom Digital

For photographers and other digital artists *460 St. Michael's Dr., Suite 401, Santa Fe, NM 87505* **Voice:** 505-820-2307 **Fax:** 505-820-2927 **E-mail:** andrew4059@aol.com **Web Site:** www.camera-darkroom.com. **Contact:** Andrew Rodney, Digital Dog **Founded:** 1995 **Admission:** Application form **Cost:** $350 per day for customized instruction; $250 per day for others from same group

CAMERA & Darkroom Digital is New Mexico's leading distributor of digital imaging hardware and software and a resource for anyone looking to move into the digital arena. It offers training in the use of Adobe Photoshop on a customized basis, for up to 4 people from a single organization at a time. Otherwise, all training is one-on-one. C & DD also teaches other facets of digital imaging. It has been working with the technology since 1990, so it has about as much experience as anyone else in mastering the complex equipment and techniques of this field.

Helene Wurlitzer Foundation

For photographers and artists in selected other disciplines *2½ hr. N of Albuquerque — P.O. Box 545, Taos, NM 87571* **Voice:** 505-758-2413 **Fax:** 505-758-2559 **Contact:** Kenneth G. Peterson, Exec. Dir. **Founded:** 1954 **Open:** Apr. 1–Sept. 30 **Admission:** Project outline, samples of work, references **Cost:** Transportation, meals **Size-Attendees:** 11 at a time **Handicapped Access**

THIS FOUNDATION sponsors artists in the creative, as opposed to interpretive, arts. Eleven artists at a time occupy a series of studio-residences for periods of up to 6 months, with an average stay of 3 months. There is no charge for rent or utilities; artists are responsible for their own meals and supplies.

This is a competitive program: residencies tend to be reserved 3 or 4 years in advance. Historically it has been open for only the summer half of the year, but the Wurlitzer Foundation is planning to offer wintertime occupancy as well in the near future.

Taos, in the shadow of the Sangre de Cristo mountains in northern New Mexico, enjoys the clear air and brilliant light of the high desert. From the 800-year-old adobe village of the Tewas to today's diverse creative community, it has always been a jewel in the artistic and cultural life of the Southwest.

Jim Bones Photographic Workshop

For nature and landscape photographers *Big Bend National Park (TX) and other Southwest locations — P.O. Box 22, Tesuque, NM 87574* **Voice:** 505-988-1762 **E-mail:** jimbones@rt66.com **Web Site:** www.rt66.com/~jimbones **Contact:** Jim Bones **Open:** Selected weeks, spring–fall **Cost:** $425–$545 for week **Size-Attendees:** 10

QUALITY OF LIGHT and care for the natural environment are Jim Bones's 2 passions. He pays particular attention to recognizing the attributes of natural light and using them to their best photographic advantage. His reverence for the fine details of the natural world sets the stage for thoughtful outdoor workshops where an emotional relationship with the subject and the light falling on it leads to stronger, deeper pictures.

Bones's Biodiversity Photo Workshop in Big Bend National Park, run under the auspices of the Big Bend Natural History Association, explores this dramatic, largely unknown corner of southwest Texas, a land of stark landscapes and exquisite light. The workshop includes daily field assignments and on-site slide processing for rapid feedback. Other workshops in the Southwest follow a similar format.

Bones, who worked with Eliot Porter in the 1970s, is an established landscape photographer with many years of teaching experience.

All the artists are longtime professionals who enjoy teaching. The Santa Fe area has long been a gathering place for artists and is a spectacular environment in which to pursue one's private muse. (Accommodations and living expenses are the responsibility of the participant.)

New Mexico Artists' Association

For photographers and artists and craftspeople in selected other disciplines *Santa Fe area — 4320 Airport Rd., Santa Fe, NM 87505* **Voice:** 505-982-5639 **Contact:** Winona Garmhausen, Dir. **Founded:** 1987 **Admission:** By application **Cost:** $775 per week **Size-Attendees:** Individual or very small group

THIS UNIQUE PROGRAM offers photographers and other artists the opportunity to study with a professional Santa Fe–based artist in his or her own studio.

Each student spends a week (or more) working directly with the professional artist, either one-on-one or in concert with 1 or 2 other students. Instruction is personalized, shaped by the artist's style and the student's needs. The artist might discuss the use of light in a student's photos or suggest how to enhance their emotional impact.

The process of matching students and teachers is highly individualized as well. Upon receipt of a detailed letter of application, the NMAA chooses the 1 of its 50-plus members who seems best suited to that applicant. The student then gets to look over the chosen artist's work ahead of time, to decide if the fit is a good one. If it is not, he or she asks for another choice, and the process begins again.

Roswell Artist-in-Residence Program

For photographers and artists in selected other disciplines *High plains, 200 mi SE of Albuquerque — 100 W. 11th, Roswell, NM 88201* **Voice:** 505-622-6037 **Fax:** 505-624-6765 **Founded:** 1967 **Open:** Year-round **Admission:** Application ($15), slide portfolio, references, statement of intent **Deadlines:** Apply Sept. 15–Oct. 15 (only) for following fall **Financial Aid:** Stipend **Size-Attendees:** Up to 6 **Handicapped Access**

THE ROSWELL MUSEUM & Art Center brings a slice of the greater world of art to the high plains of southeastern New Mexico with a series of 6-month to 1-year residencies for photographers, painters, sculptors and printmakers. These residencies are oriented toward contemporary art, in counterpoint to the traditional Southwestern forms, and serve to enhance the artistic vitality of this small (pop. 50,000) and fairly isolated community.

Artists work, live and interact in a complex of well-lighted studios and simply furnished private houses that can accommodate artists' families. There is no on-site darkroom. Each resident receives a $500 monthly stipend, plus $100 per live-in dependent, to cover expenses. Because of the rural nature of the area, a car is recommended.

Santa Fe Workshops

For photographers, filmmakers and digital artists *Overlooking Santa Fe — P.O. Box 9916, Santa Fe, NM 87504* **Voice:** 505-983-1400 **Fax:** 505-989-8604 **E-mail:** sfworkshop@aol.com **Web Site:** www.sfworkshop.com **Contact:** Roberta Koska **Founded:** 1989 **Open:** Most workshops in summer; a few in fall and winter **Admission:** Varies with experience level **Cost:** $600–$900 for workshop and lab fees; $400–$700 living expenses; $1,000–$1,200 per week for digital courses **Financial Aid:** Scholarship; Work/Study **Size-Attendees:** 70–100 photographers per week; classes 12–16

IT'S LITTLE WONDER that so many of America's leading photographers teach weeklong workshops in Santa Fe. The location is serene, the air clear, the light magnificent. SFW offers master classes with the likes of Sam Abell, Mary Ellen Mark and Robert Ketchum. Photographers work closely with the master teachers, in groups of no more than 16. Most classes are scheduled for the summer months, when half a dozen take place simultaneously, although SFW has recently added fall and winter workshops.

Subjects covered include people photography, color, landscape, photojournalism, art and figure studies, and developing your personal vision. A couple of workshops address business issues. In addition to the master classes, courses in basic craft are offered for beginners, as is black & white darkroom instruction. Digital photography, using Adobe Photoshop and Live Picture, is the fastest-growing part of the SFW curriculum.

A sample of recent work is required for admission to (and proper placement in) many of the master classes, says founder/director Reid Callanan. A work-study program is available, but only to those willing to commit for the whole summer.

SFW is set on a 25-acre campus just east of downtown Santa Fe, with a view toward the Jemez Mountains. Five buildings house classrooms, a studio, darkrooms, the dining hall and dormitories. On-campus accommodations are simple and clean. Those desiring deluxe hotels can find them in town a few minutes away. The mandatory meal program—lunch every day plus a couple of dinners—is designed to stimulate camaraderie and dialogue during the short, intensive week of work.

Santa Fe, the city, is a magical location. Artists of all kinds have long been inspired by the rugged New Mexico landscape and characteristic adobe architecture. Callanan says, "We create a safe and tranquil ambiance in which each photographer can nurture his or her own creative spark."

SFW's home page on the World Wide Web is especially clear and informative.

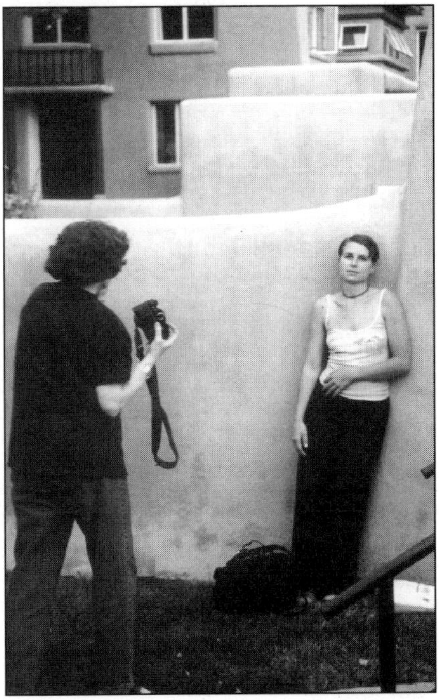

SANTA FE WORKSHOPS

Instructor Joyce Tenneson and model, Santa Fe Workshops.

Taos Institute of Arts

For photographers and artists and craftspeople in selected other disciplines *Historic town 2½ hr. N of Albuquerque — Box 5280 NDCBU, Taos, NM 87571* **Voice:** 505-758-2793 **Fax:** 505-758-2793 **E-mail:** tia@taosnet.com **Web Site:** www.taosnet.com/TIA **Founded:** 1988 **Open:** June–Oct. **Admission:** Application ($20) **Cost:** $225–$450 **Financial Aid:** Scholarship; Work/Study **Size-Attendees:** 20–50 total; classes 8–12

Taos Institute of Arts seeks to weave the cultural spirit of this historic mountain town into its offering of multidisciplinary arts courses. Six to 8 photography workshops per year combine standard art subjects, such as nature photography and special-process printing, with courses that concentrate on the light, architecture and spirit unique to northern New Mexico.

Twice during the summer, classes stop and artists of all types embark on a weekend expedition to camp and work together in an undeveloped region near Taos. TIA also offers a series of "significant other" workshops in arts-related subjects for the benefit of partners of participants.

Scholarships are available only to residents of Taos County. Participants arrange their own housing and meals.

Visual Journeys

For travel photographers *Varies — P.O. Box 9916, Santa Fe, NM* **Voice:** 505-983-1400 **Fax:** 505-989-8604 **E-mail:** sfworkshop@aol.com **Web Site:** http://webart.com/visualjourneys **Open:** Jan.–Mar. **Admission:** Application form **Cost:** $69 preregistered; $79 at the door **Size-Attendees:** 200–400

Questions to Ask in Choosing a Workshop

Workshops are a wonderful way to improve your photographic skill and vision. An intense week of study in a concentrated learning environment can lead you toward a depth of understanding about the medium of photography that would take years to achieve on your own.

It is also a big commitment of your time, money and vital energy. You want to make sure the class will be productive before you make the commitment. Here is a list of questions you might ask to help find out if a particular workshop is the right one for you.

- What is the reputation of the organization offering the workshop? Have other photographers been satisfied with their study there?
- How about the individual teacher? Is the teacher a good enough photographer to have something to offer you? How often has the teacher taught in this environment? Is the photographer skilled as a communicator (in words!) so you can anticipate receiving the benefit of his or her ability and experience?
- What is the chance of the class being canceled, either because of a shortage of participants or because the teacher gets called away?
- Do workshop owners and administrators teach classes? (Those who do will probably be unable to evaluate their own teaching skill. Better to ask, "What do you emphasize in your classes?" or "What has teaching this course taught you?" or "What is your philosophy of teaching?" The ensuing discussion will shed light on the approach and style of the teacher.)
- If in doubt, ask for referrals: previous participants who can offer opinions about the content and style of the class.

WORLD-CLASS TRAVEL photographers Lisl Dennis and Nevada Wier have packaged a ton of travel photography know-how into a full-day seminar that they take to 10 different cities around the country each year. Dennis's signature style features bold design and brilliant colors, in locations from the Southwest to Asia, to Morocco. Her pictures have appeared in magazines such as *Travel & Leisure* and *Architectural Digest,* and she has taught travel photography workshops for over a decade. Wier, who has a picture book on Vietnam to her credit, specializes in adventure travel and people photography. Together, the 2 women show slides and videos to teach photographers at all levels how to approach this most alluring photographic subject.

Outdoor Photographer magazine sponsors these auditorium-size presentations. Interested photographers should call or e-mail Santa Fe Workshops (at the numbers/address listed here), which handles reservations, for this year's schedule of cities and to check on space availability.

New York

Art/Omi International Artists' Workshop

For photographers and other visual artists *Omi, NY, 25 mi. SE of Albany — 55 Fifth Ave., 15th floor, New York, NY 10003* **Voice:** 212-206-6060 **Fax:** 212-727-0563 **Contact:** Linda Cross, Exec. Dir. **Open:** 3 weeks in July **Admission:** By invitation or application; application should include 6 slides and resume **Deadlines:** Mar. 1 **Cost:** Transportation only **Size-Attendees:** 12–20

ART/OMI CASTS a wide net to bring together outstanding artists from as many countries as possible for a 3-week residency in a bucolic village near the New York–Massachusetts border. Many of the artists are referred by Art/Omi's network of friends, which includes professional artists and arts administrators, and then are invited to attend. Individuals may also apply.

The purpose of Art/Omi is to allow artists time and space to work while encouraging interaction with peers. Group activities, such as meetings with art critics or other guests, and meals are communal events. Housing is made available in the surrounding community. The facility includes studios for those who need them, though there is no darkroom on site. Participants are asked to donate a work of art created at Omi for fund-raising purposes.

Blue Mountain Center

For photographers, writers and visual artists *Adirondack Mtns., 2 hr. N of Albany — Blue Mountain Lake, NY 12812* **Voice:** 518-352-7391 **Contact:** Admissions Committee **Open:** June 15–Oct. 15 **Admission:** Application ($20), resume, letter of intent, 10 slides **Deadlines:** Feb. 1 **Cost:** Transportation only **Size-Attendees:** 14 at a time

BLUE MOUNTAIN Lake in the Adirondacks is a quiet place, well suited for the photographer, writer or artist to spend a 4-week residency in concentrated work. Residents at the Blue Mountain Center live in private rooms in an old Victorian mansion and share daily breakfasts and dinners. Some private studios are available for those who require them. The lake and a network of hiking trails through the mountains are there to inspire creativity or to let hardworking artists kick back and take a break. The selection committee is particularly interested in fine work that evinces social and ecological concern and is directed at a general audience.

Center for Photography at Woodstock

For photographers interested in fine art *Catskill Mtns., 50 mi. S of Albany — 59 Tinker St., Woodstock, NY 12498* **Voice:** 914-679-9957 **Fax:** 914-679-6337 **E-mail:** CPWphoto@aol.com **Web Site:** http://users.aol.com/cpwphoto **Contact:** Lawrence Lewis **Founded:** 1978 **Open:** June–Oct. **Admission:** Application ($40) **Cost:** $300–$350 for weekend workshops (lab and model fees incl); $550–$650 for weeklong travel workshops; discounts for members **Financial Aid:** Work/Study **Size-Attendees:** 12–15

THE NONPROFIT Center for Photography (see "Joining Up") offers 20 to 25 workshops and lectures annually, mostly on weekends. Workshop topics extend beyond mere craft and business subjects to emphasize stretching your personal vision and deepening your relationship with photography as a medium of creative expression. Many of the teachers are accomplished artists and photographers from New York City, including Bruce Davidson, Maggie Steber and Antonin Kratochvil.

Two or 3 weeklong travel workshops in the U.S. or overseas are scheduled each year. CPW also sponsors innovative events, such as visits to the studios of some of New York's better-known photographer/artists. Darkrooms can be rented on an hourly basis year-round. A busy exhibition gallery in Woodstock is available to even the least well known photographers whose work qualifies. A number of summer-long internship positions are available.

While best known for its '60s rock festival, Woodstock has been a cultural center in the middle of Catskill farmland for decades. It is a year-round tourism center, replete with inns, cafes, restaurants and art galleries.

Desktop America

For photographers and digital artists *Midtown Manhattan — 250 W. 57th St., Suite 730, New York, NY 10019* **Voice:** 212-245-9391 **Contact:** Robert Farrell, Dir. **Founded:** 1993 **Cost:** $699 for 24-hr. individual training; $349 for 15-hr. group course; package plans available

DESKTOP AMERICA prides itself on providing concentrated training for users of Adobe Photoshop and other desktop software. Rather than just present the software and show what it can do, instructors teach individuals what they most want and need to learn. One-on-one sessions permit maximum learning in the allotted time. Small-group sessions and supervised computer rental are also available.

Eddie Adams Workshop

For young photojournalists: students and beginning professionals *Jeffersonville, NY, 2½ hr. NW of New York City — P.O. Box 4182, Grand Central Station, New York, NY 10163* **Voice:** 212-880-1613; 914-482-4112 **Fax:** 212-880-1610 **Contact:** Shauna Lyon, Workshop Producer **Founded:** 1987 **Open:** 4 days over Columbus Day weekend **Admission:** Application and portfolio **Cost:** Students are asked to contribute approximately $180 toward room and board **Size-Attendees:** 100 total; 10 per "team"

FOUR DAYS WITH the absolute top people in American photojournalism is the prize for the 50 early-career photographers (2 years or less) and 50 students who gain admission to the annual Eddie Adams Workshop. Pulitzer Prize–winning photographer Adams created this program in order to allow

Digital Imaging: The Basics

Digital imaging refers to the use of electronic devices rather than silver-based film to record images, as well as the processes of retouching, altering, combining and changing images on a computer.

When an image is scanned digitally, either in taking the picture on a digital camera or when an existing photo is transferred to a computer, millions of electronic sensors record the density and color of each tiny picture element (pixel) onto a disk. From there the picture can be viewed on a computer screen and electronically retouched or altered, transferred via disk or over the phone, or dropped into a layout for publishing. Already most printed images pass through a digital stage at one point or another. In digital media, such as the Internet or other electronic publishing, many photographs are never printed on paper at all.

A few digital cameras are currently available for convenient, filmless, ready-to-view picture taking. Unfortunately these cameras are still expensive, and they cannot record information at the high resolution and low cost of conventional film. But digital technology is catching up rapidly. As the technology continues to improve, digital picture taking will surely replace conventional cameras for most applications of both amateur and professional photographers.

Digital manipulation of images starts with a picture in digital form that has been fed into a computer. On the screen the computer operator uses image manipulation software, such as Live Picture or Adobe Photoshop or Photo Deluxe, to subtly retouch or dramatically change the image. On the computer you can combine, or "morph," together two or more images and adjust or radically change colors. Unwanted pieces of the picture can be eliminated, and desirable details added. Shapes and textures can be modified in previously unimaginable ways. The last few years have seen an explosion in the use of computers to alter existing images and as a creative tool to produce entirely new ones.

Adobe Photoshop is far and away the most popular software used by photographers for digital imaging. It offers an astonishing array of ways to create and modify images. Photoshop costs about $600 and comes in both a PC and a Macintosh version. Experienced users tend to prefer the Mac version because the internal structure of the Apple system is more conducive to working with imagery rather than text. Images consume a tremendous amount of computer memory, so Photoshop users need a lot of RAM to be able to work with detailed pictures. The basics of Photoshop can be learned in a day or two, though it is likely to take many months to become skilled enough at it to make professional-grade images.

Digital photographic technology, for all its aesthetic benefits, has raised the moral issue of what is "true" in the traditional photographic sense versus what is not. Can the photo, and by extension the photographer, be trusted any more to render a fundamentally accurate picture of reality? This has been a topic of hot debate in the photographic community. While there are no clear answers, it is fair to say that, for better or worse, the line between fiction and reality in photographic images is forever blurred.

young photographers to learn from experienced professionals about the storytelling power and social importance of photography.

Participants are divided into 10 teams, each headed by a photographer and an editor. The teams venture out with assignments to document some aspect of life in a designated town in New York State. Film is processed constantly. Daily editing and critiquing help each student to hone skills and learn about the visual, technical and emotional components of creating strong journalistic images.

This workshop is unique among photography workshops in 2 ways. First, it is free of charge, supported by sponsors and staffed by volunteers. Second, its faculty members are among the most distinguished photographers and editors in the world and represent many of America's leading newspapers and magazines.

The 100 participants are chosen from some 800 applicants.

First Light Photo Workshops & Safaris

For photographers at all levels

Workshops on Long Island; safaris across U.S. and overseas — P.O. Box 246, Sayville, NY 11782 **Voice:** 516-563-0500 **Fax:** 516-563-0694 **E-mail:** photours@aol.com **Contact:** Bill Rudock **Founded:** 1989 **Open:** Varies **Admission:** Application form **Cost:** $49 for 4-hr. workshop, $89 for 8-hr.; up to $5,500 for international safaris; $149 for aerial workshop over NYC **Size-Attendees:** 12–15

FORMER WEDDING and portrait specialist Bill Rudock—now focusing on outdoor photography—teaches a series of workshops in his studio on Long Island and leads "safaris" to nearby destinations and around the world.

Half- and full-day studio workshops teach camera and photographic technique. The "safaris" go to nearby Fire Island for a day, New England or Virginia for a weekend, or National Parks in the West for a week. The foreign trips, two 2- to 3-week adventures each year, range from Mexico to East Africa, to Nepal. Rudock's attitude toward photographing the world is reflected in his slogan "Experience life's greatest adventure ... through the eye of your camera." A licensed pilot, he also leads bimonthly aerial photography workshops in the New York area.

Image Experience Workshops

For outdoor photographers

Eastern U.S. from Maine to Florida — 55 Bobwhite Dr., Glenmont, NY 12077 **Voice:** 518-432-9913 **Fax:** 518-439-1159 **E-mail:** peterf5388@aol.com **Contact:** Peter Finger, Dir. **Founded:** 1986 **Open:** Summer and fall **Admission:** Application form **Cost:** $95 for weekends; $350 for weeklong workshops **Size-Attendees:** 6–12

OUTDOOR photographer Peter Finger personally leads about 10 workshops in beautiful Eastern locations, including the Maine coast, the White Mountains and the Florida Everglades. The workshops focus on camera technique and taking advantage of the best light. Finger sees to it that participants have fun along the way. On-site E-6 slide processing is available for some workshops.

Indian River Photo Workshops

For nature photographers

Adirondack Mtns. — P.O. Box 7, Antwerp, NY 13608 **Voice:** 716-475-2785; 315-659-8544 **Fax:** 716-475-5804 **E-mail:** swdpph@ritvax.isc.rit.edu **Contact:** Stephen Diehl **Founded:** 1981 **Open:** May and Sept. **Admission:** Application form **Cost:** $155 **Size-Attendees:** 12

IN MAY THE Adirondacks of New York State burst forth with wildflowers, and waterfalls are tumultuous with the melting snow. In late September the mountains blaze with the reds and yellows of autumn leaves. These are the 2 times that photographer Vici Zaremba and RIT professor Stephen Diehl lead photographers to view and record nature's splendor. The trips are designed as intensive learning experiences in nature photography. Dawn-to-dusk shooting and lively evening discussions fill the 5 days of the workshop. Accommodations at the rustic Covewood Lodge and home-cooked meals cost an additional $395.

International Center of Photography

For photographers at all levels
Upper Fifth Avenue, Manhattan — 1130 Fifth Ave., New York, NY 10128 **Voice:** 212-860-1776, ext. 156 **Fax:** 212-360-6490 **Contact:** Registration **Founded:** 1974 **Admission:** Some courses require portfolio review or other prerequisites **Cost:** $250–$325 for weekend workshops; $385 for 10-week evening classes; slight discount for members; $7,500 plus $600 lab fee for yearlong program **Financial Aid:** Work/Study **Size-Attendees:** 12–15 **Degree or Certification:** Two 1-year certificate programs; MFA program in association with NYU

THE MISSION OF the International Center of Photography, the premier institution in New York City devoted entirely to photography, is to nurture and advance the field of photography at all levels. Its uptown museum and midtown gallery exhibit the work of legendary photographers of yesteryear and the cutting-edge innovators of today. Its library and bookstores provide a feast of images and information for everyone from the serious researcher to the casual visitor who just loves to look at good pictures.

In keeping with its role as the most important photographic institution in the world's capital of photography, ICP's workshops, classes and seminars are some of the most advanced and thought-provoking programs anywhere. While the workshops and classes cover a broad range of subjects, from beginning black & white to special techniques and commercial skills, their principal focus is on artistic growth and the photographer's personal development. Many of the courses seek to break new ground with such provocative titles as "The Intuitive Portrait," "The Self and the Significant Other," "The Visual Diary, Opening Up" and "The Poetics of Color." Teachers are drawn from among top New York–based photographers and educators.

Workshops may last a week, a weekend, or 2 weekends. Classes meet once a week, mostly in the evenings, for 5 or 10 weeks. All courses are reasonably priced (though living in New York even for a few days can be quite expensive). A selection of 60 to 70 courses is offered 3 times per year. A few of them require a portfolio for admission. In addition, 1 or 2 travel workshops to U.S. or overseas destinations are scheduled each summer.

ICP also offers 2 full-time 1-year courses leading to certificates—one in General Photographic Studies and one in Documentary Photography and Photojournalism. Students range in age from just out of high school to well into midlife. ICP staff and selected local professionals teach. A 2-year Master's program is available in conjunction with New York University's Tisch School of the Arts. The program's principal focus is on photographic theory and criticism, though some studio work is included.

Classes and most workshops take place in ICP's classrooms and state-of-the-art darkrooms at the headquarters on Fifth Avenue, near the Metropolitan Museum of Art. The midtown gallery and bookstore are on the Avenue of the Americas at 43rd Street.

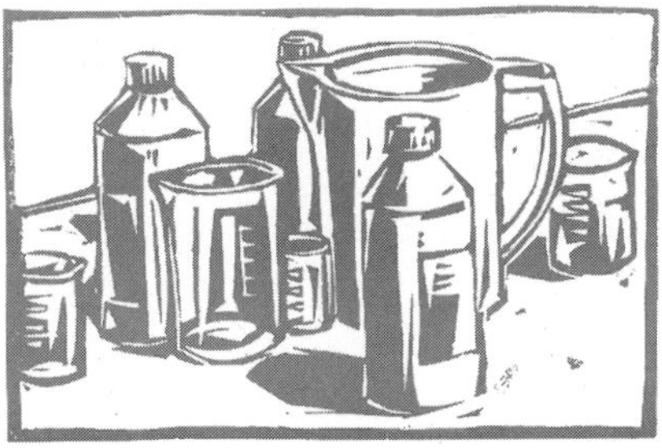

Ireland with Ron Rosenstock

For photographers at all levels *Western Ireland — Voyagers International, P.O. Box 915, Ithaca, NY 14851* **Voice:** 607-257-3091; 800-633-0299 **Fax:** 607-257-3699 **E-mail:** voyint@aol.com **Web Site:** www.gorp.com/voyagers.htm **Contact:** Mary Rachun **Founded:** 1981 **Open:** Late Apr.–Oct. **Admission:** Application form **Cost:** $1,995 (lodging, local transportation, and 2 meals per day incl.) **Size-Attendees:** 11

Where the land marries the sea in the west of Ireland, Ron Rosenstock takes photographers on a visual and cultural exploration. Rosenstock's own Hillcrest House in County Mayo serves as the base for eight 11-day photo workshops each year to the villages, hillsides and abbeys of this mystical green land.

The itinerary is a wandering one, emphasizing both photography and Irish culture. Rosenstock has decades of experience as a photographer and teacher, and a deep knowledge of and love for the place. The change of seasons from spring to fall brings variations in colors and conditions in the always unpredictable Irish weather.

"I tell my students that all of us, from the most experienced photographer to the beginner, are equals. We all have the same creative spark within us. The master photographers are simply the ones who have worked hardest and longest at their craft," Rosenstock explains. "Beginners must first learn what it really means to make an effort. The questions will be there after the effort is made. Too often they simply have not had enough experience to be able to ask the right questions. Once they have the questions then the answers will have real meaning, and progress becomes a reality."

J&J Computing

For photographers interested in digital imaging *30 mi. NW of New York City — 400 Rella Blvd., Suffern, NY 10901* **Voice:** 914-357-6381 **Fax:** 914-357-0658 **Contact:** Susan Chin, ext. 717 **Founded:** 1988 **Admission:** Application form **Cost:** $600 for 2-day course **Size-Attendees:** 4

An Apple Macintosh training facility/computer store/service bureau, J&J offers a basic 2-day course in the use of Adobe Photoshop each month, and on demand, an advanced Photoshop course. J&J teaches other graphics, design, and media production computer software as well.

The orientation here is not photographic per se but is suitable for the photographer who wants to learn computer skills applicable to a range of visual media.

John Hart's Portrait Lighting

For portrait and headshot photographers *Manhattan's Upper West Side — 344 W. 72nd St., New York, NY 10023* **Voice:** 212-873-6585 **Fax:** 212-245-2659 **E-mail:** wcress@ix.net.com **Contact:** John Hart **Founded:** 1982 **Open:** Year-round **Admission:** Application form **Cost:** $75

John Hart's claim to fame is headshots: pictures that actors use to publicize themselves and get work—big business in New York and Los Angeles. In this 3-hour seminar given every other Wednesday evening, he teaches classic and trendy lighting techniques that will bring out each subject's strongest points and create a headshot that will grab a casting director's attention. Lighting ideas for headshots are equally applicable to traditional portraiture.

Hart is the author of *Professional Headshots* and *Portrait Lighting Techniques for Pictures That Sell*, both published by Amphoto.

Light Work

For photographic artists *Syracuse University campus — 316 Waverly Ave., Syracuse, NY 13244* **Voice:** 315-443-1300 **E-mail:** cdlight@summon2.syr.edu **Contact:** Jeffrey Hoone, Dir. **Founded:** 1973 **Open:** Year-round **Admission:** Project description, resume, 20 slides **Cost:** None **Financial Aid:** Stipend **Size-Attendees:** 12–15 per year **Handicapped Access**

LIGHT WORK's artist-in-residence program invites artists working in photography to spend a month in Syracuse, concentrating on personal projects. Artists work independently, each with a private darkroom and 24-hour access to superb facilities, including an advanced digital imaging workstation. While there is no obligation to teach, residents are asked to be accessible to local artists and to leave a few pieces of work created during their stay. Each resident artist will be featured in Light Work's quarterly publication, *Contact Sheet.*

Light Work, an independent organization loosely affiliated with Syracuse University, interprets the word "photography" in broad terms and encourages the submission of all types of work. Resident artists receive a $1,200 stipend and housing in a shared apartment.

Maine Photographic Workshops/New York

For advanced and professional photographers *In and around NYC — Box 200, Rockport, ME 04856* **Voice:** 207-236-8581 **Fax:** 207-236-2558 **E-mail:** MEWorkshop@aol.com **Web Site:** www.MEWorkshops.com **Contact:** Christy Smith **Founded:** 1973 **Open:** Fall through spring **Admission:** Application form **Cost:** $425 for weekend master class; $325 for 1-day seminar **Size-Attendees:** 15

BASED IN ROCKPORT, Maine, Maine Photographic Workshops offers a series of weekend master classes in New York City with locally based photographers. Courses may use the streets of New York as the studio or may take place in the teacher's own facility. Each of these classes is narrowly focused on a particular aspect of photography, and all are designed for advanced and professional photographers only. Registration is through the MPW office in Maine. For detailed information about individual courses in New York, call 212-689-6383. (See also, in *Maine,* "Maine Photographic Workshops.")

Millay Colony for the Arts

For photographers and artists in selected other disciplines *30 mi. SE of Albany — P.O. Box 3, Austerlitz, NY 12017* **Voice:** 518-392-3103 **E-mail:** ann-ellen@millaycolony.org **Contact:** Ann Ellen Lesser, Dir. **Founded:** 1973 **Open:** Year-round **Admission:** Application, resume, 6–10 slides, reference **Deadlines:** May 1 for Oct.–Jan.; Sep. 1 for Feb.–May; Feb. 1 for June–Sept. **Cost:** Transportation only **Size-Attendees:** 6–10 **Handicapped Access**

EDNA ST. VINCENT Millay named her estate "Steepletop" after the flower of the steeplebush, which grows here. The poet's spirit still seems to hover over this place, feeding the artists and writers who come for 4-week residencies.

The Millay Colony is a quiet place, well suited to contemplative artistic production. Residents have separate living quarters near their studios. Photographers will appreciate the north light of the visual artists' studios and the darkroom in the new (1997) handicapped-accessible building. Food is included in the residency at no cost: weekday dinners are prepared by the staff, and plenty is available at other mealtimes. The grounds cover 600 acres of former berry farm in the culturally rich area near the Berkshires of Massachusetts.

Nancy Brown Hands-on NY Workshop

For commercial fashion, beauty, illustrative and stock photographers *Flatiron district of Manhattan and area locations — 6 W. 20th St., New York, NY 10011* **Voice:** 212-924-9105 **Fax:** 212-633-0911 **Contact:** Jonathan Greene, Studio Mgr. **Founded:** 1987 **Open:** 1 week in late summer–early fall **Cost:** $1,000 (2 meals incl.) **Size-Attendees:** 8–12

NEW YORK PHOTOGRAPHER and former model Nancy Brown leads an intensive weeklong workshop in how to shoot commercial people photography for magazines, the fashion industry and stock. Participants learn how to set up, light and shoot beauty and glamour as well as lifestyle images. Brown and her staff of assistants, models, stylists, and hair and makeup artists show every step of what it takes to produce top-flight professional photographs.

The workshop runs from Sunday to Saturday, either in the studio or on location in the New York City area, and is suitable for aspiring professionals, as well as working photographers. Brown, who is the author of *Photographing People for Stock,* published by Amphoto, will also arrange one-on-one training for any photographer who wants that level of concentrated instruction.

Neversink Photo Workshops

For nature photographers *In the Catskills, 2 hr. N of NYC — 13 E. 17th St., New York, NY 10003* **Voice:** 212-929-0008; 914-434-0575 **Fax:** 212-929-2689 **Web Site:** www.apogeephoto.com/neversink.html **Contact:** Lou Jawitz **Founded:** 1988 **Open:** Aug. weekends **Cost:** $175 (2 lunches incl.); $95 for Sat. only; $65 for Sun. only.

THE NEVERSINK RIVER, which flows past Lou Jawitz's barn in Woodbourne, New York, gives its name to the weekend workshops conducted by photographers Jawitz and Ed Bohon every August. Students meet at the barn on Friday evening to view and critique photos. Most of Saturday and Sunday is spent exploring the woods and hills, observing the light, and taking pictures. (Inexpensive lodging is available at local hotels.)

Instruction is geared to the intermediate to advanced photographer, primarily on techniques of pictorial photography. Jawitz and Bohon are experienced commercial and stock photographers who know about equipment and can offer guidance on business and marketing issues.

Northern Short Course in Photojournalism

For news photographers *Different northeastern city each year — 187 Hodge Ave., Buffalo, NY 14222* **Voice:** 716-884-8844; 800-289-NPPA **E-mail:** 72640.21@compuserve.com **Web Site:** http://sunsite.unc.edu/NPPA **Contact:** Joe Traver **Founded:** 1981 **Open:** Feb.–Mar. **Cost:** $180 ($115 for NPPA members) for 3 days; lower fee for individual days; contest fee extra **Size-Attendees:** 500

EVERY YEAR IN MARCH, photojournalists gather at a different city in the Northeast for 3 days of lectures, seminars and hands-on demonstrations on the subject of still and TV news photography. Individual courses vary from year to year and may cover photographic and lighting techniques or the use of new technologies to shoot and transmit pictures. There is also likely to be a discussion of editing and publishing issues or perhaps some guidance on how to work more effectively with editors and colleagues in the deadline-sensitive arenas of newspapers and television news.

Teachers and lecturers are all working photojournalists and editors. The Northern Short Course is sponsored by the National Press Photographers Association (see "Joining Up"), though nonmember photojournalists are also welcome. NPPA, which will accept reservations for the conference, puts on a photography contest open only to its members.

Northlight Photo Workshops

For nature photographers
Wilderness areas in North America — 362 Bullville Rd., Montgomery, NY 12549 **Voice:** 914-361-1017; 800-714-1375 **Fax:** 914-361-1017 **Contact:** Brent McCullough, Dir. **Founded:** 1981 **Open:** Varies **Cost:** $585 –$645; $175 for weekends **Size-Attendees:** 8

BRENT MCCULLOUGH leads photographers on about a dozen week-long photography workshops into pristine natural areas every year. Workshop locations include National Parks from the Rockies to Maine plus coastal areas, mountains and desert regions throughout North America.

Workshop time is organized around the best light at each location. McCullough, whose nature images have appeared in books, posters and Sierra Club and Audubon calendars, makes a point of giving each participant as much as an hour's individual instruction per day.

With over 15 years teaching experience, McCullough is fastidious in his preparation, providing a detailed pre-workshop kit and itinerary for each trip. Some on-site processing is available. Lodging can be arranged at local motels.

Several weekend workshops, to natural areas in the East, are also offered.

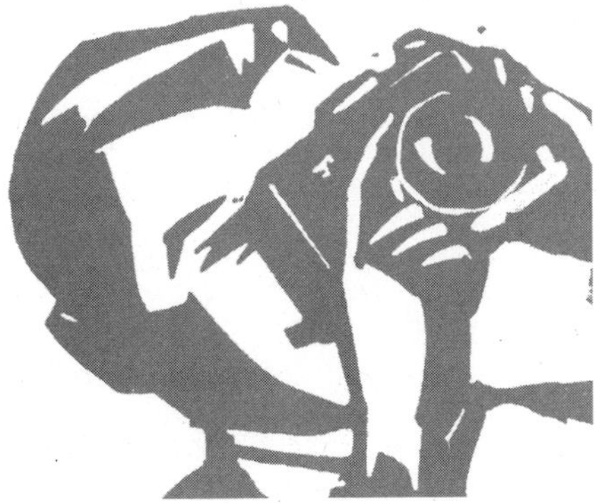

Photographics Unlimited

For photographers and digital artists
Flatiron district of Manhattan — 17 W. 17th St., New York, NY 10011 **Voice:** 212-255-9678 **Fax:** 212-620-0999 **Contact:** Rana Weaver **Founded:** 1995 **Open:** Year-round **Cost:** $295 **Size-Attendees:** 6 **Handicapped Access**

A CUSTOM PHOTO LAB, Photographics Unlimited offers a beginning and a more advanced class in Micrografx's Picture Publisher software. Picture Publisher is a Microsoft Windows- (rather than Macintosh/) based program that includes all the typical image management and manipulation functions (see page 107). The 8-hour sessions, offered frequently throughout the year, may be taken on 1 Saturday or on consecutive weekday evenings.

Pratt Institute

For student photographers and artists in many disciplines *200 Willoughby Ave., Brooklyn, NY 11205* **Voice:** 718-636-3669; 800-331-0834 **Fax:** 718-636-3670 **Contact:** Admissions **Open:** Year-round **Admission:** Application ($35), portfolio, goals essay, transcript, reference **Cost:** $16,000 per year, plus $11,000 room, board, supplies and fees **Financial Aid:** Scholarship; Fellowship **Degree or Certification:** 4-year BFA, 2-year MFA

THE MEDIA ARTS Department at Pratt encourages a hell-bent dedication to original seeing and interpretation through still and moving images. Photographers receive a basic grounding in photographic techniques and methods, but the overriding imperative is toward creating art. The theory is that an individual who has developed his or her own creative side will be able to produce artistic, commercial or editorial images at a consistently high level.

Pratt faculty are working artists, and students receive the wonderful benefit of being able to meet with, and sometimes intern with, many of the top practicing arts professionals in New York City. Other art and architecture courses, combined with a liberal arts curriculum, provide a broad choice of course material for the Pratt student.

Professional Photographers Society of NY Photo Workshop

For wedding & portrait photographers *Hobart College, Geneva — 121 Genesee, Avon, NY 14414* **Voice:** 716-226-8351 **Contact:** Lois Miller **Open:** 1 week in Aug. **Admission:** Application form **Cost:** $475 (dorm room and meals incl.); $100 discount for early registration **Financial Aid:** Scholarship **Handicapped Access**

THIS WINONA-AFFILIATED school (see *Georgia*) offers 5 weeklong courses in August on portraiture, weddings and the business of running a studio. Each participant takes 1 course for the week. The campus of Hobart College overlooks Seneca Lake in upstate New York, about an hour's drive west of Syracuse.

GEORGE EASTMAN HOUSE

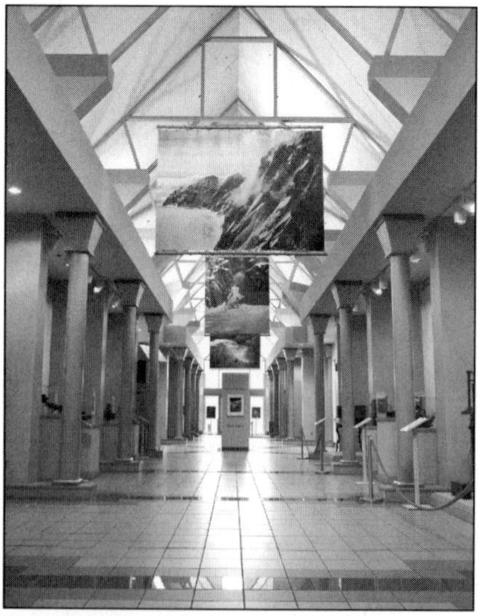

Photographic galleries, George Eastman House, Rochester.

Rochester Institute of Technology

For student photographers *1,300-acre campus 10 mi. S of Rochester — 70 Lomb Memorial Dr., Rochester, NY 14623* **Voice:** 716-475-7401 **Fax:** 716-475-5804 **E-mail:** info@RIT.edu **Web Site:** www.RIT.edu **Contact:** Nancy Stuart, Assoc. Dir. **Admission:** Academic application **Cost:** $18,000 per year, plus room and board **Financial Aid:** Scholarship; Work/Study **Size-Attendees:** 800 undergraduates in photo program **Degree or Certification:** AAF, BFA, BS, MFA **Job Placement:** Yes

ROCHESTER INSTITUTE of Technology offers comprehensive instruction in photography at both undergraduate and graduate levels.

The RIT School of Photographic Arts and Sciences has been recognized for decades as a leader in providing thorough training in photographic methods and technology. About 800 undergraduates and 100 graduate students attend the 4-year Bachelor's and 2-year Master's programs. Many RIT graduates go on to successful careers as photographers or photography-related technical experts.

The undergraduate program is vocationally oriented, with emphasis in applied photography (commercial or photojournalism), fine art or digital/technical. Students can also specialize in Film/Video, Computer Animation, Biomedical Photography, and Imaging Systems Management. The 2-year graduate program is directed primarily to the fine arts. Students have the choice of working with traditional methods or using modern electronic technology.

The school has state-of-the-art facilities, with 180 fully equipped darkrooms, 30 photo studios, a holography lab and a high-speed video lab. Digital imaging courses, on high-powered workstations, are part of the required curriculum for undergraduates. Some 150 photo courses are offered every quarter.

Though not directly affiliated with nearby Kodak, RIT students do take advantage of their proximity to the photography giant. They also have access to Rochester's outstanding photography museum and archive, the George Eastman House, named for Kodak's founder.

A full-time job placement counselor helps students find employment after graduation. About 80 percent of RIT's graduates find work in their preferred field within 2 years.

(The Technical and Education Center, which provides digital training for professionals, is described separately in this section.)

School of Visual Arts

For photographers and visual artists *Gramercy Park area of Manhattan — 209 E. 23rd St., New York, NY 10010* **Voice:** 212-592-2055 **Fax:** 212-592-2060 **Contact:** Deborah Vazquez **Founded:** 1968 **Open:** Workshops in summer; degree programs year-round **Admission:** Application for degree programs; registration only for continuing-ed workshops **Cost:** $300–$425 for summer workshops; $14,700 per year for graduate school; $13,000 per year for undergraduate; $5,000 per year for room and board **Financial Aid:** Scholarship **Size-Attendees:** 18 for studio classes **Degree or Certification:** BFA, MFA **Job Placement:** Yes

THIS NEW YORK CITY arts college has full 4-year undergraduate and 2-year graduate programs leading to degrees in photography and other commercial and fine arts. Undergraduates choose to specialize in either commercial photography or documentary/fine art, and are encouraged to experiment with developing their own photographic vocabulary and style. The facilities are first-rate, and students enjoy the benefit of living and studying in the photography capital of the world.

The SVA has an interesting summer program of 3- to 5-day photo workshops on topics that address the needs of up-and-coming working photographers, such as studio lighting or being a professional photographer's assistant. There are also courses in landscape and travel photography. Darkroom space is available for rent during the summer term.

Southampton College Master Photography Workshop

For intermediate to advanced photographers *LIU Southampton campus, Eastern Long Island — 239 Montauk Hwy., Southampton, NY 11968* **Voice:** 516-287-8427 **Fax:** 516-283-4081 **E-mail:** caglioti@sand.liunet.edu **Web Site:** www.southampton.liunet.edu **Contact:** Carla Caglioti **Founded:** 1985 **Open:** July–Aug. **Cost:** $450 (lab fee incl.) for weekend and 4-day classes **Size-Attendees:** 15 for most classes

THE FASHIONABLE summer vacation area of the Hamptons is the setting for this concentrated series of photo workshops offered by Long Island University. About a dozen weekend and weekday courses for the intermediate to advanced photographer address issues of personal vision and craftsmanship, as well as color and black & white darkroom and some digital work. The blend of Asian and Western faculty brings a cross-cultural influence to several of the workshops in this program.

One course is specifically geared to photography instructors.

The Hamptons, near the tip of Long Island, offer a wide variety of outdoor activities, from tennis to strolling on the many beaches. The area has a lively arts community and plenty of fine restaurants. LIU can arrange housing for $200 to $300 per week ($40 to $50 per night) and provides an optional meal plan.

Technical and Education Center of the Graphic Arts and Imaging at RIT

For graphic and digital arts professionals *On RIT campus — P.O. Box 422, E. Rochester, NY 14445* **Voice:** 716-475-2759; 800-724-2536 **Fax:** 716-475-7052 **E-mail:** dct1020@RIT.edu **Web Site:** www.RIT.edu **Contact:** David Tontarski **Founded:** 1951 **Cost:** $675 for 2-day Photoshop courses; $895 for 3-day **Size-Attendees:** 15

The Technical and Education Center is a professional training center within RIT that offers digital photography classes in Adobe Photoshop and Live Picture to photographers and other visual arts professionals. Other courses and seminars explore the intricacies of the electronic imaging process and teach the use of graphic design and publishing software. All hands-on workshops take advantage of RIT's advanced equipment and experienced teachers.

Every August the T & E Center offers a one-of-a-kind seminar: "Preservation of Photographs in a Digital World." This weeklong event, run in association with George Eastman House, presents the most thorough and detailed information available on the subject. The fee for the seminar is $1,050.

SUE WEISLER

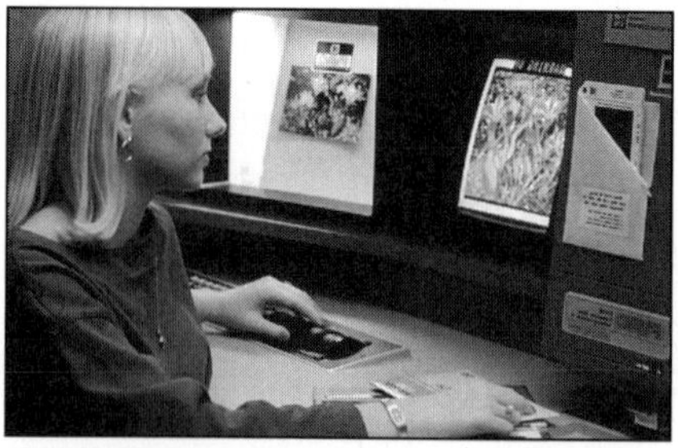

The digitized image, Rochester Institute of Technology.

Tisch School of the Arts/NYU

For students of photography *Greenwich Village area of Manhattan — 721 Broadway, 8th floor, New York, NY 10003* **Voice:** 212-998-1930 **Web Site:** www.nyu.edu **Contact:** Thomas Drysdale, Chair **Founded:** 1965 **Open:** School year plus summer programs **Admission:** Academic application plus samples of work **Cost:** $20,000 per year, plus fees and living expenses **Financial Aid:** Scholarship; Fellowship; Work/Study **Degree or Certification:** BFA, MFA **Handicapped Access**

The NYU program mixes scholarly consideration of photography with practical training for students who seek to enter the profession. The faculty includes critics and historians, as well as photographers who teach the skills and methods of the trade.

Undergraduate students choose to specialize in fine art photography, documentary practices and/or computer imaging. Graduate students may take their degree in association with the International Center for Photography (see above). All students benefit from being in New York, the world center for photography and the arts.

Tuscany Color Photography Workshop

For experienced photographers working in color *Near Siena, Italy — 561 Hudson St., Box 98, New York, NY 10014* **Voice:** 212-366-0601 **Fax:** 212-366-1107 **E-mail:** jmworks@angel.net **Contact:** Joel Meyerowitz, Dir. **Founded:** 1996 **Open:** 2 weeks in June **Admission:** Portfolio **Deadlines:** Early May **Cost:** $2,500 (shared accommodations and meals incl.) **Size-Attendees:** 16–18

THE FIRST LINE OF the brochure for this workshop says it all: "There is nothing like two weeks in the beautiful Tuscan countryside to refresh your way of looking at the world." The workshop takes place at Castelnuovo Tancredi, a large estate near Siena, in north central Italy. Experienced American and European photographers spend a fortnight together under the guidance of Joel Meyerowitz, one of the world's foremost color visionaries. (Meyerowitz is a successful commercial and art photographer, well known for his book *Cape Light* and other color projects.)

The purpose of the workshop is to enhance each photographer's passion for the medium. Participants spend their days photographing the exquisite towns and landscapes of Tuscany. Evenings are filled with discussions and viewing images. There are day trips to many famous and historic sites, and 3 home-cooked meals a day are included in the fee. This workshop is new as of this writing and may be subject to change in coming years.

United Digital Artists

For photographers, digital artists and multimedia artists *Midtown Manhattan — P.O. Box 548, FDR Station, New York, NY 10150* **Voice:** 212-777-7200; 800-227-4935 **Fax:** 212-777-7222 **E-mail:** UDIGART@applelink.apple.com **Web Site:** www.uda.com **Contact:** Maryalice Quinn **Founded:** 1994 **Cost:** $645 for 2-day classes; $1,850 for Certification in Imaging (4 courses) **Size-Attendees:** 15 **Handicapped Access**

NEW-MEDIA EXPERT Stewart McBride founded United Digital Artists as an agency to represent a broad array of artists working individually and in teams on producing CD-ROMs, Web sites, and whatever other kinds of cyber-products the market may want or artists can dream up. UDA offers courses in leading-edge software and electronic techniques, with a new catalogue coming out every 4 months. By next year, UDA may be offering training in imaging technology that does not exist today.

Most classes run for 2 days, including access to the computers during the evening of the first day if the student wishes. The teachers are all working professionals. The Imaging Certificate Program includes beginning, intermediate and advanced classes in Adobe Photoshop and some exposure to related programs. All classes are held at the Apple Market Center in the Citicorp building in midtown Manhattan.

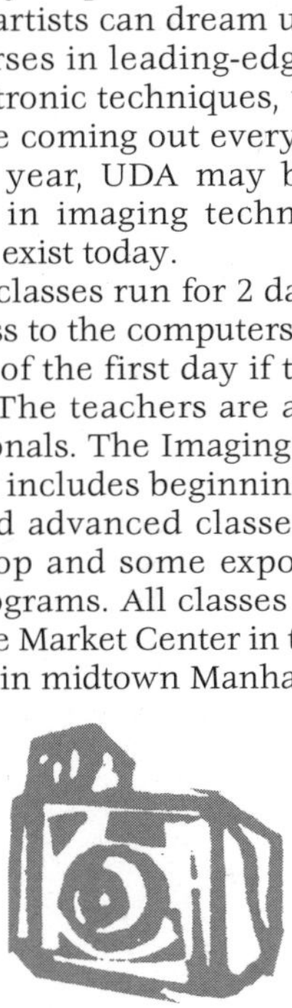

VISCOMM

For photographers, multimedia artists, designers *Javits Convention Center, Manhattan — 1420 MacArthur Dr., Suite 104, Carrollton, TX 75007* **Voice:** 203-852-0500, ext. 288; 800-243-3238 **Fax:** 203-838-3710 **E-mail:** viscomm@tradeshow.com **Contact:** Andrea Cassello, Marketing Mgr. **Founded:** 1985 **Open:** 3 days in Oct.–Nov. **Admission:** Intended for trade only; under 18 must be accompanied by qualified adult **Deadlines:** 1 mo. ahead for early registration **Cost:** $25 entry (free with seminars); $90 for most seminars; $645 for hands-on digital workshops **Size-Attendees:** 10,000+; seminars vary, up to 200 **Handicapped Access**

EVERY YEAR AROUND Halloween, thousands of professional photographers descend on the Javits Convention Center on Manhattan's West Side for 3 days of the largest photographic trade show in the country.

VISCOMM has 2 parts: an exhibit hall full of products and services for the photographer, and a seminar series. The exhibit hall is immense, with displays of all the latest in cameras, lighting, accessories and electronic equipment. Here you can fiddle with a new camera or see a demonstration of the most advanced photo manipulation software. Manufacturers' representatives are eager to answer any and all questions. This is an information event: products are not for sale on site.

Seminars, most lasting 1½ to 2 hours, run throughout the trade show. There are over 100 of them, covering an enormous range of topics. VISCOMM seminars, more than anywhere else, address the most forward-looking concerns of the photo industry, including the assessment of current trends and new technology. The program also offers studio tours and hands-on digital workshops, run by United Digital Artists (see above).

The greatest value of attending the VISCOMM show may be the creative boost you receive just by being around the best and most advanced that photography has to offer. Besides photography, the show includes exhibits on photo lab equipment, multimedia and advanced design technology. Students get free admission and discounts on seminars. Discounts are also available for early enrollees and those attending multiple seminars. There's a western VISCOMM, too—see *California*.

Visual Studies Workshop

For photographers, digital artists and videographers *Museum district, downtown Rochester — 31 Prince St., Rochester, NY 14607* **Voice:** 716-442-8676 **Fax:** 716-442-1992 **Contact:** Cathy Higgins, Adm. Asst. **Founded:** 1982 **Open:** July–Aug. **Cost:** $385 for week (lab fee incl.); surcharge for academic credit **Size-Attendees:** 30–60; classes 12 (digital 8) **Degree or Certification:** Credit can be arranged through the State University of New York

THE VISUAL STUDIES Workshop offers a series of 6 intensive week-long summer courses to the photographer interested in learning new techniques and enhancing his or her artistic vision, as well as 6 courses in digital imaging. There are courses for early-stage as well as advanced photographers in traditional image making, non-silver printing and photographic publishing.

Housed in an imposing stone building in Rochester's museum district, VSW is an internationally known center for media studies, which includes film and video and visual books, as well as photography and digital imaging. It publishes books and posters by artists and writers and maintains several galleries and a bookstore. Its Research Center houses a large and diverse collection of primary and secondary materials in visual media, and it offers an MFA program in association with New York State University at Brockport. VSW's artist-in-residency program supports research and artistic creation with monthlong residencies in photography, book arts and video.

Voyagers International

For photographers at all levels *Ireland, Africa, Nepal, South America, Alaska, China — P.O. Box 915, Ithaca, NY 14851* **Voice:** 607-257-3091; 800-633-0299 **Fax:** 607-257-3699 **E-mail:** voyint@aol.com **Web Site:** www.gorp.com/voyagers.htm **Contact:** Nancy Grossman, Adm. Dir. **Founded:** 1981 **Open:** Year-round **Cost:** $2,000–$6,000; some fees include airfare **Size-Attendees:** Mostly 10–18

VOYAGERS International coordinates photographic tours all over the world. The tours are specifically designed for photographers, and all are led by experienced professionals, most of whom have been leading groups overseas for years. Many of the photographer/instructors who work with Voyagers, such as John Gerlach, Ron Rosenstock, Joe McDonald and Dewitt Jones, also conduct their own independent photo tours (and have separate listings here).

Groups are kept small to allow each participant plenty of personal access to the instructor. Itineraries are planned around visually appealing places that are suitable for photography, not just general sightseeing. The schedule is flexible to permit plenty of time for waiting out pictures. Voyagers International administers literally dozens of photo tours to 5 continents and provides especially comprehensive pre-departure materials.

Women's Studio Workshop

For photographers and artists in selected other disciplines *Mid-Hudson Valley, 100 mi. N of New York City — P.O. Box 489, Rosendale, NY 12472* **Voice:** 914-658-9133 **E-mail:** wsw@mhv.net **Web Site:** www.webmark.com/wsw/wswhome.htm **Contact:** Tatana Kellner for fellowship program, Ann Kalmbach for book grants, Laura Moriarty for summer program and internships **Founded:** 1974 **Open:** Workshops in summer; residency and internships year-round **Admission:** Artists' Fellowships by jury: application, resume, letter of interest, 6–10 slides. Book grants: written description of project, resume, 6–10 slides. **Deadlines:** Fellowships: May 15 for Sept.–Feb.; Nov. 1 for Mar.–June. Book Grants: Nov. 15. Internships: Mar. 15 for summer; July 15 for fall; Nov. 15 for spring. **Cost:** $425 for 5-day workshop; $200 per week plus materials for Fellowship recipients **Financial Aid:** Fellowship; Work/Study; Stipend

A MULTIDISCIPLINARY arts organization, the Women's Studio Workshop offers several photography workshops during the summer, plus artist-in-residence fellowships during the rest of the year. The orientation is strictly toward the creation of fine art, and especially handmade artists' books.

Reading WSW's brochures, you can almost hear summer's crickets chirping in this popular retreat area near Woodstock. The small towns of the Hudson Valley seem to lend themselves especially well toward personal contemplation and artistic creation. WSW attracts artists from across the country, whose work and ideas blend to give rise to a culturally rich and stimulating atmosphere.

Photography workshops here explore alternative processes and the way photography can play a part in personal well-being. Fellowship programs during the non-summer months last from 2 to 6 weeks and give artists open use of the facilities, including darkrooms, to create as they see fit. Though run entirely by women and catering primarily to women artists, WSW welcomes men as well.

Artists' book residency grants, which support the production of limited-edition books at WSW, include a stipend of $1,800 plus up to $450 in materials. Book production grants, for artists working off-site, help with production costs up to $750.

The Summer Arts Institute engages 3 interns each year to provide general assistance to the staff and to do maintenance work. Interns can attend workshops at no charge when not working, and receive $75 per month stipend plus housing and access to facilities.

Yaddo

For photographers and artists in selected other disciplines *25 mi. N of Albany — P.O. Box 395, Sarasota Springs, NY 12866* **Voice:** 518-584-0746 **Fax:** 518-584-1312 **Founded:** 1900 **Open:** Year-round, except certain weeks in Sept. **Admission:** Application ($20), resume, 7 slides, references **Deadlines:** Jan. 15 for May–Feb.; Aug. 1 for Oct.–May **Cost:** Voluntary contributions encouraged **Size-Attendees:** 35 in summer; 15 off-season **Handicapped Access**

YADDO'S MISSION AS an art center was born out of tragedy. Financier Spencer Trask, who built the 55-room mansion that serves as principal residence, lost all 4 of his children and thus had no one to whom he could pass on the 400-acre estate. So in 1900 he and wife, Katrina, designated that the place should serve the needs of artists who would "make gifts useful to the world."

Yaddo is a busy place—especially in summer, when the number of residents is more than double that of the rest of the year. Established artists work intensively during the declared "quiet hours," 9 a.m. to 4 p.m. and after 10 p.m., but mingle freely in the afternoons and evenings. The cross-fertilization of ideas from different disciplines, and often different countries, makes Yaddo a stimulating place for residents, who spend an average of 5 weeks on the premises.

Breakfast and dinner are taken communally, and each artist has a private bedroom and studio. There is a black & white darkroom. Recreational facilities are ample both on the estate and in nearby Saratoga Springs.

Yaddo residents tend to be among the most accomplished artists and writers anywhere. Expect that work samples will be judged by rigorous standards.

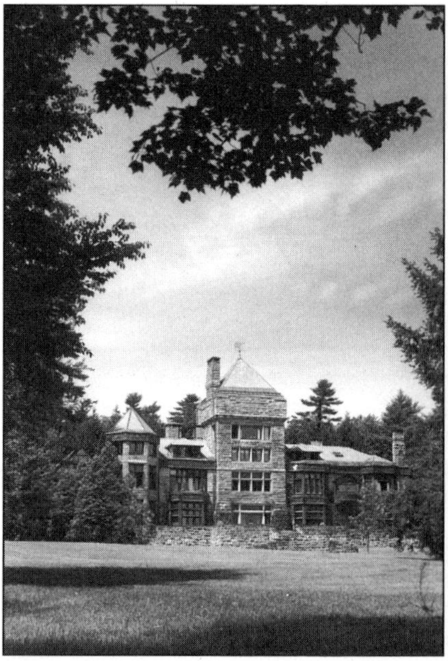

Yaddo Mansion, Yaddo, Saratoga Springs

North Carolina

NPPA Electronic Photojournalism Workshop

For newspaper, magazine and television photographers *Varies — 3200 Croasdaile Dr., Durham, NC 27705* **Voice:** 919-383-7246; 800-289-NPPA **E-mail:** 72640.21@compuserve.com **Web Site:** http://sunsite.unc.edu/nppa **Contact:** Charles Cooper, Exec. Dir. **Founded:** 1988 **Open:** 1 week in Sept. **Admission:** Application **Cost:** Under $500 **Group Size:** 125

EVERY YEAR AN intrepid group of photojournalists, designers and news editors get together for a week in September to explore the electronic frontier. They work with digital cameras, scanners and computers to produce on paper and over the Internet a one-of-a-kind newspaper called "The Electronic Times."

The workshop was created for the membership of the National Press Photographers Association, though some freelancers and a number of foreign-based photographers usually attend. Participants work in teams of photographers and editors, learning how to use the latest technology as it relates to magazines, newspapers and television. They gather news, edit images, create stories and prepare them for print and transmission. They work long hours. "Pixels never sleep" is the battle cry. At every turn, the emphasis is on doing familiar jobs in high-tech ways.

The volunteer teaching staff of 35 includes some of the sharpest television and newspaper technology users in the country. An annual theme of the workshop is to go beyond last year's boundaries to the very edges of the technology envelope. The workshop is held in a different small to medium-size city each year. While this event is oriented to the news photographer, anyone may apply.

No direct financial aid is available, but EPW does count on a few hardworking college interns. For details about this year's program, call John Cranfill at the *Dallas Morning News*, 919-977-8361, or e-mail at jcranfill@ix.net.com.

NPPA Flying Short Course

For news photographers and photojournalists *Five different cities each year — 3200 Croasdaile Dr., Durham, NC 27705* **Voice:** 919-383-7256; 800-289-NPPA **E-mail:** 72640.21@compuserve.com **Web Site:** http://sunsite.unc.edu/nppa **Contact:** Charles Cooper, Exec. Dir. **Open:** Early Oct. **Admission:** Application form **Cost:** $50 **Group Size:** 250–300

EXPERTS IN photojournalism and in subjects of interest to news photographers embark on a whirlwind jaunt every October to 5 cities across the country. At each stop, they present a daylong series of lectures to a few hundred photographers and news professionals. The topics vary with the speakers, which generally include the NPPA newspaper and television Photographers of the Year. The cities change annually. Check with NPPA for this year's presenters and the day's content.

Penland School of Crafts

For photographers and artists in selected other disciplines *Blue Ridge Mtns., 50 mi. N of Asheville — Penland, NC 28765* **Voice:** 704-765-2359 **Fax:** 704-765-7389 **E-mail:** pnlndschl@aol.com **Contact:** Robert Chiarito, Coord. (workshops), or Dana Moore, Prog. Dir. (residencies) **Founded:** 1929 **Open:** Spring, summer, and fall **Admission:** Workshops: application ($25). Residents: application, references, 15–20 slides, personal statement. **Deadlines:** Work/study and studio assistants: Feb 20. Residencies: Oct. 28. **Cost:** $265–$630 for 1–2½ weeks; room and board $200–$500 per week; $1,200–$4,000 for 2- to 8-week spring and fall concentration programs. Residents: $150 per month for housing. **Financial Aid:** Scholarship; Work/Study **Group Size:** 7 residencies, 15 in workshops **Degree or Certification:** Credit through East Tennessee State Unversity and West Carolina University **Handicapped Access**

IN THE QUIET mountains of western North Carolina, the Penland School of Crafts has been providing instruction and studio opportunities to artists for over half a century. Many workshops are available to everyone from the beginner to the working professional. The majority of Penland's summer courses run for 2 weeks, time enough to immerse yourself in a topic and explore many of its subtleties. This is significant since workshops in photography (and other fields) often address just the creative periphery of the medium. Penland's spring and fall "Concentration" sessions can run as long as 8 weeks.

The residency program offers independent working artists at transitional points in their careers 2 or 3 years to work on their projects. Residents have no official responsibility to teach but are expected to interact with participants in the regular programs. Those seeking resident status should have prior experience at Penland in some capacity.

Penland is a tranquil place, organized around intensive creative endeavor. Housing is simple but comfortable, with choices ranging from dormitory to private rooms. Studios are open 24 hours a day. Students do not work in isolation, however. An on-campus coffee house, occasional volleyball games and frequent evening activities provide ample opportunity for social interaction and discussion. Summer studio assistants and work/study students exchange labor for a whole or partial reduction in tuition.

Professional Photographers of North Carolina/ Summer Short Session

For wedding and portrait photographers *NC State University, Raleigh — 705 Randolph St., #E, Thomasville, NC 27360* **Voice:** 910-476-4938 **E-mail:** clatruell@aol.com **Contact:** Rex Truell **Founded:** 1958 **Open:** 4 days in mid-Aug. **Cost:** $395–$450 for most courses; $750 for digital; discounts for early registration **Group Size:** 100 total; classes 10–25; digital 10 **Handicapped Access**

THIS WINONA-AFFILIATED school (see *Georgia*) offers a series of six or seven 4-day classes on wedding and portrait technique, plus business issues for the studio photographer. It has also offered a digital imaging class that covers the use of Adobe Photoshop to rework and retouch images and of digital cameras for direct digital image capture.

Ohio

Nature's Light

For novice to advanced amateur photographers *Scenic locations across America; also Galapagos — 7805 Lake Ave., Cincinnati, OH 45236* **Voice:** 513-793-2346 **Fax:** 513-793-2342 **Web Site:** www.apogeephoto.com/natures_light.html **Contact:** William Manning, Dir. **Founded:** 1993 **Open:** Year-round **Admission:** Application form **Cost:** $185 for weekend workshops, $115 for 2-day extension; $650–$1,100 for tours (lodging incl.); $3,375 for trip to Galapagos (airfare from Miami incl.) **Group Size:** Workshops 22 maximum; tours 8 maximum

SHARING THE pleasure of photographing beautiful places is the aim of the Nature's Light programs. Friday evening to Sunday afternoon workshops, with optional 2-day extensions, take place in scenic locations from Maine to Texas, Yellowstone to the Smokies. The tours consist of 5 to 7 days spent hiking and shooting in the Tetons, in Bryce Canyon or at Mt. Rainier. Participants spend most of their time in the field, enjoying nature and the camaraderie of photographers and instructors.

The Galapagos trip focuses on the unique species that inhabit these isolated islands.

DOUG BOYLAN

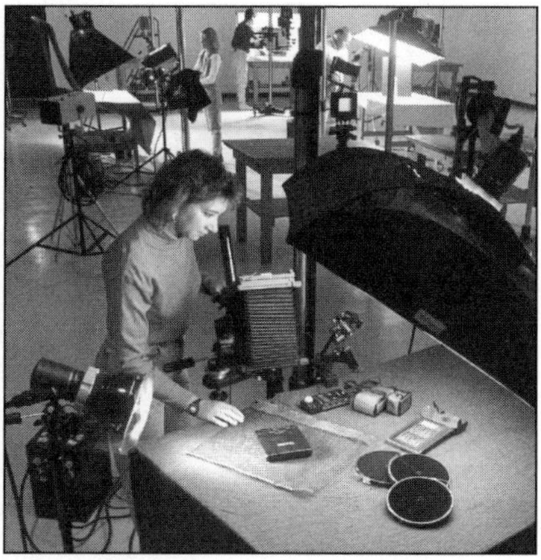

Fine-tuning a shot, Ohio Institute of Photography and Technology, Dayton.

Ohio Institute of Photography and Technology

For student photographers *3 mi. S of downtown Dayton — 2029 Edgefield Rd., Dayton, OH 45439* **Voice:** 513-294-6155; 800-932-9698 **Fax:** 513-294-2259 **Contact:** Alycia Falkner **Founded:** 1970 **Open:** 4 quarters yearly **Admission:** Application ($100) **Cost:** $10,000 per year **Financial Aid:** Scholarship **Group Size:** 150 photography students **Degree or Certification:** Associate's degree, diploma **Job Placement:** Yes

A TECHNICAL SCHOOL owned by a medical group, OIP&T trains high-school graduates to become professional photographers and computer imaging specialists. Students may concentrate on general applied photography, commercial, portrait or biomedical photography, or in imaging technology. The course of study, which includes general education classes, lasts 2 years for an Associate's degree or 18 months for a diploma.

OIP&T's own 18,000-square-foot building in Dayton houses studios, classrooms and darkrooms, plus computer facilities. Housing and all meals are the responsibility of the students. Non-matriculated photographers who qualify may take selected courses along with full-time students.

Ohio University School of Visual Communication

For student photographers, especially in documentary photography *1½ hr. SE of Columbus — 301 Siegfred Hall, Athens, OH 45701* **Voice:** 614-593-4894 **Fax:** 614-593-0190 **E-mail:** vicodept@ouvaxa.cats.ohiou.edu **Web Site:** www.viscom.ohiou.edu **Contact:** Larry Nighswander, Dir. **Admission:** Application; portfolio for graduate program **Deadlines:** Feb. for fall admission **Financial Aid:** Scholarship; Fellowship; Work/Study **Group Size:** 200 undergraduate; 25 graduate students **Degree or Certification:** BS (Visual Communications), MA, MFA **Job Placement:** Yes **Handicapped Access**

THE OHIO UNIVERSITY program has a rich tradition of preparing students for careers in photography, especially in the areas of documentary photography and photojournalism. Six full-time faculty members with impressive professional credentials teach photo editing and illustration, digital imaging, and multimedia, as well as providing thorough training in still photography.

Graduate students may seek either an MA, which is oriented toward documentary photography, or an MFA in the College of Arts & Sciences.

A 5-week summer workshop in Edinburgh, Scotland, gives students a chance to operate as working journalists in another country. The photography program is open to non-Ohio U. students as well, at the undergraduate and graduate levels.

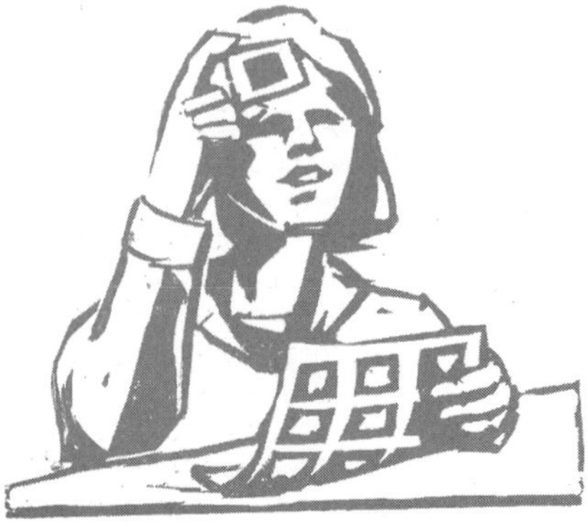

Oklahoma

David Halpern Photography Workshops

For landscape photographers *Oklahoma and Rocky Mtns. — 7420 E. 70th St., Tulsa, OK 74133* **Voice:** 918-252-4973 **Fax:** 918-252-5710 **E-mail:** david_halpern@msn.com **Contact:** David Halpern **Founded:** 1984 **Open:** June and July **Cost:** $95–$125 for Park-sponsored weekends; up to $1,000 for weeklong workshops

IN ASSOCIATION WITH the Rocky Mountain National Park in Colorado and several art/educational institutions in Oklahoma, David Halpern teaches photographers to enhance their visual skills and make pictures of the natural landscape. Workshops vary considerably from year to year, and may range from youth programs to large-format explorations of the natural world. Halpern has been a commercial photographer and has exhibited his landscape work for over 20 years.

Oklahoma Fall Arts Institutes

For photographers and artists in selected other disciplines *Quartz Mtn. Arts & Conference Center, 125 mi. W of Oklahoma City — P.O. Box 18154, Oklahoma City, OK 73154* **Voice:** 405-842-0890 **Fax:** 405-848-4538 **E-mail:** okarts@telepath.com **Web Site:** www.telepath.com/okarts **Contact:** Linda DeBerry, Ass't Prog. Dir. **Founded:** 1985 **Open:** Fall **Cost:** $450 for 4-day weekend (room and board incl.) **Financial Aid:** Scholarship **Group Size:** 80–100 total; classes 20 **Handicapped Access**

SOME OF AMERICA'S most renowned photographers, such as Mary Ellen Mark and Jay Maisel, lead these 4-

day-weekend workshop retreats under the auspices of the Oklahoma Arts Institute. Instruction, discussion and critique of previous work take place in the studio pavilions overlooking Lake Lugert in Quartz Mountain State Park in southwest Oklahoma. Daily assignments, in the studio or out, are up to the individual instructor. These are hands-on workshops, designed to promote rapid growth in your photographic vision in a very short time.

Five programs are scheduled during the fall, each one reserved for a single art medium, so that all 4 or 5 photography courses meet at the same time. This format provides a superb opportunity for photographers enrolled with different instructors to mingle and share impressions. Instructors present their own work and discuss their artistic philosophies during the evenings.

Participants share lodge or cabin accommodations and Thursday evening through Sunday morning meals. These workshops are open to amateur and professional artists and educators on a first-come, first-served basis. Some scholarships are available to Oklahoma residents and teachers.

Oklahoma School of Photography

For student photographers *Suburb of Oklahoma City — 2306 N. Moore Ave., Moore, OK 73160* **Voice:** 405-799-1411 **Fax:** 405-799-2923 **Contact:** Jerry Cockrell, Dir. **Founded:** 1973 **Open:** Year-round **Admission:** Personal interview **Cost:** $6,000 (most materials incl.) **Group Size:** 50–75 total; classes up to 20 **Degree or Certification:** Certificate **Job Placement:** Yes

ASPIRING photographers receive training in the basic theory and techniques of photography in this 30-week course. Lectures, demonstrations and personal instruction introduce subjects; hands-on studio and darkroom work allows students to learn the various skills and procedures.

Students may enter any Monday and have 45 weeks to complete the 24-hour-per-week course. While the school offers instruction in many aspects of photography, it emphasizes portraiture and weddings.

Oregon

Duckworth Forensic Photography

For police and forensic photographers *Varies — 2495 Maple Ave. NE, Salem, OR 97303* **Voice:** 503-364-9570 **Contact:** John Duckworth **Founded:** 1970 **Open:** As requested **Admission:** Application form **Cost:** Varies with location and size of group **Group Size:** 12–24

JOHN DUCKWORTH, author of the textbook *Forensic Photography,* teaches a 30-hour course (usually over the course of 4 days) in all aspects of the subject, including crime scene, surveillance, autopsy and other aspects of police/forensic work.

Rather than schedule regular classes in Oregon, Duckworth travels to conduct his workshop wherever demand merits. The sponsoring group pays his transportation and expenses, plus the instructor's fee of $250 per day.

Oregon School of Arts & Crafts

For photographers and artists in selected other disciplines *8245 SW Barnes Rd., Portland, OR 97225* **Voice:** 503-297-5544 **Fax:** 503-297-9651 **Founded:** 1979 **Open:** Residencies June–Aug. **Admission:** Application, resume, statement of intent, samples of work, references, portfolio **Deadlines:** Dec. 1 for following summer **Financial Aid:** Fellowship **Group Size:** 2 **Degree or Certification:** Degree and certificate programs as part of 3-year art college

BESIDES ITS 3-year art college program, the Oregon School of Arts & Crafts offers 2 summer residencies for mid-career photographers and other artists in a variety of craft-related media.

Residents receive on-campus housing, a $1,200 fellowship, $300 for materials, and up to $500 transportation reimbursement. Residents are invited to share their work with students at ongoing workshops and classes, and they may audit all classes.

Photographers may use the photography department studios and black & white and color darkrooms. Applicants must be U.S. nationals or permanent residents.

Philip Augustin Workshops

For landscape photographers *Yellowstone and southern Utah — P.O. Box 5387, Salem, OR 97304* **Voice:** 503-588-1654 **Fax:** 503-588-1654 **E-mail:** augustin-photo@worldnet.att.net **Contact:** Philip Augustin **Founded:** 1989 **Open:** Winter and fall **Admission:** Application form **Cost:** $1,500 (lodging, meals, and local transportation incl.) **Group Size:** 16

LANDSCAPE photography is the subject of these weeklong workshops, which take place in Yellowstone in the winter and in the Escalante Canyon region of southern Utah during the fall. Philip Augustin and co-instructors provide instruction in translating what the photographer sees into a successful image, in color or black & white. Photographers have plenty of time during long days in the field to concentrate on the natural beauty before them. Evening presentations and portfolio reviews supplement the hands-on instruction.

Sitka Center for Art & Ecology

For photographers, naturalists and artists in selected other disciplines *90 mi. SW of Portland — Neskowin Coast Foundation, P.O. Box 65, Otis, OR 97368* **Voice:** 541-994-5485 **Contact:** Randall Cook **Founded:** 1971 **Open:** Residencies: fall and spring **Admission:** Application, project description, resume, samples, references **Deadlines:** June 20 **Cost:** Meals and transportation **Group Size:** 2

THE SITKA CENTER, located in the Cascade Head National Scenic Research Area on the coast of Oregon, is dedicated to the expression of the strong relationship between art and nature. Photographers and other artists and naturalists may apply for a 4-month residency in the fall or spring, to work in semi-isolation at a privately owned ranch.

Artists/naturalists in 3 categories—emerging, mid-career and on sabbatical—are eligible for the residency program. Those accepted may teach workshops and are required to spend 20 hours per month in community service on behalf of Sitka. Residents live in a private house, where they are responsible for their own meals, and have the use of studio space and the great outdoors, where the Cascade Mountains meet the Pacific Ocean. Applicants must not have participated in an arts residency within the previous 2 years.

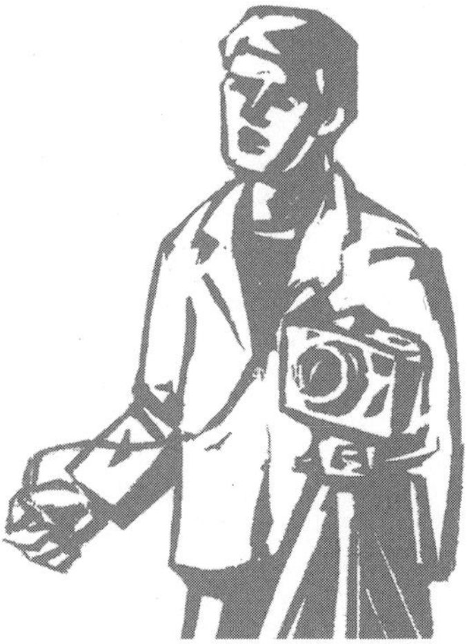

Pennsylvania

Fabric Workshop & Museum Artist-in-Residence Program

For photographers and artists in selected other disciplines *Center City — 1315 Cherry St., 5th fl., Philadelphia, PA 19107* **Voice:** 215-568-1111 **Fax:** 215-568-8211 **Contact:** Steven Beyer, Asst. Artistic Dir. **Founded:** 1977 **Open:** Year-round **Admission:** Resume, 10–20 slides, statement of interest **Cost:** Transportation only **Financial Aid:** Stipend **Group Size:** Usually 1 **Handicapped Access**

THE VARIED possibilities of working with fabric begin with photo-silkscreen and extend to wherever an artist may take them. Each year the Fabric Workshop and Museum, a nonprofit organization devoted to experimental design and printing, invites about a dozen artists, including photographers, to work with its own artistic staff in experimental and artistic creations. Most artists-in-residence stay for only a week or two, though they may continue on for a couple of months if the project merits. Artists receive a $1,000 honorarium, an apartment, a per diem for meals and the cost of materials. Because most projects are collaborative with the museum's staff, visiting artists are requested to leave an example of the work they have completed during the residency.

Joe McDonald Wildlife Photography

For wildlife and nature photographers *Central PA, scenic places in U.S., and some overseas, especially Africa — 73 Loht Rd., McClure, PA 17841* **Voice:** 717-543-6423 **Fax:** 717-543-6423 **Web Site:** www. apogeephoto.com/joe_mcdonald.html **Contact:** Joe or Mary Ann McDonald **Founded:** 1985 **Open:** Varies **Cost:** $1,000–$1,250 for weeklong workshops around U.S.; $400 for 3-day in PA; $800 for weeklong Nature Photo School in PA; $6,000 for southern Africa; all include lodging, some meals **Group Size:** 12

WILDLIFE AND NATURE are the focus of Joe and Mary Ann McDonald's workshops and tours. They offer 3 types of programs: intensive weeklong courses at their curiously named Hoot Hollow Institute; workshops at Hoot Hollow and in the Everglades, Bryce Canyon, the Tetons and the like; and tours to such places as Africa or the Galapagos.

The McDonalds are both veteran nature photographers whose work has been published in many leading magazines (*Natural History, Wildlife Conservation, Ranger Rick*). They personally lead all the workshops, often together. For the domestic workshops and the classes in Pennsylvania, the emphasis is on teaching more than on free shooting. Workshop days often start before dawn to take advantage of the light and proceed well into the evening hours. Overseas tours are geared to giving photographers as much time as possible to shoot.

Joe McDonald is the author of the Amphoto book *The Complete Guide to Wildlife Photography* and other titles on the subject of photographing animals.

Michael A. Smith/ Paula Chamlee Apprenticeships

For black & white fine art photographers *Bucks County, 1 hr. N of Philadelphia — P.O. Box 400, Ottsville, PA 18942* **Voice:** 610-847-2005 **Fax:** 610-847-2373 **E-mail:** smitcham@epix.net **Contact:** Michael Smith or Paula Chamlee **Open:** Varies **Admission:** Phone call first; then portfolio and letter stating interest **Cost:** Living expenses

MICHAEL A. SMITH and spouse Paula Chamlee are 2 of America's most prolific and accomplished fine art photographers. They work only in large-format (8 x 10 and up) black & white, making their living exclusively by publishing books and selling contact prints of images of nature and the built world. They need apprentices to assist them in the darkroom and sometimes in the field.

Photographers who are passionate about learning fine art photography will find that the apprenticeship method, with its extended period of work and observation, provides a much deeper understanding of the medium than a brief workshop or school program can. Apprentices may work for a year or more and are paid a small salary if they prove successful, though they are not allowed to use the facilities for their own work.

PAULA CHAMLEE

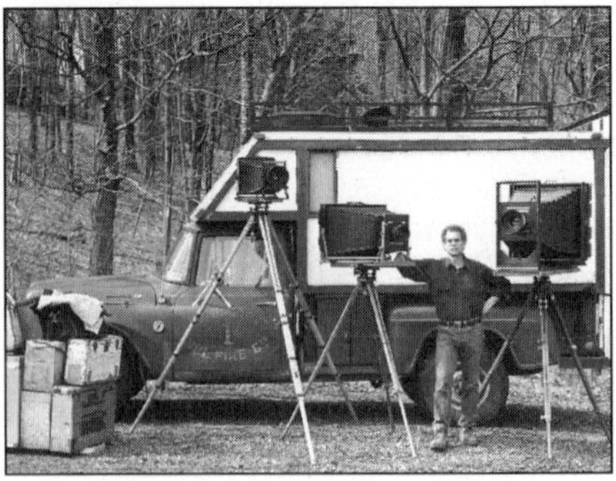

Large **large-format cameras, Michael A. Smith/Paula Chamlee Apprenticeships, Ottsville, PA.**

School of Evidence Photography

For forensic, scientific and medical photographers *Varies — EPIC, 600 Main St., Honesdale, PA 18431* **Voice:** 717-253-5450; 800-356-3742 **Fax:** 717-253-5011 **Contact:** Robert Jennings, Dir. **Founded:** 1968 **Open:** Weekend in fall; sometimes in spring **Cost:** $295; discount for early registration

THIS 3-DAY COURSE, held once or twice per year, teaches all aspects of legal and forensic still photography and videography. Six to 8 instructors cover the business of legal photography, lighting and surveillance techniques, courtroom considerations, digital imaging applications and more. There are demonstrations of new technologies and specialized equipment.

Useful for those already working in forensic photography, this course also provides a good introduction for photographers looking to branch out into this field.

STUDIO for Creative Inquiry

For photographers and artists in all media *E of center city — College of Fine Arts, Carnegie Mellon University, Pittsburgh, PA 15213* **Voice:** 412-268-3451 **Fax:** 412-268-7817 **E-mail:** mmbm+@andrew.cmu.edu **Contact:** Marge Myers, Ass't Dir. **Founded:** 1989 **Open:** Year-round **Admission:** Concept proposal, resume, work samples **Cost:** Room and board **Financial Aid:** Fellowship; Stipend **Group Size:** 20–30 total **Handicapped Access**

THE STUDIO for Creative Inquiry is an interdisciplinary center within Carnegie Mellon University, serving as a focus for experimental activities in the arts. It sponsors projects that blend the intellectual and the creative, with the goal of incubating new knowledge that will benefit the university and the greater community. Recent projects have included a multimedia presentation of the workings of body cells, a virtual-reality multicultural art museum and a robotic marine craft built to circumnavigate the Earth.

Many of the STUDIO's staff are university professors and researchers. Visiting artists ordinarily work with staff and researchers to execute projects, which may take advantage of the university's technological and scientific expertise and facilities.

Stipends and fellowships are granted according to the needs of a project and available funding. Two salaried full-time research positions are available each year; other residencies may last only a week or two. Housing is not provided. Proposals are judged on the appropriateness to the STUDIO's overall mission. The director says that he looks forward to receiving proposals that surprise him.

Triangle Institute of Professional Photography

For wedding and portrait photographers *Greentree Marriott Hotel, Pittsburgh — 441 State St., Baden, PA 15005* **Voice:** 412-869-9281 **Fax:** 412-869-5455 **Contact:** Samuel Pelaia **Founded:** 1968 **Open:** 1 week in late Jan. **Deadlines:** Dec. 31 for enrollment preference **Cost:** $460 for week (lunches and dinners incl.) **Financial Aid:** Scholarship **Group Size:** 350 **Handicapped Access**

THIS WINONA-AFFILIATED school (see *Georgia*) offers photographers a choice of 2 half-week courses in a variety of more than a dozen portrait, wedding and studio management classes. The other option is a full week's concentration on 1 subject. One of the weeklong classes is an introduction to Adobe Photoshop digital imaging software (a real bargain here). This is a large gathering of photographers, and a good place to meet and talk shop with colleagues.

Rhode Island

Rhode Island School of Design

For student photographers and artists in many disciplines *Near downtown Providence — 2 College St., Providence, RI 02903* **Voice:** 401-454-6300; 800-364-7473 **Fax:** 401-454-6309 **E-mail:** admissions@risd.edu **Founded:** 1875 **Admission:** Application ($35) **Cost:** $17,600, plus $6,600 room and board **Group Size:** 1,850 undergraduate; 150 graduate students; most classes under 20 **Degree or Certification:** BA, MA

ONE OF THE PREMIER art and design universities in the world, RISD (pronounced riz-dee) is a cauldron of creativity, with some 2,000 students and 300 full-time faculty. The photography program stresses both developing a unique form of visual expression and understanding the role photography plays in the modern culture. Undergraduate photography majors learn the technical aspects of the medium, as they would at any career-oriented school, in preparation for finding their own creative voice. The 2-year graduate program encourages artists to explore related media, such as video and digital imaging, in the quest of advancing personal vision and artistic expression.

At RISD one is never far from the investigative urge that drives students in all creative media. Students benefit from distinguished guest lectures by such renowned innovators as Maya Angelou and Ted Turner. RISD is especially suitable for students who seek the cross-fertilization of ideas found in a community of dedicated artists.

Tennessee

Arrowmont School of Arts & Crafts

For pre-professional photographers, visual artists and artisans *40 mi. SE of Knoxville — P.O. Box 567, Gatlinburg, TN 37738* **Voice:** 423-436-5860 **Fax:** 423-430-4101 **Open:** Sept.–Aug. **Admission:** Application ($10), 20 slides, references **Deadlines:** Apr. 30 **Cost:** $175 per mo. for housing and studio **Financial Aid:** Scholarship **Group Size:** 3–5

ARROWMONT SCHOOL is an internationally known visual arts complex located in Gatlinburg, near the entrance to Great Smoky Mountains National Park. Its artist-in-residence program provides an opportunity for self-directed beginning-career artists to concentrate for 9 to 11 months on building a substantial body of work. Residents have the use of private studios and can take advantage of superb art and craft facilities and full-time and visiting faculty in an environment of ongoing workshops, seminars and classes.

Residents live in a group home on the wooded 70-acre campus. They are responsible for their own meals and supplies, and must commit to 8 hours work per week doing maintenance or office work, or assisting instructors or staff. The residency program lasts for the better part of a year and is designed to launch young artists and photographers into professional careers.

Arrowmont also runs a variety of workshops, including several photography workshops, throughout the year.

Cory Nature Photography

For nature photographers *Mostly in TN; some workshops in scenic U.S. locations — P.O. Box 42, Signal Mountain, TN 37377* **Voice:** 423-886-1004; 800-495-6190 **Contact:** Tom or Pat Cory **Founded:** 1985 **Open:** Mar.–Nov. **Admission:** Application form **Cost:** $65 for 1-day intensives; $300–$1,300 for location workshops (lodging and some meals incl.)

TOM AND PAT CORY help photographers to explore the beauty of nature and bring home technically correct, striking pictures. They offer several 1-day intensives in cities in Tennessee and conduct photo tours in the Smoky Mountains. Other U.S. destinations may include Maine, the Upper Peninsula of Michigan or Yellowstone. They co-teach all workshops, providing as much or as little hands-on instruction as participants want.

The Tennessee workshops feature delicious homemade food. The Corys' last brochure included a recipe for poppyseed muffins.

Great Smoky Mountains Institute

For nature photographers *35 mi. SE of Knoxville — 9275 Tremont Rd., Townsend, TN 37882* **Voice:** 423-448-6709 **Fax:** 423-448-9250 **E-mail:** nancy@smoky.igc.apc.org **Contact:** Nancy Condon, Prog. Dir. **Open:** 1 workshop in spring and fall **Admission:** Application form **Cost:** $335 for 4 days (meals and lodging incl.)

EACH SPRING AND fall, Great Smoky Mountains Institute at Tremont hosts some of the top nature photographers in the country for 3 half-day workshops of photography, exploration and fun. Field shooting takes place amid the ample wildlife and splendid scenery of the Great Smoky Mountains National Park on the Tennessee/North Carolina border. The rest of the time is spent in lectures and presentations by the instructors, plus critiquing of participant work. Meals and dormitory living are included in the fee, or participants can pay $260 for tuition only.

Like Rocky Mountain Institute, Great Smoky Mountains Institute is an organization dedicated to finding ways to care for a natural resource and to involve and educate people about that resource.

Texas

Hill Country Arts Foundation

For photographers and artists in selected other disciplines *65 mi. NW of San Antonio — P.O. Box 176, Ingram, TX 78025* **Voice:** 210-367-5120; 800-318-4223 **Fax:** 210-367-5725 **Founded:** 1959 **Open:** Summer **Admission:** Application form **Cost:** $225–$360 for workshops (lab fees incl.) **Financial Aid:** Scholarship **Group Size:** Varies

KERR COUNTY, in the hills west of San Antonio, is the setting for this nonprofit arts and crafts center, which teaches everything from glassmaking and fabrics to folk art. Photography offerings are limited to a few courses each summer on darkroom technique, art photography and non-silver printing. Courses are taught by working artists and photographers. A digital imaging class teaches 2 days of Adobe Photoshop.

The Hill Country Arts Foundation also boasts a gallery and a theater that presents Broadway shows during the summer.

Southwest Craft Center

For photographers and artists in selected other disciplines *Downtown — 300 Augusta, San Antonio, TX 78205* **Voice:** 210-224-1848 **Fax:** 210-224-9337 **Contact:** Nancy Heneghan, Reg. **Founded:** 1965 **Open:** Year-round **Cost:** $70 for 5 weeks; $180 for 10 weeks (lab fees incl.) **Group Size:** 6–12

THE SOUTHWEST CRAFT Center, located in a former Ursuline academy and convent, teaches a variety of fine arts and crafts, including photography, to members of the San Antonio community. Photography courses cover basic camera technique, the use of studio lighting, and black & white darkroom at introductory to advanced levels. Its darkrooms can handle negatives from 35mm to 8 x 10. A few courses are devoted to artistic expression and include classes in alternative methods. Most classes meet for 1 evening per week over the course of 5 to 10 weeks. Photography studio chair Tim Summa will answer questions about specific courses.

Texas School of Professional Photography

For wedding and portrait photographers *Sam Houston State University, Huntsville — 1501 W. 5th St., Plainview, TX 79072* **Voice:** 806-296-2276 **Fax:** 806-293-5124 **E-mail:** ddickson@lonestardbs.com **Contact:** Don Dickson **Founded:** 1977 **Open:** 3rd week in Apr. **Admission:** Application form **Cost:** $360 (dinners incl.); digital courses may include rental fee **Financial Aid:** Scholarship **Group Size:** 300 **Handicapped Access**

THE TEXAS EDITION of the Winona-affiliated schools (see *Georgia*) is one of the largest, naturally, with some 14 weeklong courses offered each year. Wedding photography, portraiture and the business of running a studio are the topics covered. Photographers wishing to take the class in Adobe Photoshop can bring their own computers or pay several hundred dollars in lab fees to use rented computer equipment.

Turning Backgrounds into Dollars

For portrait photographers and studio owners *Between Austin and San Antonio — EPS Photographic, P.O. Box 1745, San Marcos, TX 78666* **Voice:** 512-353-3111; 800-647-3777 **Fax:** 512-353-0611 **Contact:** Jim Wilson, Dir. **Founded:** 1987 **Open:** Year-round **Admission:** Application form **Cost:** $325 (lunches and materials incl.) **Group Size:** 12

SPECIAL-EFFECTS backgrounds is the subject of this monthly 3-day workshop geared to the studio portrait photographer. Jim Wilson and his staff discuss and demonstrate a special piece of equipment called The Scene Machine, which projects images into a portrait background. Portrait subjects can appear to be standing in front of the pyramids, on stage at a nightclub or on the ocean floor. Wilson promotes this workshop as a creative profit-making tool for portrait photographers. The workshop is sponsored by the manufacturer of The Scene Machine, which sells for $6,500 and up, depending on configuration.

Two Coyotes Workshops

For nature and landscape photographers *The Southwest — 1701 River Run Rd., #702, Ft. Worth, TX 76107* **Voice:** 817-339-8889 **Fax:** 817-339-8818 **Contact:** Karee Galloway **Founded:** 1990 **Open:** Varies **Admission:** Application form **Cost:** $400 for 3 to 5 days **Group Size:** 8–16

PHOTOGRAPHER/philosopher/psychologist Richard Fenker focuses on taking better pictures based on more careful and complete seeing. His workshops, for photographers at all lev-

RICHARD M. FENKER

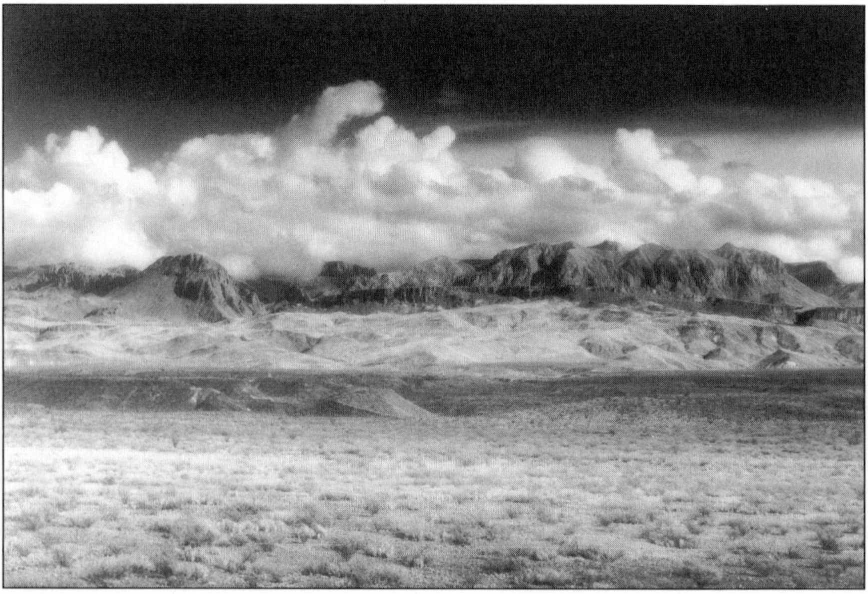

Western Sky, Two Coyotes Workshops, Ft. Worth.

els, mix the pursuit of ideal subjects in Texas and the Southwest with the quiet watching and listening it takes to make the best pictures.

Fenker is concerned with documenting the landscape, especially where development and human occupation cause subtle or significant change. The workshop schedule varies from year to year to allow for the best seasons to shoot in a variety of locations.

Workshops in the West

For nature photographers

The West, Canada, and overseas; darkroom sessions in Manchaca, just outside Austin — P.O. Box 1261, Manchaca, TX 78652 **Voice:** 512-295-3348 **Fax:** 512-295-3348 **Web Site:** http:// www.apogeephoto.com/winthewest.html **Contact:** Joe Englander, Pres. **Founded:** 1981 **Open:** Year-round; darkroom sessions Jan.–Mar. **Admission:** Application form **Cost:** $400 for 2-day darkroom intensive; $600–$950 for weeklong domestic workshops; up to $3,650 for overseas workshops **Group Size:** 10–12 **Handicapped Access**

Joe Englander thrives on teaching photography. And clearly he is good at it, because his students attest time and again to learning more in his travel and darkroom workshops than they have elsewhere.

The Workshops in the West schedule starts each year with 2 months of 2-day darkroom sessions at his studio in the hill country of Texas, each custom-designed to the photographers' needs and skill levels. Englander provides personal instruction in the fine points of color and black & white printing techniques.

During the summer and fall, 15 to 20 location workshops venture out into the American West. Five days of exploring and photographing such glorious places as Zion Canyon, the Tetons and the Olympic Peninsula provide ample opportunity for everyday concerns to subside and focused attention on image making to emerge. Special workshops, lasting 1 to 2 weeks, take place in Alaska's Denali National Park and 2 or 3 overseas locations annually.

Joe Englander has been a commercial and industrial photographer for over 20 years. His images have appeared in the pages of *American Photo, Camera and Darkroom, View Camera* and elsewhere. Prints of his work are in museum collections around the country. The majority of his students are amateurs, though the customized attention and opportunity to build a stock portfolio make his workshops suitable to the professional as well.

Utah

Utah Canyons Workshops

For outdoor photographers

Canyons of southern Utah — P.O. Box 296, Springdale, UT 84767 **Voice:** 801-772-3748 **Fax:** 801-772-3021 **Contact:** Michael Plyler **Founded:** 1991 **Open:** Spring and fall **Admission:** Application form **Cost:** $325 for 4 days **Group Size:** 12

Michael Plyler has a love affair with Zion National Park. His intimate familiarity with the terrain allows him to take photographers to lesser-known spots where they can devote more time to photographing the dramatic landscape of southern Utah. Plyler and his assistant, Jim McGlasson, provide personal guidance on both art and technique during the morning and afternoon shooting sessions. Lectures during the harsh light of midday and portfolio reviews in the evening fill out a busy 4-day schedule. Other workshops visit the Capitol Reef area to the east of Zion.

Vermont

Art New England Summer Workshops

For art photographers and artists in selected other disciplines *SW corner of VT — Bennington College, Bennington, VT 05201; 425 Washington St., Brighton, MA 02135* **Voice:** 617-232-1604 **Fax:** 617-782-4218 **E-mail:** artne@tiac.net **Founded:** 1981 **Open:** Aug. **Admission:** Application form **Deadlines:** June 1 **Cost:** $825 (room and board incl.); $535 for tuition and lunch only **Group Size:** 12

TWO COURSES MAKE up the photography component of the Art New England summer program held annually at Bennington College. One workshop is about developing and enhancing your personal vision; the other concerns the use of alternative photographic processes such as hand coloring and printing on non-paper surfaces.

Dormitory living among artists working in many different media makes this a fine late-summer retreat for photographers who want to develop their fine art sensibilities.

Bennington is a 550-acre campus in the rolling hills of southern Vermont, within an hour's drive of the many arts activities of the Berkshires and the Saratoga (NY) area.

Fred Picker Vermont Photo Workshop

For serious photographers working in black & white *Marlboro College, near Brattleboro — RR 2, Box 1170, Putney, VT 05346; RFD 1, Box 156, Brattleboro, VT 05301* **Voice:** 802-257-3397; 802-387-4334 **Contact:** John Willis **Open:** 1 week in Aug. **Admission:** Application form **Cost:** $1,185 (lodging and meals incl.); $850 for instruction only

SERIOUS PHOTOGRAPHERS, from novices to seasoned professionals, gather for a week with Fred Picker and his associate instructors to pursue technical, aesthetic, emotional and intellectual aspects of black & white photography. The workshop covers the Zone system and the use of different kinds of equipment, printing theory and practice and critiques of students' and instructors' work.

Picker is the founder of Zone VI Studios, the author of *The Zone VI Workshop,* published by Amphoto, and a veteran photographer and teacher. The weeklong workshop is carefully planned to give personal attention to each student's particular interests. Many students work with view cameras, though smaller formats are acceptable. Participants are required to read certain books and to view 2 of Picker's videos prior to attending the workshop.

Marlboro College, which also hosts the famous Marlboro Music Festival, has recreational facilities for tennis, swimming and canoeing. Cultural activities in southern Vermont spring to life each summer with local theater, antiques auctions and gorgeous Green Mountains scenery.

JMC Eye Photo

For eye-oriented medical specialists and photographers *Orlando (Jan.), Dallas (Mar.), Atlanta (May), Mt. Snow, VT (Sept.), Chicago (Nov.), San Francisco (Dec.), plus 3 variable U.S. locations — Rt. 1, Box 21A, Shaftsbury, VT 05262* **Voice:** 802-442-2907 **Fax:** 802-442-3725 **E-mail:** jmceye20@sover.net **Contact:** Mike Coppinger, Dir. **Founded:** 1978 **Open:** 9 sessions per year **Admission:** Application form **Cost:** $625 for 3-day course; $50 for 4th day on digital cameras **Group Size:** 32 **Handicapped Access**

THESE 3-DAY courses, offered around the country, teach the specialized skills of ophthalmic photography. Working with low-power microscopes and equipment provided by manufacturers, students learn the many facets and dimensions of photographing the human eye for medical purposes. The basic course, half lecture and half hands-on work, is open to anyone, though most participants are medical people already involved with vision and eye disease. The advanced course helps prepare students for certification. Both courses include instruction in the use of digital cameras.

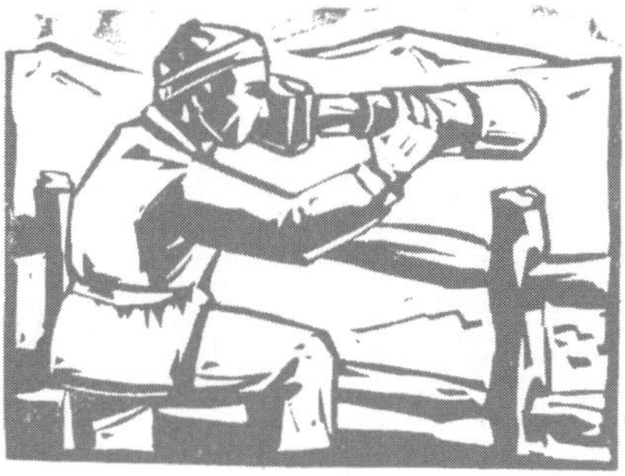

Vermont Studio Center

For photographers and artists in selected other disciplines *40 mi. NE of Burlington — P.O. Box 613, Johnson, VT 05656* **Voice:** 802-635-2727 **Fax:** 802-635-2730 **E-mail:** vscvt@pwshift.com **Founded:** 1984 **Open:** Year-round **Admission:** Application ($25), resume, references, work samples **Deadlines:** Applications anytime; fellowship deadlines 3 times yearly **Cost:** $1,500 for 2-week residency; $2,600 for 4-week; room and board incl. **Financial Aid:** Fellowship; Work/Study **Group Size:** 50–60 **Degree or Certification:** Undergraduate credit through University of the Arts, Philadelphia; MFA program with Johnson State College

A THRIVING ARTS CENTER in the northern Green Mountains, the Vermont Studio Center accepts 1 photographer per month to join with a host of other writers and visual artists in serious creative work away from the normal pressures of daily life. VSC invites mid-career as well as talented emerging artists to apply. Each artist receives simple but comfortable housing, along with a studio and 3 meals per day. The photography darkroom, new in 1994, is well equipped for negatives up to 4 x 5.

VSC is one of those places where artists working in different media support and learn from each other. Each month VSC also invites 5 or 6 prominent visiting artists to share their skills and enthusiasm as a part of the typical interaction of the community.

Residencies last from 4 to 12 weeks, with a limited number of shorter stays available. Several forms of financial aid are available, including grants, work exchange, and a limited number of full fellowships, awarded based on need. Residents may use the cultural and recreational facilities at Johnson State College nearby.

Virginia

Bob Shell Photo Workshops

For glamour and figure photographers *In studio or woods in VA, or on location elsewhere in U.S. — P.O. Box 808, Radford, VA 24141* **Voice:** 540-639-4393 **Fax:** 540-633-1710 **E-mail:** 76750.2717@compuserve.com **Contact:** Bob Shell **Founded:** 1982 **Open:** Varies **Admission:** Application form **Cost:** $350–$400 for 2-day workshop (lunch incl.); $500 per day plus model fees for individual instruction **Group Size:** 15 in studio; 20 outdoors **Handicapped Access**

GLAMOUR PHOTOGRAPHY and figure studies are Bob Shell's specialty. His weekend workshops in the studio or in nearby private wooded areas give photographers 2 days of working with top models under the tutelage of a veteran glamour and beauty photographer.

One or 2 group workshops per year take place on location in the West, on the beach in Florida or wherever a large enough group requests. Individualized instruction is also available.

Virginia Center for the Creative Arts

For photographers and artists in selected other disciplines *Central VA near Lynchburg — Mt. San Angelo, Sweet Briar, VA 24595* **Voice:** 804-946-7236 **Fax:** 804-946-7239 **E-mail:** vcca@artswire.org **Founded:** 1971 **Open:** Year-round **Admission:** Application ($20), resume, work samples, references **Deadlines:** May 15 for Sept.–Dec.; Sept. 15 for Jan.–Apr.; Jan. 15 for May–Aug. **Cost:** Minimum contribution of $30 per day **Group Size:** 24 at a time

DEEP IN HORSE country in the foothills of the Blue Ridge Mountains, the Virginia Center for the Creative Arts is one of the largest and best artists' retreats in the country, with a full year-round calendar. Visual artists, writers and composers come here on 2-week to 2-month fellowships. Fellows enjoy private studio space in the modern Studio Barn, where they receive lunch—delivered quietly so as not to interrupt—each day. A darkroom is available for photographers.

VCCA is set on the lovely 450-acre Mt. San Angelo estate, which is owned by nearby Sweet Briar College. Artists live in private rooms in a comfortable modern facility and dine together in the mornings and evenings. When not working they have the use of a library and game room, as well as access to the cultural and recreational facilities at Sweet Briar, a few miles away.

VCCA's size—24 residents at a time—provides an unusually rich opportunity for artists in different fields to meet and learn from one another. Mt. San Angelo is closed to the public to minimize distractions, and fellows have no obligations other than to their work. The small financial contribution requested of each artist is a tiny price to pay for the privilege of working on your art in this environment.

Washington

Black & White Photographic Workshops

For black & white fine art photographers *Ballard section of Seattle — 2911 NE 60th St., Seattle, WA 98115* **Voice:** 206-525-5836; 206-784-2060 **Contact:** Mark Griffith, Dir. **Founded:** 1989 **Open:** Mar.–Sept. **Admission:** Application form **Cost:** $150 for weekend workshops; $350 for 4 days in the field **Group Size:** 4 for darkroom; 8 for others

THE FINE ART OF black & white is the sole focus of Mark Griffith's workshops. Six times per year he teaches printing techniques in his own, very large, darkroom (materials are included in the fee). On other occasions, he and guest instructors lead classes in the Zone system, which include field shooting and may be coordinated with processing and printing in the darkroom.

The purpose of these workshops is not merely to teach technique, but to train and evoke each photographer's unique photographic voice.

Center for Inner Focus

For photographers and artists in selected other disciplines *Anacortes and natural locations in the Northwest — 619 Commercial Ave., Suite 34, Anacortes, WA 98221* **Voice:** 360-299-2471 **E-mail:** cif@halcyon.com **Contact:** Jane Kennedy or Larry Bullis, Dir's. **Founded:** 1992 **Open:** Apr.–Sept. **Admission:** Application form **Cost:** $320–$450 for workshops; $150 for 8-week class **Financial Aid:** Work/Study **Group Size:** 12

LARRY BULLIS IS A fine art photographer and Jane Kennedy a psychotherapist and former dancer with a special interest in creativity. Together they lead 4 or 5 workshops and classes that seek to develop the participants' personal photographic vision and artistry. In a workshop they call "Intuitive Photography," Bullis and Kennedy stress that each photographer turn inward to discover the roots of personal creativity. Through this introspective approach, photographers are able to achieve more spontaneous picture taking, unencumbered by habitual ways of looking at subject matter and photographing.

Some classes take place in the Center's studio and gallery in Anacortes; others travel to pristine locations in Washington and Oregon. While all formats are welcome, those working in 35mm color negative will be able to have film processed quickly and available for group discussion. Besides the 5-day location workshops, Bullis and Kennedy teach an 8-week evening class on creative vision.

Centrum Artist in Residency Program

For photographers and artists in selected other disciplines *On the Olympic Peninsula — P.O. Box 1158, Port Townsend, WA 98368* **Voice:** 360-385-3102 **Fax:** 360-385-2470 **Contact:** Marlene Bennett **Open:** Sept.–May **Admission:** Application ($15), resume, 15–20 slides, project description **Deadlines:** Oct. 1 for following year **Cost:** None **Financial Aid:** Stipend

Fort Worden State Park, at the northeast corner of the Olympic Peninsula overlooking the Strait of Juan de Fuca between Seattle and Victoria, BC, is the setting for these 1-month fully subsidized artists' residencies. Residents are housed in simple cottages, have the use of a studio and receive a $300 stipend. With no phone, radio or television, photographers and other artists are free to engage their creative souls with the foggy mornings and ancient trees of this 445-acre park.

The Olympic Peninsula is one of America's richest and most varied natural treasures. Snow-capped mountains give way to lush forests that meet the Pacific Ocean along miles of beach and sea-sculpted headlands. For Centrum residents who need a bit more of civilization, the nearby town of Port Townsend is an arty community of Victorian-era charm.

RANDY GREEN

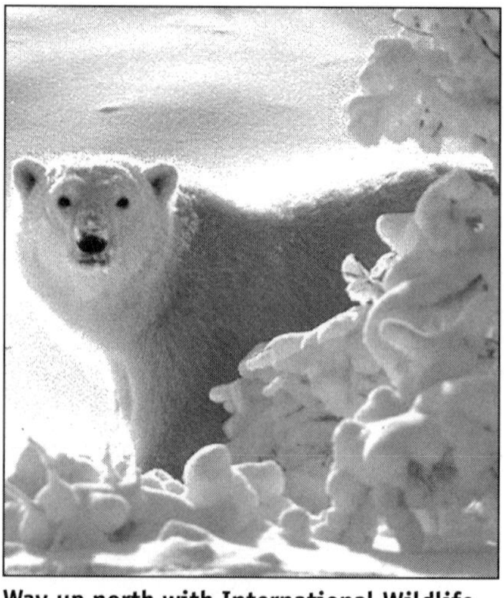

Way up north with International Wildlife Adventures, Vashon, WA.

Coupeville Arts Center

For photographers and artists in selected other disciplines *Rural island setting — 15 NW Birch, P.O. Box 171, Coupeville, WA 98239* **Voice:** 360-678-3396 **Fax:** 360-678-7420 **E-mail:** cac@whidbey.net **Contact:** Judy Lynn, Dir. **Founded:** 1986 **Open:** Apr.–Sept. **Admission:** Application form **Cost:** $225–$350 for 2- to 3-day workshops; $325–$400 for 3- to 5-day location workshops; discounts for members **Financial Aid:** Scholarship **Group Size:** 20

On idyllic Whidbey Island in the middle of Puget Sound, about halfway between Seattle and Victoria, BC, Coupeville Arts Center offers one of the Northwest's foremost arts education programs.

About a dozen photography workshops are offered, with such well-known photographers as Gary Braasch, Martha Casanave and David Hiser. The subject matter tends toward artistry, personal expression and vision. A few of the workshops venture off-island to visit and photograph the natural areas of the Oregon coast or the Olympic Peninsula.

Besides photography, Coupeville offers beginner and advanced courses in visual arts, sculpture, fabrics and a variety of fine crafts.

International Wildlife Adventures

For wildlife photographers *Worldwide — P.O. Box 15, Vashon, WA 98070* **Voice:** 206-463-1943; 800-593-8881 **Fax:** 206-463-4081 **E-mail:** 70400.2004@compuserve.com **Web Site:** http://www.wildlifeadventures.com **Contact:** Randy Green **Open:** Year-round **Admission:** Application form **Cost:** $1,500–$5,000 for 7- to 10-day workshops; $12,000 for Antarctica **Group Size:** 8–16

International Wildlife's tours are just what the name suggests: photographic journeys to view and take pictures of some of the world's most spectacular wildlife. Amateurs as well as professionals go on their frequent trips to the Galapagos, as well as their 5- to 15-day tours to Manitoba for polar bears, Antarctica for penguins, Kenya, Japan and several animal-rich areas in North America. Director Dan Guravich's work has appeared in *Smithsonian* and *Life* magazines. Trip leaders are all naturalists and accomplished wildlife photographers as well.

Joseph Van Os Photo Safaris

For outdoor, nature and wildlife photographers *Destinations on all 7 continents — P.O. Box 655, Vashon Island, WA 98070* **Voice:** 206-463-5383 **Fax:** 206-463-5484 **Contact:** Nancy Morgan Barnes, Registrar **Founded:** 1985 **Admission:** Application form **Cost:** $1,700–$7,000 for most 1- to 3-week trips (lodging, most meals, some airfare incl.); $11,500 for 3½ weeks in Antarctica **Group Size:** 7–25

JOE VAN OS HAS built one of the largest and most successful nature/travel photography organizations in the U.S. His 40 to 50 trips per year go just about everywhere and cover an enormous variety of wildlife and landscapes. There's a trip to photograph pandas in China and one to shoot penguins in Antarctica. You can journey to Alaska to view musk oxen, grizzly bears or humpback whales, or to India for monkeys and tigers. There is even a trip to Indonesia, home of the bizarre Komodo dragon.

For those who prefer to concentrate on the landscape, the Van Os organization takes groups to the Canadian Rockies in the north and as far south as the magnificent rock towers of Torres del Paine in Chile. A special group of tours feature the great national parks of the world, on 4 continents.

For photographers who prefer concentrated skill training, Van Os offers a few advanced photo workshops in select National Parks in the U.S. Advanced workshops cost $695, with lodging at recommended hostelries and meals the responsibility of participants.

All trips are led by experienced photographer/naturalists, including the likes of John Shaw and Rod Planck. Many of the tour leaders have been piloting these kinds of expeditions for years. Accommodations are generally in comfortable, if not luxurious, hotels and inns. Participants should be in good health but need not be especially fit for most tours. The Van Os organization is completely professional, from its brilliant color brochure to its meticulous pursuit of new and exciting destinations for its tours.

Northern Exposures

For nature photographers *Scenic locations in the Northwest and western Canada — 11221 9th Pl. W., #4, Everett, WA 98204* **Voice:** 206-347-7650 **Fax:** 206-347-7650 **Contact:** Linda Moore, Dir. **Founded:** 1985 **Open:** Most of the year **Admission:** Application form **Cost:** $275–$400 for 3- to 5-day workshops; $175 per day for tours in Canada (lodging, some meals incl.) **Group Size:** 12

LINDA MOORE TAKES photographers on rafting trips to the largest winter gathering of bald eagles and leads workshops and tours to photograph the dramatic landscape and wildlife of the Northwest. Tours into Canada, which last a week or two, visit remote scenic locations where few other workshops go. Three- to 5-day workshops in Washington and Oregon include more photographic instruction and focus on wildflowers, waterfalls and the landscape.

(Northern Exposures' telephone area code is scheduled to change to 425 in November 1997.)

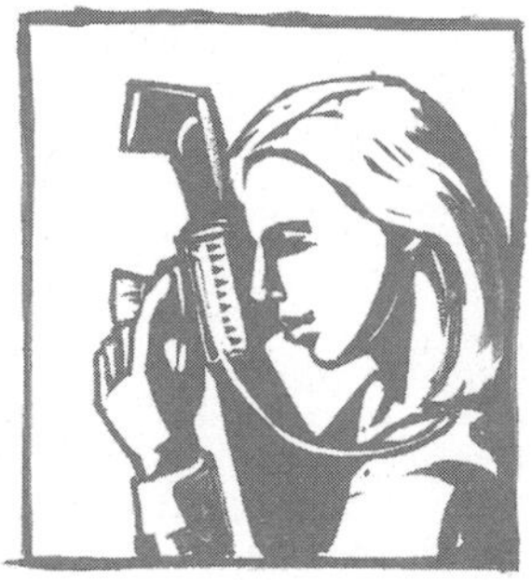

Pacific Northwest School of Professional Photography

For wedding and portrait photographers *Seattle Pacific University in Seattle — 6203 97th Ave. Ct. W., Tacoma, WA 98467* **Voice:** 206-565-1711 **Contact:** Ginny Rodgers **Founded:** 1978 **Open:** 1 week in June **Admission:** Application form **Cost:** $450 (discount for members); room and meal package available **Group Size:** 75; classes 20–30

ONE OF THE Winona-affiliated schools (see *Georgia*), the Pacific Northwest School runs a few courses directed to the wedding and portrait photographer every June. The content of the weeklong courses varies from year to year and may include demonstrations of photographic technique, advice on business issues, and instruction on working with subjects to produce the best photos.

Photographic Arts Workshops

For fine art photographers *Washington and the Southwest, France, Mexico — P.O. Box 1791, Granite Falls, WA 98252* **Voice:** 360-691-4105 **Fax:** 360-691-4105 **Contact:** Bruce Barnbaum, Dir. **Founded:** 1975 **Open:** Year-round **Admission:** Application form **Cost:** $600–$650; $1,100–$1,500 for overseas

FROM HIS BASE IN the Cascade Mountains of Washington, Bruce Barnbaum conducts his 5-day workshops in black & white process several times each year. This workshop is an intensive study of photographic technique, from exposing negatives to the fine points of printing. The program is oriented exclusively to the fine art of photography (as are all his workshops) and includes field and darkroom instruction. The color workshop, taught once during the summer, covers similar subjects with color film. Workshops in the Canyon Country and in Mexico and Provence, France, taught by Barnbaum and others, all emphasize the sheer joy of creating elegant images in black & white and color.

Barnbaum received the Sierra Club's Ansel Adams Award for Conservation Photography in 1972 and has published 2 photography books.

Photographic Center School

For students of photography *2617 Fifth Ave., Seattle, WA 98121* **Voice:** 206-441-7030 **Fax:** 206-441-8583 **E-mail:** 75054.3010@compuserve.com **Web Site:** www.speakeasy.org/photocen **Contact:** Peggy Jacobson, Dir. of Ed. **Founded:** 1987 **Open:** Year-round **Admission:** Application **Cost:** $175–$350, plus lab fees, for 10-week classes; $85–$125 for weekend workshops; $215–$275 for youth summer classes; approximately $2,400 per year, plus supplies, for 3-year program **Financial Aid:** Scholarship **Group Size:** 8–12 **Degree or Certification:** Certificate **Job Placement:** Yes **Handicapped Access**

THE PHOTOGRAPHIC CENTER School is Seattle's educational resource for people who love photography. It offers a full series of introductory 1-day and weekend workshops and a slate of 5- to 10-week evening classes for beginning through advanced photographers. Workshops cover camera technique and the use of flash plus basic darkroom in color and black & white. Evening classes enhance photographic skills in such areas as lighting, darkroom work and the use of large-format equipment.

For those interested in a career in photography, the school has a comprehensive 3-year professional training course. The course starts with a core curriculum of black & white and color, the history of photography and the study of how to see and control light. By the third year, students choose to specialize on a commercial or fine art track, which culminates in a thesis project and a 1-person exhibit in the school gallery.

Though the school is based in downtown Seattle, the majority of courses are taught at their facility in the Greenlake area. Color and black & white darkroom space is available for rent. The school occasionally brings in nationally known artists such as Duane Michaels and Joyce Tenneson for lectures and exhibits or to jury print competitions. During the summer quarter there are special classes for high school and junior high students.

Port Townsend Photography Immersion Workshops

For photographers at all levels *On the Olympic Peninsula — 1005 Lawrence St., Port Townsend, WA 98368* **Voice:** 604-469-1651 **Contact:** Ron Long, Dir. **Open:** Summer **Admission:** Application form **Cost:** $450; lodging $240

TWICE EACH SUMMER, Canadian commercial photographer and photographic educator Ron Long encourages photographers to immerse themselves in a week of thinking, breathing and doing photography. Set in the delightful Olympic Peninsula town of Port Townsend on the Strait of Juan de Fuca, north of Seattle, these workshops include lectures, demonstrations and a great deal of time shooting outdoors. Overnight E-6 processing permits daily critiquing of each student's pictures.

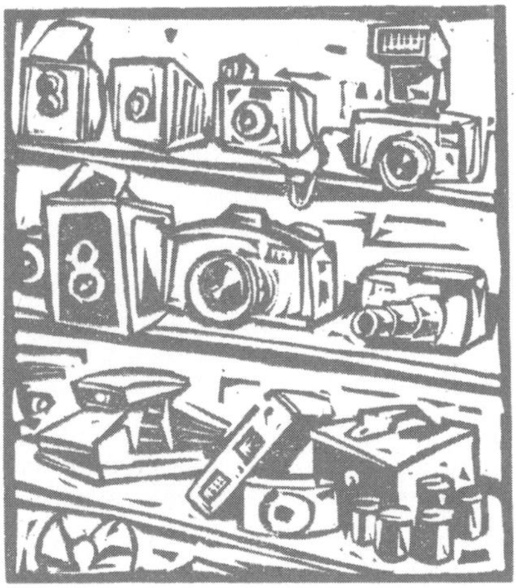

West Virginia

Mexico Photography Workshops

For photographers at all levels *Oaxaca or Veracruz areas in Mexico — Otter Creek Photography, Rte. 1 Box 3, Hendricks, WV 26271* **Voice:** 304-478-3586 **Web Site:** www.apogeephoto.com/mexicophoto.html **Contact:** John Warner **Founded:** 1992 **Open:** Year-round **Admission:** Application form **Cost:** $1,300 for 8 days (all meals, lodging, guides, and some film processing incl.) **Group Size:** 5–8

MEXICO'S COLOR, charm and history are the subjects of photographer/anthropologist John Warner's photo adventures south of the border. These trips explore remote locations, including archaeological sites, as well as local markets and the cities and towns of the southern Mexican states of Oaxaca and eastern Veracruz. In 8 days there is also plenty of time to discover the culture of this beautiful and friendly nation, and to enjoy the wonderful Mexican food. Warner has been visiting and photographing Mexico for 25 years. Anyone who recruits a tour group of 5 or more receives a substantial discount.

Your World in Color

For photographers interested in color darkroom work *Central WV, 140 mi. S. of Pittsburgh, PA — Stone Cellar Darkroom, P.O. Box 253, Buckhannon, WV 26201* **Voice:** 304-472-1669 **Contact:** Jim Stansbury, Dir. **Founded:** 1985 **Open:** Summer **Admission:** Application form **Cost:** $295 (supplies incl.) **Group Size:** 5

JIM STANSBURY'S home in the hills of West Virginia is the base of operations for this specialized weeklong course in color negative photography and printing. Each day is divided between photographing the natural landscape and darkroom work, including film developing and color printing. The week finishes on Saturday with a critique and evaluation of each student's work.

The workshop fee includes lunches; participants are responsible for other meals and accommodations in local motels.

Stansbury is a self-taught fine art photographer and printmaker, with over 2 dozen 1-man shows to his credit. He also co-teaches a general color photography workshop at the Bluestone Conference Center, near Hinton, WV, in the fall.

Wisconsin

High-Speed Motion Analysis Systems & Techniques

For photographers, photo-technicians and engineers *University of Wisconsin–Milwaukee, 161 W. Wisconsin Ave., STE 6000, Milwaukee, WI 53203* **Voice:** 414-227-3125; 800-399-4896 **Fax:** 414-227-3146 **Contact:** Richard Albers, Prog. Dir. **Founded:** 1975 **Open:** 1 week in Oct. **Admission:** By application **Cost:** $1,290 (lunches incl.) **Group Size:** 80

This highly specialized weeklong session presents state-of-the-art technique and equipment for still and video imaging of objects that move too fast for the eye to follow. Participants divide their time between practical and theoretical classroom lectures and lab work. The majority of attendees are engineers who use these techniques for industrial applications.

Sell & ReSell Your Photos

For current and aspiring stock photographers *Around the U.S. — Pine Lake Farm, Osceola, WI 54020* **Voice:** 715-248-3400; 800-624-0266 **Fax:** 715-248-7394 **E-mail:** psi1@ix. netcom.com **Founded:** 1976 **Open:** Year-round **Admission:** Application form **Cost:** $125; discount for early registration and groups **Group Size:** 12

Rohn Engh spends more time telling others how to sell stock photos these days than he spends on selling his own. His half-day seminar, which travels all around the country, deals with finding the markets for stock photographs, the business and legal aspects of talking to buyers, and making the sale. Engh publishes print and electronic information about stock photography in general and markets in particular through his company, PhotoSource International.

Wisconsin Indianhead Photographers School at Treehaven

For wedding and portrait photographers *University of Wisconsin, Stevens Pt., 110 mi. N of Madison — 55 S. Brown St., Rhinelander, WI 54501* **Voice:** 715-369-2535 **Contact:** Dennis McGill, Dir. **Open:** 5 days starting Mother's Day **Admission:** Application form **Deadlines:** Apr. 15 **Cost:** $450 (room and board incl.); $150 equipment rental for digital course **Financial Aid:** Scholarship **Group Size:** 100; classes 20

This Winona-affiliated photography program (see *Georgia*) offers 5 courses for the midwestern wedding/portrait photographer each year.

Courses are kept small to give each student maximum attention. With all the PPA programs in the Midwest, director Dennis McGill makes a special effort each year to bring in teachers who do not appear at other PPA-affiliated schools for a fresh point of view.

Wyoming

Snake River Institute

For outdoor and nature photographers *Near Jackson Hole — P.O. Box 128, Wilson, WY 83014* **Voice:** 307-733-2214 **Fax:** 307-739-1710 **E-mail:** snakeriverinst@wyoming.com **Web Site:** www.wyoming.com/~jacksonhole/SRI/ **Contact:** Samantha Strawbridge, Prog. Dir. **Founded:** 1988 **Open:** Summer and fall **Admission:** Application form **Cost:** $850 for 4-day workshop (lodging and 2 meals per day incl.); $40 for 1-day workshop **Group Size:** 15; 24 for 1-day events

THE SNAKE RIVER Institute is a regional nonprofit organization whose mission is to celebrate the landscape and culture of the American West. From May to September it offers a series of courses on the history, art, mythology and peoples of the Jackson Hole and northern Rockies area. Each fall, the Institute conducts a 4-day photography workshop in the Grand Tetons and Yellowstone Park during the peak of the fall foliage season. Three instructors assist photographers at all levels to develop their interpretive and technical photographic skills. Park fees, transportation, simple lodging and 2 meals per day are included.

During the summer, the Institute also offers 4 single-day photo workshops that focus on the beauty and grandeur of nature in the spectacular Teton region.

Ucross Foundation

For photographers and artists in selected other disciplines *27 mi. SE of Sheridan — 2836 U.S. Hwy 14–16 E., Clearmont, WY 82835* **Voice:** 307-737-2291 **Fax:** 307-737-2322 **E-mail:** ucrossfdn@aol. com **Founded:** 1983 **Open:** Feb.–early Dec. **Admission:** Application ($20), resume, samples of work, references **Deadlines:** Oct. 1 for Feb.–June; Mar. 1 for Aug.–Dec. **Cost:** None **Group Size:** 8

THEY CALL THE complex of buildings in the Wyoming high plains "Big Red." Once the headquarters of the Pratt & Ferris Cattle Company, today it serves as the home of the Ucross Foundation's artist-in-residence program.

Ucross accepts some 60 artists and writers each year for periods of 2 to 8 weeks. Each resident has a private studio and living quarters, and communal meals are provided in the remodeled company schoolhouse. The clear, dry air and stark landscape of the northern Rockies provide a peaceful yet vibrant atmosphere in which photographers and other artists can devote themselves to their work.

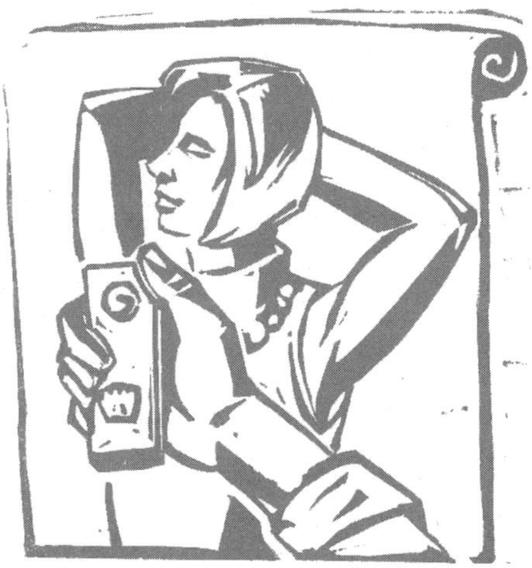

Canada

Ampro Photo Workshops

For student photographers *Central Vancouver — 636 E. Broadway, Vancouver, British Columbia, Canada V5T 1X6* **Voice:** 604-876-5501; 800-565-4750 **Fax:** 604-876-5502 **Web Site:** www.ampro-photo.com **Contact:** Ralph Baker, Pres. **Founded:** 1974 **Open:** Year-round **Admission:** By application **Cost:** C$4,900 (plus C$2,500 for materials) for photojournalism; C$5,900 (plus C$1,000 materials) for digital imaging; C$6,700 (plus C$3,000 materials) for commercial photo course; C$180–$C500 for individual workshops **Financial Aid:** Scholarship **Group Size:** 12 **Degree or Certification:** Diploma

A MAJOR CANADIAN photographic educational institution, Ampro offers many specialized workshops in a broad range of photographic subjects, plus career courses in photojournalism (6 months), commercial photography (9 months) and electronic imaging (5 months). Some of the career courses are made up of a specific series of individual workshops.

The school has good darkroom facilities, a studio and photofinishing and computer equipment. Students provide their own cameras and certain other materials. The electronic imaging curriculum teaches Photoshop, Quark Xpress and Pagemaker, as well as a more general understanding of the use of computers in photography.

Ampro also offers technical career courses in photofinishing, camera repair and minilab machine processing.

Freeman Patterson Workshops

For photographers at all levels *Shampers Cove Ltd./Clifton Royal, Clifton Royal, New Brunswick, Canada E0G 1N0* **Voice:** 506-763-2189 **Contact:** Lynda Titus **Founded:** 1973 **Open:** June– Oct. **Admission:** Application form **Cost:** C$600; lodging and meals C$415 (camping available) **Group Size:** 15

FREEMAN PATTERSON calls his workshops "Photography and Visual Design," and he bases them on his well-known books *Photography and the Art of Seeing* and *Photographing the World Around You.*

Five workshops per year take place over 6 days in a rural area of New Brunswick. Patterson and his co-teachers encourage each photographer to strive toward a personal way of seeing that resonates within and can be transmitted onto film. They have found that a mix of newer photographers and seasoned amateurs and professionals provides the most stimulating and productive workshop environment.

Toronto Image Works

For photographers and graphic and multimedia artists *80 Spadina Ave., Suite 207, Toronto, Ontario, Canada M5V 2J4* **Voice:** 416-703-1999 **Fax:** 416-703-7659 **E-mail:** TIW@astral.magic.ca **Web Site:** www.magic.ca/tiw **Founded:** 1986 **Open:** Year-round **Admission:** Application form **Cost:** C$120–C$295 for photo workshops; C$495 for Photoshop; C$325 for Live Picture

TORONTO IMAGE WORKS mixes workshops in traditional photography with a full slate of digital imaging courses. The photography workshops vary from the most basic to classes in lighting and people photography. Digital courses cover Adobe Photoshop, Live Picture and other graphics, publishing and Internet programs, plus in-depth training in multimedia.

Western Academy of Photography

For student photographers and photojournalists *755 A Queens Ave., Victoria, British Columbia, Canada V8T 1M2* **Voice:** 604-383-1522 **Fax:** 604-383-1534 **Contact:** Paul Smyth, Man. Dir. **Founded:** 1984 **Open:** School year **Admission:** Application form **Cost:** C$7,200 for photography program; C$5,200 for photojournalism program **Financial Aid:** Loans; Scholarships **Group Size:** 36 **Degree or Certification:** Diploma

THE 10-MONTH photo course in photography at Western Academy teaches a full range of basic photographic skills from color and black & white darkroom, to lighting, to many kinds of location photography. The photojournalism program is divided between photography and writing courses. Both teach the fundamentals of operating a business as part of the curriculum, and both include an introduction to appropriate digital techniques.

Instructors are working professionals who bring real-life experience to classroom teaching. Facilities include professionally equipped studios and color and black & white darkrooms. Victoria is called "the Garden Capital of Canada" and enjoys mild weather year-round, with less rain than nearby Seattle and Portland.

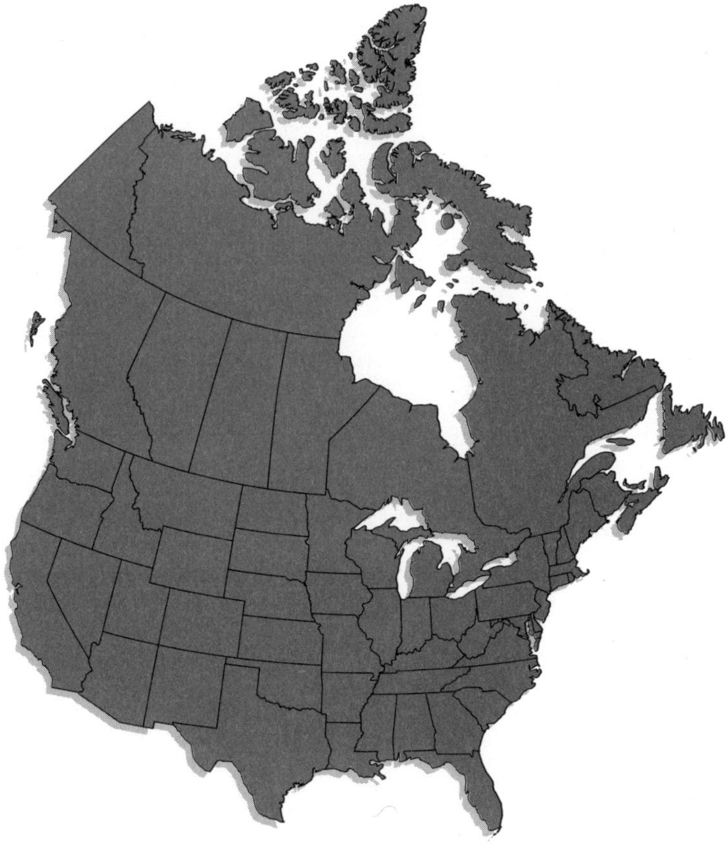

PART THREE

The Business of Photography

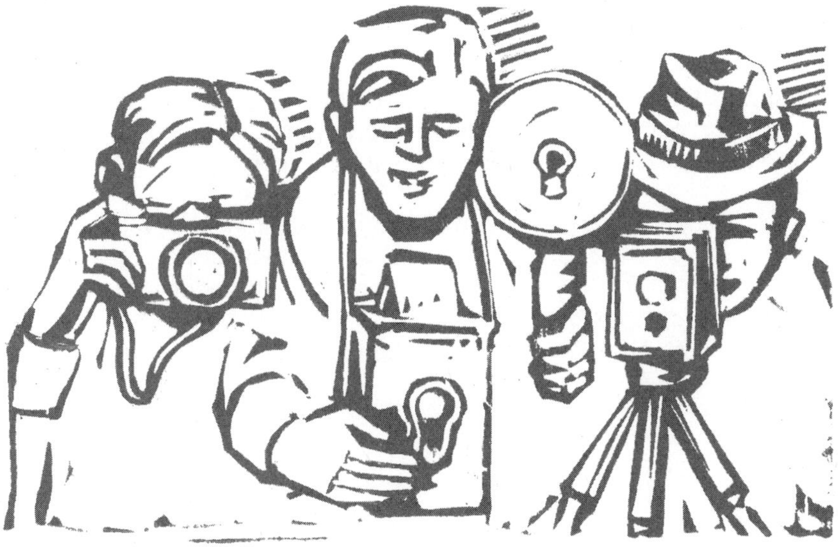

Equipped to Do the Job

Cameras and Lenses

Vision, in both literal and figurative senses, is the key to all photography. But that does not translate into pictures without a camera and a lens.

There is an enormous selection of cameras and lenses available today. Most are well made and reliable, with sophisticated technological gimmickry that really works. But you shouldn't buy a camera just because of what it can do. You must choose your equipment on the basis of what *you* want to do.

Fine art landscape photographers need to use large-format cameras, at least 4 x 5 inch, to render a scene in fine enough detail and small enough grain to make the image work aesthetically. Wedding and portrait photographers usually use medium-format cameras, 6 x 6 cm or similar, to get the rich picture quality suitable for lifelong mementos and large prints. Most personal and stock photography, news photos, and many assignments are shot on 35mm film to take advantage of the convenience and versatility of small-format camera systems.

Which brand you buy—at first, anyway—makes little difference. Although Nikon and Canon dominate the professional photography world, a host of other manufacturers—Minolta, Olympus, Konica, Yashica, Pentax and others—make top-quality equipment and enough accessories to suit most photographers' needs. Secondary lens manufacturers, such as Sigma, Tamron and Tokina, make lenses that will do the job for all but the most demanding standards. If you are serious about your photography, you probably should avoid very cheap and house-brand lenses and cameras.

Which one to buy? The best idea is to visit several camera stores and handle as many cameras as you can that have the features you seek and are in your price range. Change lenses and play with the dials. Find out about the electronic features, and see if they are easy to use. If one camera feels especially good in your hands in the store, it will probably be comfortable to use in the field as well.

Choose lenses on the basis of how many you intend to own. The 50mm lens that comes with most cameras is not all that useful. If you start with two fixed-focal-length lenses, better to begin with one in either 28 or 35mm, and another of about 85 to 105mm. This gives you tremendous versatility in a compact, lightweight package. Zoom lenses offer the benefit of many focal lengths in one lens, but they can cause confusion and framing uncertainty that rob a photographer of the clarity needed to compose a picture properly.

Do-everything zooms, from wide angle to moderate telephoto with macro capability, permit you to work with only one lens. But they have their drawbacks as well. They tend to be heavy, not all that sharp because of the complex optics and very slow. Experienced photographers find that lens speed (that is, maximum aperture) is an important advantage that you simply cannot find in a 28–135mm macro zoom, no matter how expensive it is.

Point-and-shoot cameras, those with integrated lenses and non-reflex viewing, have come a long way since the Instamatic days. Some of them are quite sophisticated, permitting top-quality pictures from a package that weighs only a few ounces. They are best suited to photographing on the go, when circumstances do not permit a more deliberate approach.

Accessories

A tripod is a must for all serious photographers. You can often tell who is the professional and who is the amateur because the professional is the one using a tripod, even in good light. Tripods can be cumbersome and heavy. They can whack you in the legs and trip you. But they give you more control over the photographic process and help produce better, sharper pictures.

All the rest of your accessories depend entirely on what you want to do. A flash is a good thing to carry, especially a modern electronically controlled unit that works with your camera's computer to balance ambient light and fill in shadows without the telltale harshness of direct flash. Bigger flash units, such as high-powered portable or studio strobes, permit you to set up any kind of lighting and control the illumination as you see fit.

A few basic filters—UV to protect your lenses, and warming filters to take the blue out of shadows—are helpful accessories. A polarizer is useful less often than one might think, and expensive. It distorts color and cuts reflections only in certain limited situations and at certain angles. Other filters, such as half-color filters or starbursts, create special effects that only rarely improve a well-composed, properly exposed picture.

A good light meter is less important in today's world of electronic multi-segment metering, but it may be useful when you're shooting very light or very dark areas, or in tricky light. A spot meter is a valuable accessory for fine art work or for shooting high-contrast subjects.

Finally, take care in selecting the right camera bag. A camera bag holds and protects your valuable equipment, like an assistant ready to hand you exactly what you need. Whether the bag sits on your hip or hangs from your shoulder, it should be quick to use and large enough to hold everything you need, including film. The hard-shell camera cases sold by camera manufacturers are a waste of money if you have a good camera bag.

Buying vs. Renting

You should own anything that you are sure you will use more than ten or fifteen times. However, there may be many things you need infrequently that are much cheaper to rent than to buy. A medium-format camera to shoot a wedding, for example, or studio lights (or the complete studio) are often better rented as needed. Major camera stores oriented to professional photographers rent a broad selection of equipment, and some commercial photographers rent out their studios by the day.

When you rent, you can pick the best equipment and facilities for each individual task, rather than being tied to what you have already bought (and may still be paying for). The huge caution about renting is that you will not be as familiar with the gear you rent as you are with your own. *Always* test and practice with rented equipment before you use it on important images. Shooting an assignment with rented equipment is a little like driving a race in someone else's car. You will probably manage all right, but you vastly increase your chances of winning the race if you have taken the car for a spin and gotten the feel of it before you approach the starting line.

When doing a professional photographic job, perhaps the most valuable single commodity you can rent is an assistant. Assistants set up lights, check cameras, load film and permit photographers to concentrate on what they are hired to do: take pictures. Assistants are usually up-and-coming photographers who learn and earn by helping professionals on the job. Many an assistant has prevented disaster. They often know more in some areas than the photographers they are working for.

Film

Today's films are wonderful, and the intense competition among the leading manufacturers is making them even better. You can pick virtually any film from the leading manufacturers and be assured of fine grain and good color.

Color negative films have a wider exposure latitude than slide (transparency) films, but slides are preferred for publication because they are first-generation images—they do not suffer even the minimal loss of image quality that occurs in the step from negative to print. Stock usage and commercial assignments usually require transparencies. Of course, if the purpose of the pictures is a photo album or a print for the wall, color negative would be the right choice. Good color prints from slides are more expensive than prints from negatives.

Black & white is still a hallowed choice among art and some editorial photographers. So little of it is done by amateurs today that you pretty much have to process it yourself or bring it to a professional lab. Journalistic black & white can get by with gritty-looking grainy pictures shot on small-format cameras with high-speed films. Art, in the classic sense of photographic art, needs virtually invisible grain not to interfere with the aesthetics of the image.

In both color and black & white, slower-speed films have a finer grain structure and slightly higher contrast than higher-speed films. Beware of going above ISO 200 if you don't want the grain to be too visible in your images.

Selling Pictures vs. Selling Yourself

NOT LONG AGO, the photography business was based entirely on assignments: photographers worked on assignment from publishers, advertisers, corporations and private clients, shooting the pictures requested and being paid for their labor. It wasn't until the 1970s that the whole notion of stock photography—selling already existing images—became a significant part of the industry. Today stock accounts for a huge portion of the total photography business. And while stock is meaningless for breaking news, weddings, portraits and product illustration, it is a legitimate component of the photography mix that will only grow as electronic media consume thousands of images for distribution over computer networks and CD's worldwide.

The Stock Photography World

It is a buyer's market for all but the highest-end, hardest-to-find subjects. Millions of pictures sit waiting to be purchased in the files of hundreds of stock agencies and thousands of individual photographers. Still, the number of pictures purchased each year as stock is large enough that opportunity exists for any talented and savvy photographer.

If you are interested in selling your own stock images, here is an exercise you might try: Imagine yourself as the buyer who uses the kind of pictures you take. Where does that buyer work, and what are the demands of the job? What is that buyer likely to do when a particular picture is needed? How could that person find you? This is a difficult problem for all photographers in light of the competitive nature of the business. It is especially challenging for those who have a comparatively small number of really first-rate pictures that cover heavily photographed themes. Sunsets, beautiful scenics, wildlife and common travel destinations are everyday commodities in stock photography. So why would the buyer opt for *your* pictures?

This is where stock photo agencies come in. Stock agencies are marketing organizations. They house the work of a few (or a few hundred) photographers and spend their time, effort and resources marketing those images to buyers around town and around the world. They publish lavish color catalogues of the images that they think will sell best and will stimulate buyers to call and inquire about what else is in the files.

Stock agencies are always seeking new photographers who can add variety to their files. Any photographer with a few thousand professional-grade pictures who wants to sell through stock should do the research and inquire about joining the agency or agencies that fit best. Just remember that the stock agency is looking for the photographer who is going to make *them* money. If they already have oodles of what you like to shoot, they are unlikely to take you on.

If you do sign a contract with a stock agency, it will expect you to produce more and more work, so as to keep the files current and the images fresh. Joining a stock agency is not simply a matter of giving it images, then sitting back and waiting for the checks to arrive.

The people who make significant money with stock agencies either have a strong specialty or shoot large numbers of pictures covering areas that the markets want. A ten-minute conversation with any stock agent will help you decide whether this is an appropriate avenue for you. The Picture Agency Council of America (800-457-7222) publishes a guide to stock photography and a listing of its member agencies.

Photographers who cannot gain acceptance into a stock agency or who prefer to market their images themselves can still make a decent income. The key is to target your efforts to those buyers who use photos of the kind you have in your files. That takes research, promotion and possibly years of building a reputation. Stock photography can have its rewards, but it is not for the dabbler who is not willing to invest what it takes to establish a position in this competitive field.

Doing Business in a Businesslike Manner

WE OPERATE IN A FIELD where anyone can buy a camera and a few rolls of film and call himself a photographer. This is terrific for the emerging serious photographer, but it also allows any hack or starry-eyed hopeful to call himself or herself a professional.

Businesses prefer to work with true professionals, those who know what they can do and what they cannot do, who present themselves fairly and uphold certain standards and unwritten rules of conduct. When dealing with professionals, clients want to be assured that transactions will flow smoothly and that the whole work environment will function efficiently and profitably.

If you want to be seen as a professional, you have to present yourself that way. You need to print up business cards and letterhead, have a business telephone number, a fax machine and if possible an e-mail address. A few editors may enjoy ferreting out passionate amateurs in order to discover heretofore hidden photo collections. But the great majority of those in position to pay for photography like to deal with someone who looks and acts like a professional.

Paperwork

Professionals keep good records. They send out written estimates for assignments and delivery memos with stock images. Their invoices are detailed, and they follow up if they remain unpaid after thirty days. They insist on written contracts for assignments and any long-term agreements. Poet Robert Frost said, "Good fences make good neighbors." Good paperwork makes for healthy business relationships and provides essential verification in the event that something goes wrong.

The American Society of Media Photographers (see "Joining Up") publishes a book of business forms that you can copy or use as a model in constructing your own.

Copyright

Place the notification of copyright on all your work by using the copyright symbol ©, your name, and the year the image was created or first published. You may write it by hand, buy a rubber stamp or use computer-printed labels. Photographers own the copyright to their images from the moment they press the shutter, unless they are employees of a company that commissioned the work or there is some other written agreement stipulating otherwise. You do not have to send a copy of a picture to some office in Washington to have a legally enforceable copyright. (The laws on this matter are changing at this time, probably in favor of individual artists. Should you run into a dispute, check on the latest version of the law. Your reference librarian can help.)

Copyright represents photographers' ownership rights to their work, what is referred to as "intellectual property rights" in legal circles. Copyright is critically important because the owner of the copyright determines who can use the picture and in what media, and what compensation is due. Copyright law also determines what statutory damages the photographer is entitled to receive in case of an infringement.

Some clients will ask photographers to sign a "work-for-hire" agreement, which means a forfeiture of copyright. I strongly encourage all photographers never to sign a work-for-hire agreement unless it is absolutely necessary (the baby is sick and your family is on the verge of eviction because of overdue rent) since the copyright you sign away could come back to haunt you. You could even end up competing against your own pictures for sales! Most clients can be persuaded to accept whatever rights to an image they really want and need without having to own the copyright. Their lawyers tell them to ask for it. All the associations of photography professionals stand united in their opposition to signing away copyright.

Do not be seduced by an attractive publication credit in return for copyright. The picture you sell for one-time use in a magazine may appear on promotional cards, calendars, even be sold to another publisher, with no gain to you if you have released the copyright. Photo labs must respect a copyright notice on a print or slide and refuse to make reprints without the written consent of the copyright holder. Copyright is a powerful tool. Guard it carefully so it can work for you.

Presentation and Labeling of Images

If your images are presented in anything less than a professional manner, they, and you, will look amateurish. Slides should be submitted in 20-up clear plastic sheets, each one neatly identified with your copyright and a caption. If you submit a significant number of slides and have a computer, it may be worth your while to buy a caption-writing program, such as Cradoc Caption Writer (see *Bibliography & Resources*). Larger transparencies should be in plastic sheets as well, and watch out for dirt and fingerprints.

The standard in prints is 8 x 10. Unless there is a reason to submit larger or smaller ones, that is the best size, especially for black & white. Small snapshots look as if they came from the drugstore. Never send a contact sheet unless someone has asked specifically for it.

Mail

Pack your pictures between two firm pieces of cardboard, preferably slightly oversize, and tape or put a rubber band around the whole thing.

Your cover letter (on letterhead) and delivery memo should be on top, where they cannot be missed. A padded envelope adds extra protection, though any strong envelope will do. It is wise to stamp or write "Photographs: Do Not Bend" in red on the outside. You would be amazed at how strong mail handlers can be when they want to cram an unlabeled photograph, however sturdily packed, into a small mailbox.

You are completely responsible for the well-being of your images until they are in the hands of the recipient. If you can get the receiver to let you use its overnight delivery service, that's the best choice. If you use the mails, send the images priority and certified to minimize the chance of loss or damage. The other party should be legally responsible for getting the pictures back to you, and your delivery memo should state that. Many publishers, especially magazine and calendar publishers, insist that all submissions be accompanied by a self-addressed stamped envelope. If you fail to follow their stated policy, they are not responsible for the return of your pictures, though they cannot throw them away without due notice.

Send valuable images only to someone who has requested them or who has acknowledged that you will be sending them (get the person's name). If you claim you sent photos to a company and nobody there admits to ever having heard of you, you will have a mighty hard time reclaiming lost or misplaced pictures.

Should you send originals or dupes? That depends on a lot of things. Many publishers request dupes to minimize their liability. That means you have to spend the extra money and find a good-quality duper who will render colors faithfully and not turn your crystal-sharp images to mush. Professionals send out (all but their most prized) originals all the time, though they do it with great care and only to legitimate buyers and clients. We are fast approaching the day when photographs will be sent out as digitized information on a computer disk or transmitted electronically over the phone lines, eliminating the risk to valuable originals.

As in all fields, be especially wary of someone you have never heard of who wants a lot of your pictures and promises great things.

Insurance

You should insure camera equipment up to its replacement value. You can do this either through a photographers' organization's group insurance plan or via a floater tacked onto your homeowner's policy.

You cannot insure individual images except at enormous cost. If a picture would be unbearable to lose, hold on to it (and get a digital scan for your archives). Photographers are entitled to compensation under certain circumstances if a potential buyer loses or damages a photo. This a legitimate loss of something of value, and claims are paid all the time, though it sometimes means the loss of a client. No postal or delivery service will accept responsibility for the declared value of photographs unless you can prove their worth, something that is most difficult to do. If you consider yourself in business as a photographer, you should have business insurance.

Money, Money, Money

ONE OF AMERICA'S LEADING stock photo agents started out in business with absolutely no idea how to price pictures for sale. When a buyer would ask him how much he charged, he would first ask all the pertinent questions about usage: how the picture was to be used, what size, number of insertions, print run, etc. Then he would say, "Well, gee ... we've sold pictures for situations like this for anywhere from $300 to $1,200." The buyer would often respond, "Twelve hundred dollars! That's ridiculous! I never pay more than $750 for a picture like this."

The low ball/high ball approach was this man's way of finding out what the buyer's budget was for a given picture. It still works in some cases. But often you simply have to have the experience to know what a picture is worth, or accept whatever price the buyer offers.

Many publications have a list of standard rates they pay for specific usage. A cover gets one fee, a half-page magazine interior another, their annual calendar something else. If you can convince someone that a given picture is unique or required slogging through a snake-infested jungle, you may be able to negotiate a higher figure. If you sell stock images regularly, the book *Negotiating Stock Photo Prices* by Jim Pickerell (see *Bibliography*) is an excellent reference that is updated every few years. It provides a good basis on which to begin negotiating. Remember, though, your aim is to receive the maximum for your pictures, not anyone's listed minimum.

In pricing yourself for assignments or weddings, you look foolish if you charge too little. But you had better be able to produce great work if you come in at a high price. One effective pricing method is to determine the lowest figure at which you could do a job without sacrificing your self-respect, then add 20 percent. If the buyer haggles, you still have a bit of room before you feel you are being squeezed. It also helps to know what others are charging for similar work (ask around when you're attending a workshop or conference).

Another way to set prices is to decide how much you want to make over the course of a year, how much work you can reasonably expect to book or sell, and what you pay for overhead, self-promotion, film and processing, insurance, and so on. With a little arithmetic, you can determine exactly what you need to charge—if your projections are accurate, of course.

Never agree to a fee that is so low that it demeans you and devalues your work. Few photographers who walk away from a too-low fee regret their decision for long.

Business Planning

MONEY CONSIDERATIONS enter into all planning in one way or another. You are planning either how to make money, how to spend money or how to have enough of it for later on. If photographers appear to charge a great deal for their time and effort, it is because it is an expensive business to operate with limited opportunities and less security. Photographers need to charge enough to sustain themselves over the long run.

Love of photography alone is not a good enough reason to be in business as a photographer (though it may be a good enough reason to stay an amateur). Making photography a career or a profession, even on a part-time basis, requires you to take into account financial issues.

Sole Proprietorship and Taxes

If it is just you, and you are in business as a photographer, you are a sole proprietor. That means you own the whole business. If you have employees who do not own any of the business, you are still a sole proprietor. For tax purposes, the business and you are one and the same. Instead of a salary, you receive all the profit from the business. At tax time you file IRS form 1040 Schedule C, and you pay quarterly estimates during the year. You may deduct all legitimate business expenses and must declare as income all monies received. You may need to collect and pay your state sales tax.

There is no law that says you need to make a profit, especially at first, but you will run afoul of the IRS if your business loses money year after year. Because photography is a popular hobby as well as a profession, the tax authorities are keenly aware of photography deductions that do not seem merited by circumstances. If you sell a few pictures or shoot a couple of assignments, be careful about declaring your photography a business just to write off a new camera, especially if you retain other employment.

If you do set up a business, consult a bookkeeper or accountant to organize your recordkeeping in such a way that you can manage your finances and keep track of accounts. This could be the best couple of hundred dollars you spend in getting going. A good computer program, such as Quicken, or the Dome Bookkeeping Record books are also a great way to organize your finances. Best to rely on your bookkeeper to get you off on the right foot, however.

When your business is properly organized, you feel more professional and are likely to project yourself to others that way. Photographers' associations or colleagues who are slightly ahead of where you are can be a great help in making your foray into business more a successful trial than a series of errors.

Incorporation

When should a photographer incorporate? Only when you have a lot to lose or a big enough operation to encounter the complexities of a larger-scale business. Corporations offer some protection from liability. If you get sued for a huge amount, the business can go bankrupt without your personal assets being attacked.

Otherwise, incorporation means complex paperwork and tax considerations, and a slew of federal laws by which you must abide. Consult an accountant and a lawyer before you jump to add "Inc." after your name.

Investing for Your Future

As a full-time non-salaried photographer, or one who plans to graduate to that level soon, you will need to plan for the long term just as would any salaried employee in a corporation. Health insurance is one issue you should attend to. A retirement plan is another. Systematic savings (for a rainy day or an emergency) should be a third.

Certain photographers' organizations provide access to group health insurance that may and may not provide better value than what you can get elsewhere.

As a self-employed person, you can have a Keogh retirement account, which allows you to sock away more money than just a standard IRA. (If you have any to spare, you can still put up to $2,000 per year in an IRA.)

Photography, in most commercial and editorial fields, tends to be a younger person's profession. As much as we would like to think that our vision and skill will mature forever, the facts are that the physical labor required and the sensibilities toward current trends are most appropriate to people between the ages of twenty-five and fifty. There are many exceptions, of course. But it is a shame to see photographers not yet into middle age who have lost their businesses because they could not compete with the dynamism and innovation of younger people. The shame becomes a tragedy if they have not set aside the financial resources to sustain them while they refocus their lives on whatever comes next.

Photographers tend to think of themselves as visual artists, and have for many years been notoriously poor businesspeople. By planning for the financial future of your business, yourself, and your family, you establish a foundation that can withstand life's inevitable crises. You may or may not have what it takes to make it in the competitive world of photography. By taking the necessary business and planning steps, at least you give yourself a fighting chance.

Feeding Your Soul

Personal Projects

The best and most successful photographers are always working on personal projects. Elliott Erwitt shoots black & white pictures of dogs. Jay Maisel is constantly experimenting with the urban landscape. Sure, some of the pictures they shoot on their own may sell as stock. But they do these pictures because they are photographers, whose mission it is to translate a visual world into pictures on film. Personal projects sustain that mission.

Photographers who shoot only assignments or only commercial stock pictures are dooming themselves to the rust-covered category of "has-beens." It is necessary for all of us to keep working on personal photography to keep our spirits and vision alive. No matter if the pictures are of flowers, portraits of your child's schoolmates, large-format landscapes, or unusual doorways, photographers should have at least one, perhaps several, personal projects cooking at all times. The freshness of vision derived from these projects spills over to better commercial images as well. The kettle that is still warm boils much faster than the one that has lain cold overnight.

Continued Learning

Photography is always changing. New equipment makes new ways of shooting possible, and digital technology is turning industry norms and underlying assumptions upside down. People get tired of looking at the same solutions to age-old image requirements, no matter how well conceived and well executed they are. Photographers who do not constantly challenge themselves grow stale.

You absolutely must continue to learn if you have any hope of maintaining yourself as a photographer. Join professional or amateur organizations of photographers, attend seminars, take some of the courses described in this book. Read the magazines that address issues of seeing and making images, not just those that promote hot new cameras and accessories. Look at your images carefully, and keep a log of what succeeds and what does not. Those that almost work but just miss can be some of your best teachers. Nothing provides more information about how *you* take pictures and what you need to do to take better ones.

Go to print exhibits and galleries. Prints on a wall are much more powerful than the same pictures reproduced in a magazine or book. Besides, just taking the time to visit a gallery or exhibit is a way of telling yourself that you are serious about photography.

Most important, look at pictures whenever and wherever you can. Writers read books, musicians listen to symphonies. A photographer looks at images. Studying them, thinking about them, and feeling them is the most important thing you can do to feed your photographic soul.

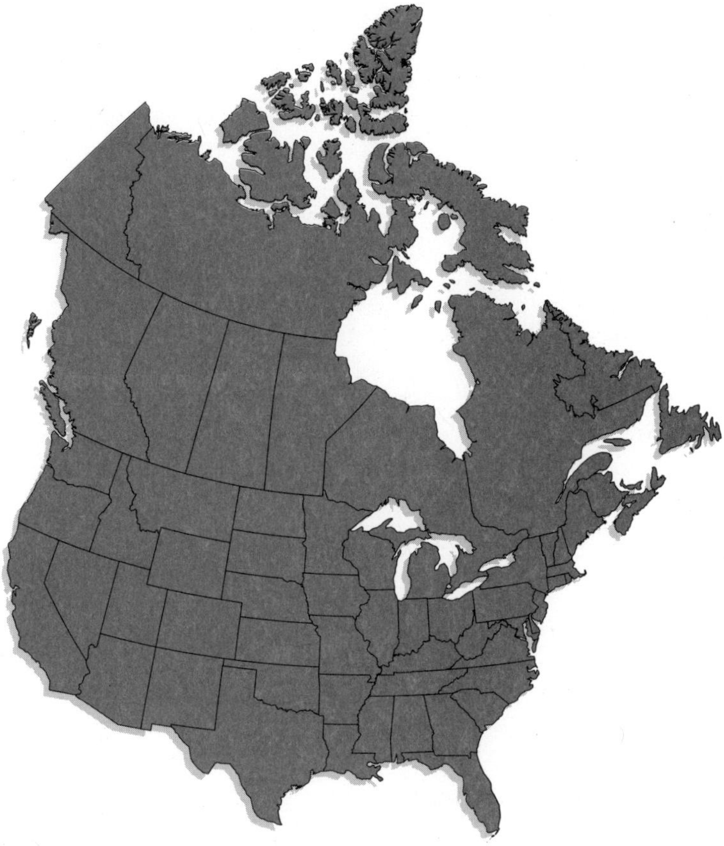

PART FOUR

Bibliography & Resources Index

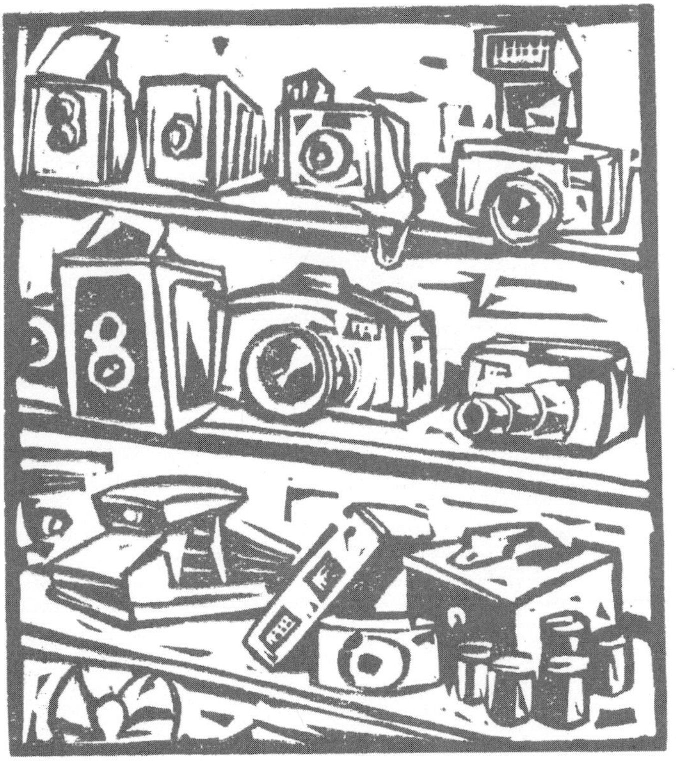

Bibliography & Resources

Bibliography

Stock Photography and Markets for Images

Photographers' Market, Writer's Digest Books, 1507 Dana Ave., Cincinnati, OH 45207; 800-289-0963.

Photo Marketing Guidebook, Images Media, 97-28 Third Ave., Brooklyn, NY 11209; 800-982-2875; fax 800-982-2874.

Negotiating Stock Photo Prices, by Jim Pickerell, 110 Frederick Ave., Rockville, MD 20850; 301-424-2455; e-mail: jim@chd.com.

Shooting for Stock, by George Schaub. Amphoto Books, Watson-Guptill Publications, 1987.

The Photographic Aesthetic

Learning to See Creatively, by Bryan Peterson and DÌAMAR Interactive (book and CD). Amphoto Books, Watson-Guptill Publications, 1995.

John Shaw's Landscape Photography, by John Shaw. Amphoto Books, Watson-Guptill Publications, 1994.

Specialized Photography Business

John Shaw's Business of Nature Photography, by John Shaw. Amphoto Books, Watson-Guptill Publications, 1996.

The Business of Wedding Photography, by Ann Monteith. Amphoto Books, Watson-Guptill Publications, 1996.

The Business of Portrait Photography, by Tom McDonald. Amphoto Books, Watson-Guptill Publications, 1996.

Professional Techniques for the Wedding Photographer, by George Schaub. Amphoto Books, Watson-Guptill Publications, 1985.

Academic Programs

Most public libraries have the annual *Peterson's Guides* —to four-year colleges, to two-year colleges, and to graduate programs in the humanities and social sciences. Another useful reference is *The College Blue Book: Occupational Education,* published by Macmillan.

Resources

Where to Find Photography Books

Three distributors:

Calumet Photographic.
Telephone: 800-CALUMET.
Images Media, 89 Fifth Ave., New York, NY 10003.
Write for a catalogue or send a fax: 212-741-3439.
Silver Pixel Press, 21 Jet Dr., Rochester, NY 14624. This publisher distributes many of the Kodak books. Telephone: 716-328-7800 or e-mail: silverpix@aol.com.

In New York City, two bookstores with a large selection:

A Photographers' Place
133 Mercer Street
International Center for Photography
1130 Fifth Avenue and 1133 Avenue of the Americas

Slide Labeling Computer Program

CRADOC Caption Writer
Perfect Niche Software
6962 E. First Ave., #03
Scottsdale, AZ 85251
voice: 602-945-2001, fax: 602-949-1707
e-mail: sales@perfectniche.com

Index

General Index

Academic programs, 11. See also Academic Programs index
Accessories, 149
Advertising Photographers of New York, 27
Advertising photography, 21
American Society of Media Photographers, 27
American Society of Picture Professionals, 27
Assisting professional photographers, 83
Buying vs. renting equipment, 149–50
Cameras, 148–49
Catalogue photography, 21
Commercial photography, 22
Conferences, 10–11. See also Conferences index
Continued learning, 158
Copyright, 152–53
Corporate photography, 20
Digital imaging: basics, 107; programs, 11–12; software, 49; specialists, 22. See also Digital Imaging Programs index
Editorial photography, 22
Equipment, 148–49
Evidence Photographers International Council, 28
Fashion photography, 21
Film, 150
Filters, 149
Financial aid, 14. See also Financial Aid index
Fine art photography, 22
Flash units, 149
FOTOFUSION convocation, 64
Freelance work, 20, 22
The Friends of Photography, 28
Handicapped access, 14. See also Handicapped Access index
Icons, 12
Incorporation, 157
Industrial photography, 20
Information display format, 12–14
Insurance, 154–55
Labeling images, 153–54
Lenses, 148–49
Light meters, 149
Mailing pictures, 153–54
Master classes, 79
National Press Photographers Association, 28–29
North American Nature Photography Association, 29
On–the–road programs, 12. See also On-the-Road Programs index
Paperwork, 152
Personal projects, 158
Photographer's assistants, 83
Photographic Society of America, 29
Photojournalism, 19–20
Picture Agency Council of America, 151
Portraits, 22
Presenting images, 153–54
Pricing, 155
Programs defined, 10–12
Professional Advancement Conference, 58
Professional Photographers of America, 29, 68
Residential programs, 11. See also Residential Programs index
Retirement plans, 157
Society for Photographic Education, 29–30
Sole proprietorship, 156
Stock photography, 21, 151–52
Taxes, 156
Tripods, 149
Underwater photography contests, 65
University Photographer's Association of America, 30
Web sites, 13. See also Web Sites index
Wedding & Portrait Photographers International, 30
Weddings, 22
Workshops: 10; choosing a workshop, 104; information on World Wide Web, 57. See also Workshops index

Photography Programs

Academy of Art College, 37
Acadia National Park Artist-in-Residence Program, 78
Adams, Eddie. See Eddie Adams Workshop
Al Weber, 37
Alden B. Dow Creativity Fellowships, 89
Allaman's Montana Photographic Adventures, 94
Ambient Light Workshops, 70

American Film Institute, 38
Ampro Photo Workshops, 144
Anchell Photography Workshops, 54
Anderson, Mary. See Mary Anderson Center for the Arts
Anderson Ranch Arts Center, 54–55
Arrowmont School of Arts & Crafts, 130
Art Center College of Design, 38
Art Ketchum Workshops, 71
Art New England Summer Workshops, 134
Art/Omi International Artists' Workshop, 105
Atlantic Center for the Arts, 60–61
Augustin, Philip. See Philip Augustin Workshops
Balthis, Frank. See Frank Balthis Photography Workshops
Bemis Center for Contemporary Arts, 98
Big Bend Natural History Association. See Jim Bones Photographic Workshop
Bike Week Workshops, 61
Birds as Art, 61
Black & White Photographic Workshops, 137
Blue Mountain Center, 105
Bob Shell Photo Workshops, 136
Bodie Photography Workshops, 38
Bond, Howard. See Howard Bond Workshops
Bones, Jim. See Jim Bones Photographic Workshop
Boston Photo Collaborative, 82
Bradley, Matt. See Matt Bradley Photography Workshops
Branson Reynolds Photographic Workshops, 55
Brooks Institute of Photography, 38–39
Brown, Nancy. See Nancy Brown Hands-on NY Workshops
California Natural Wonders Photographic Workshops, 39
Camera & Darkroom Digital, 101
Cape Cod Photo Workshops, 83
Carina House: A Monhegan Residency, 78
Center for Inner Focus, 137
Center for Nature Photography, 35
Center for Photography at Woodstock, 106
Center for Photonics Studies, 71
Centrum Artist in Residency Program, 138
Chamlee, Paula. See Michael Smith/Paula Chamlee Apprenticeships
Clayton Fogle's Hummingbirds, 40
COMPrehend Computer Education Centers, 61
Conifer Photographic Workshops, 56
Contemporary Artists Center, 83–84
Cory Nature Photography, 130
Country Photography Workshops of New Jersey, 99
Coupeville Arts Center, 138
Cousteau, Jean Michel. See Jean Michel Cousteau/Project Ocean Search
Crealde School of Visual Art, 62
Creative Computer Workshop, 40
Creative Studio Lighting, 40
Darkroom, The. See The Darkroom
David Halpern Photography Workshops, 124
Desktop America, 106
Digital Works, 84
Djerassi Resident Artists Program, 40–41
Dorland Mountain Arts Colony, 41
Dow, Alden B. See Alden B. Dow Creativity Fellowships
Dramatic Light Nature Photography, 56–57
Duckworth Forensic Photography, 125
Dynamic Graphics Educational Foundation, 71–72
Eddie Adams Workshop, 106, 108
Electronic Imaging Center, 92
Everglades Photo Safari, 62
Exfoditions, Journeys beyond Photography, 41
Fabric Workshop & Museum Artist-in-Residence Program, 127
Fine Arts Work Center in Provincetown, 84
First Light Photo Workshops & Safaris, 108
First Light Photography Tours, 57
Fitchburg State College Photoshop Workshop, 85
Florida School of Professional Photography, 62
Fogle, Clayton. See Clayton Fogle's Hummingbirds
Frank Balthis Photography Workshops, 42
Fred Picker Vermont Photo Workshop, 134
Freeman Patterson Workshops, 144
Gamma Technical Institute, 72

Georgia School of Professional Photography, 66
Gerlach Nature Photography, 89
Gilroy, Steve. See Steve Gilroy's Alaska Photo Tours
Glacier Institute, 95
Golden Gate School Professional Photographic Workshops, 42
Great American Photography Weekend, 76–77
Great Lakes Institute of Photography, 90
Great Smoky Mountains Institute, 130–31
Hallmark Institute of Photography, 85
Halpern, David. See David Halpern Photography Workshops
Hambidge Center, 66
Hart, John. See John Hart's Portrait Lighting
Headlands Center for the Arts, 42–43
Helene Wurlitzer Foundation, 101
Hidden Worlds, 43
High-Speed Motion Analysis Systems & Techniques, 142
Hill Country Arts Foundation, 131
Howard Bond Workshops, 90
Illinois Workshops, 72
Image Experience Workshops, 108
Indian River Photo Workshops, 108–9
Interactive Factory Workshops, 85
International Center for Earth Concerns/ Nature Photography, 43
International Center of Photography, 109
International Model Testing Workshops, 98–99
International Wildlife Adventures, 138–39
Ireland with Ron Rosenstock, 110
J&J Computing, 110
Jean Michel Cousteau/Project Ocean Search, 43–44
Jim Bones Photographic Workshop, 101–2
JMC Eye Photo, 135
Joe McDonald Wildlife Photography, 127
John Hart's Portrait Lighting, 110
John Sexton Photography Workshops, 44
Joseph Van Os Photo Safaris, 139
Kalani Honua Eco-Resort Artist-in-Residence Program, 69–70
Kansas Professional Photographers School, 76
Katmai Coastal Tours, 35
Ketchum, Art. See Art Ketchum Workshops
Latent Image Workshop, 81
Latigo Ranch Photography Workshops, 57–58
Lepp & Associates, 44
Light Work, 111
MAC University, 72–73
MacDowell Colony, 99
Macro Tours Photographic Workshops & Tours, 45
Macro/Nature Photography, 62–63
Maine Photographic Workshops, 79–80
Maine Photographic Workshops/New York, 111
Maria Piscopo, 45
Mary Anderson Center for the Arts, 75
Matt Bradley Photography Workshops, 36
McDonald, Joe. See Joe McDonald Wildlife Photography
McSavaney, Ray. See Ray McSavaney Photographic Workshops
Medicine Wheel Artists' Retreat, 86
Meteor Technology Education, 90
Mexico Photography Workshops, 141
Michael Smith/Paula Chamlee Apprenticeships, 128
Mid-America Institute of Professional Photography, 75
Midwest Photographic Workshops, 90–91
Millay Colony for the Arts, 111
Missouri Photo Workshop, 93
Montana Artists Refuge, 95
Monte Zucker Portrait/Wedding Classes, 63
Mountain Workshop, 77
Mt. Carroll Center for Applied Photographic Arts, 73
Nancy Brown Hands-on NY Workshop, 112
Nantucket Island School of Design & the Arts, 86–87
Natural Habitat Adventures, 58
Natural Photography, 70
Nature Images Workshops, 63
Nature One Photography & Wildlife Adventure, 100
Nature's Light, 123
Neversink Photo Workshops, 112
New England Institute of Professional Photography, 87
New England School of Photographic Arts, 59–60
New England School of Photography, 87–88
New Horizons Computer Learning Center, 67
New Mexico Artists' Association, 102

New Vision Workshops, 63–64
Nikon School of Underwater Photography. See WaterHouse Photo Tours
Northern Exposures, 139
Northern Short Course in Photojournalism, 112–13
Northlight Photo Workshops, 113
NPPA Electronic Photojournalism Workshop, 121
NPPA Flying Short Course, 121
Ohio Institute of Photography and Technology, 123
Ohio University School of Visual Communication, 124
Oklahoma Fall Arts Institutes, 124–25
Oklahoma School of Photography, 125
Oregon School of Arts & Crafts, 125–26
Osprey Photo Workshops & Tours, 82
Pacific Northwest School of Professional Photography, 140
Palm Beach Photographic Centre, 64–65
Patterson, Freeman. See Freeman Patterson Workshops
Penland School of Crafts, 122
Peters Valley Craft Center, 100
Philip Augustin Workshops, 126
Photo Explorer Tours, 91
Photo Metro Digital Workshops, 46
Photo Week Workshops, 80
PhotoCentral—Hayward Area Recreation and Park District, 46
Photographic Arts Workshops, 140
Photographic Center School, 140–41
Photographic Resource Center, 88
Photographics Unlimited, 113
Photography at the Summit & Sports Photography Workshop, 58–59
Photography Workshops International, 88
PhotoProExpo, 60
Picker, Fred. See Fred Picker Vermont Photo Workshop
Piscopo, Maria. See Maria Piscopo
Planck, Rod. See Rod Planck Presents
Point Reyes Field Seminars, 46
Port Townsend Photography Immersion Workshops, 141
Portfolio Center, 67
PPA Imaging Conference and Expo, 68
Pratt Institute, 113–14
Proam Photo Workshops, 47
Professional Photographers of North Carolina/Summer Short Session, 122
Professional Photographers Society of NY Photo Workshop, 114
Ragdale Foundation, 73
Ray McSavaney Photographic Workshops, 47
Redwood Exposure, 47–48
Reynolds, Branson. See Branson Reynolds Photographic workshops
Rhode Island School of Design, 129
Robert Winslow Photo Tours, 59
Rochester Institute of Technology, 114–15
Rocky Mountain School of Photography, 95–96
Rocky Mountain Seminars, 59
Rod Planck Presents, 91
Ron Sanford, 48
Rosenstock, Ron. See Ireland with Ron Rosenstock
Roswell Artist-in-Residence Program, 102
Samy's Digital Imaging, 48
Sanford, Ron. See Ron Sanford
Santa Fe Workshops, 103
Savannah College of Art & Design, 68
School of Evidence Photography, 128
School of the Art Institute of Chicago, 74
School of Visual Arts, 115
Sell & ReSell Your Photos, 142
Sexton, John. See John Sexton Photography Workshops
Shell, Bob. See Bob Shell Photo Workshops
Sierra Photographic Workshops, 48–50
Sitka Center for Art & Ecology, 126
Skowhegan, 80–81
Smith, Michael. See Michael Smith/Paula Chamlee Apprenticeships
Snake River Institute, 143
Southampton College Master Photography Workshop, 115–16
Southern Illinois University at Carbondale, 74
Southwest Craft Center, 131
St. Cloud State University Summer Photo Imaging Workshop, 92
Steve Gilroy's Alaska Photo Tours, 36
STUDIO for Creative Inquiry, 128–29
Studios Midwest, 75
Summer Weekend of Photography, 92
Summit Photography Workshops, 50
Superior/Gunflint Photography Workshops, 93
Taos Institute of Arts, 104
Technical and Education Center of the Graphic Arts and Imaging at RIT, 116
Texas School of Professional Photography, 131–32
The Darkroom, 50
Tisch School of the Arts/NYU, 116

Toronto Image Works, 144–45
Touch of Success Seminars, 65
Triangle Institute of Professional Photography, 129
Turning Backgrounds into Dollars, 132
Tuscany Color Photography Workshop, 117
Two Coyotes Workshops, 132–33
UC Santa Cruz Extension, 50
Ucross Foundation, 143
United Digital Artists, 117
United Digital Artists/West, 51
Utah Canyons Workshops, 133
Van Os, Joseph. See Joseph Van Os Photo Safaris
Vermont Studio Center, 135–36
Villa Montalvo Artist Residency Program, 51
Virginia Center for the Creative Arts, 136–37
VISCOMM, 118
VISCOMM West, 51–52
Visual Journeys, 104–5
Visual Studies Workshop, 118–19
Voyagers International, 119
Washington University Summer Art Study in Florence, 94
WaterHouse Photo Tours, 65–66
Weber, Al. See Al Weber
West Coast School of Professsional Photography, 52
Western Academy of Photography, 145
Wild Eyes Photo Adventure, 97
Wilderness Photographic Workshops, 52–53
Wilderness Photography Expeditions, 97
Wilderness Travel, 53
Winona International School of Professional Photography, 69
Winslow, Robert. See Robert Winslow Photo Tours
Wisconsin Indianhead Photographers School at Treehaven, 142–43
Women's Studio Workshop, 119–20
Workshops in the West, 133
Wurlitzer, Helene. See Helene Wurlitzer Foundation
Yaddo, 120
Yankee Schooner Cruises, 81
Yosemite Field Seminars, 53
Your World in Color, 141–42
Zucker, Monte. See Monte Zucker Portrait/Wedding Classes
Zzyzx, 53

Residential Programs

Acadia National Park Artist-in-Residence Program, 78
Alden B. Dow Creativity Fellowships, 89
Anderson Ranch Arts Center, 54–55
Arrowmont School of Arts & Crafts, 130
Art/Omi International Artists' Workshop, 105
Atlantic Center for the Arts, 60–61
Bemis Center for Contemporary Arts, 98
Blue Mountain Center, 105
Carina House: A Monhegan Residency, 78
Centrum Artist in Residency Program, 138
Contemporary Artists Center, 83–84
Djerassi Resident Artists Program, 40–41
Dorland Mountain Arts Colony, 41
Fabric Workshop & Museum Artist-in-Residence Program, 127
Fine Arts Work Center in Provincetown, 84
Hambidge Center, 66
Headlands Center for the Arts, 42–43
Helene Wurlitzer Foundation, 101
Kalani Honua Eco-Resort Artist-in-Residence Program, 69–70
Light Work, 111
MacDowell Colony, 99
Mary Anderson Center for the Arts, 75
Medicine Wheel Artists' Retreat, 86
Michael Smith / Paula Chamlee Apprenticeships, 128
Millay Colony for the Arts, 111
Montana Artists Refuge, 95
Nantucket Island School of Design & the Arts, 86–87
New Mexico Artists' Association, 102
Oregon School of Arts & Crafts, 125–26
Penland School of Crafts, 122
Peters Valley Craft Center, 100
Ragdale Foundation, 73
Roswell Artist-in-Residence Program, 102
Sitka Center for Art & Ecology, 126
Skowhegan, 80–81
STUDIO for Creative Inquiry, 128–29
Studios Midwest, 75
Ucross Foundation, 143
Vermont Studio Center, 135–36
Villa Montalvo Artist Residency Program, 51
Virginia Center for the Creative Arts, 136–37

Visual Studies Workshop, 118–19
Women's Studio Workshop, 119–20
Yaddo, 120

Workshops

Al Weber, 37
Allaman's Montana Photographic Adventures, 94
Ambient Light Workshops, 70
Ampro Photo Workshops, 144
Anchell Photography Workshops, 54
Anderson Ranch Arts Center, 54
Art Ketchum Workshops, 71
Art New England Summer Workshops, 134
Bike Week Workshops, 61
Birds as Art, 61
Black & White Photographic Workshops, 137
Bob Shell Photo Workshops, 136
Bodie Photography Workshops, 38
Boston Photo Collaborative, 82
Branson Reynolds Photographic Workshops, 55
California Natural Wonders Photographic Workshops, 39
Cape Cod Photo Workshops, 83
Center for Inner Focus, 137
Center for Nature Photography, 35
Center for Photography at Woodstock, 106
Center for Photonics Studies, 71
Clayton Fogle's Hummingbirds, 40
Conifer Photographic Workshops, 56
Contemporary Artists Center, 83
Cory Nature Photography, 130
Country Photography Workshops of New Jersey, 99
Coupeville Arts Center, 138
Crealde School of Visual Art, 62
Creative Studio Lighting, 40
David Halpern Photography Workshops, 124
Dramatic Light Nature Photography, 56
Duckworth Forensic Photography, 125
Eddie Adams Workshop, 106
Exfoditions, Journeys beyond Photography, 41
First Light Photo Workshops & Safaris, 108
First Light Photography Tours, 57
Florida School of Professional Photography, 62
Frank Balthis Photography Workshops, 42
Fred Picker Vermont Photo Workshop, 134
Freeman Patterson Workshops, 144
Georgia School of Professional Photography, 66
Gerlach Nature Photography, 89
Glacier Institute, 95
Golden Gate School Professional Photographic Workshops, 42
Great American Photography Weekend, 76
Great Lakes Institute of Photography, 90
Great Smoky Mountains Institute, 130
Hidden Worlds, 43
High-Speed Motion Analysis Systems & Techniques, 142
Hill Country Arts Foundation, 131
Howard Bond Workshops, 90
Illinois Workshops, 72
Image Experience Workshops, 108
Indian River Photo Workshops, 108
International Center for Earth Concerns/Nature Photography, 43
International Center of Photography, 109
International Model Testing Workshops, 98
International Wildlife Adventures, 138
Ireland with Ron Rosenstock, 110
Jean Michel Cousteau/Project Ocean Search, 43
Jim Bones Photographic Workshop, 101
JMC Eye Photo, 135
Joe McDonald Wildlife Photography, 127
John Hart's Portrait Lighting, 110
John Sexton Photography Workshops, 44
Joseph Van Os Photo Safaris, 139
Kansas Professional Photographers School, 76
Katmai Coastal Tours, 35
Latent Image Workshop, 81
Latigo Ranch Photography Workshops, 57
Lepp & Associates, 44
Macro Tours Photographic Workshops & Tours, 45
Macro/Nature Photography, 62
Maine Photographic Workshops, 79
Maine Photographic Workshops/New York, 111
Maria Piscopo, 45
Matt Bradley Photography Workshops, 36
Mexico Photography Workshops, 141
Midwest Photographic Workshops, 90
Missouri Photo Workshop, 93

Monte Zucker Portrait/Wedding Classes, 63
Mountain Workshop, 77
Mt. Carroll Center for Applied Photographic Arts, 73
Nancy Brown Hands-on NY Workshop, 112
Nantucket Island School of Design & the Arts, 86
Natural Habitat Adventures, 58
Natural Photography, 70
Nature Images Workshops, 63
Nature One Photography & Wildlife Adventure, 100
Nature's Light, 123
Neversink Photo Workshops, 112
New England Institute of Professional Photography, 87
New England School of Photographic Arts, 59
New Vision Workshops, 63
Northern Exposures, 139
Northlight Photo Workshops, 113
Oklahoma Fall Arts Institutes, 124
Osprey Photo Workshops & Tours, 82
Pacific Northwest School of Professional Photography, 140
Palm Beach Photographic Workshops, 64
Penland School of Crafts, 122
Peters Valley Craft Center, 100
Philip Augustin Workshops, 126
Photo Explorer Tours, 91
Photo Week Workshops, 80
Photocentral—Hayward Area Recreation and Park District, 46
Photographic Arts Workshops, 140
Photographic Center School, 140
Photographic Resource Center, 88
Photography at the Summit & Sports Photography Workshop, 58
Photography Workshops International, 88
PhotoProExpo, 60
Point Reyes Field Seminars, 46
Port Townsend Photography Immersion Workshops, 141
Proam Photo Workshops, 47
Professional Photographers of North Carolina/Summer Short Session, 122
Professional Photographers Society of NY Photo Workshop, 114
Ray McSavaney Photographic Workshops, 47
Redwood Exposure, 47
Robert Winslow Photo Tours, 59
Rocky Mountain School of Photography, 95
Rocky Mountain Seminars, 59
Rod Planck Presents, 91
Ron Sanford, 48
Santa Fe Workshops, 103
School of Evidence Photography, 128
School of Visual Arts, 115
Sell & ReSell Your Photos, 142
Sierra Photographic Workshops, 48
Snake River Institute, 143
Southampton College Master Photography Workshop, 115
Southwest Craft Center, 131
St. Cloud State University Summer Photo Imaging Workshop, 92
Steve Gilroy's Alaska Photo Tours, 36
Summer Weekend of Photography, 92
Summit Photography Workshops, 50
Superior/Gunflint Photography Workshops, 93
Taos Institute of Arts, 104
Texas School of Professional Photography, 131
The Darkroom, 50
Toronto Image Works, 144
Touch of Success Seminars, 65
Triangle Institute of Professional Photography, 129
Turning Backgrounds into Dollars, 132
Tuscany Color Photography Workshop, 117
Two Coyotes Workshops, 132
UC Santa Cruz Extension, 50
Utah Canyons Workshops, 133
Visual Journeys, 104
Visual Studies Workshop, 118
Voyagers International, 119
WaterHouse Photo Tours, 65
West Coast School of Professsional Photography, 52
Wild Eyes Photo Adventure, 97
Wilderness Photographic Workshops, 52
Wilderness Photography Expeditions, 97
Wilderness Travel, 53
Winona International School of Professional Photography, 69
Wisconsin Indianhead Photographers School at Treehaven, 142
Women's Studio Workshop, 119
Workshops in the West, 133
Yankee Schooner Cruises, 81
Yosemite Field Seminars, 53
Your World in Color, 141

Conferences

Northern Short Course in Photojournalism, 112–13
NPPA Electronic Photojournalism Workshop, 121
NPPA Flying Short Course, 121
Photography at the Summit & Sports Photography Workshop, 58–59
PhotoProExpo, 60
PPA Imaging Conference and Expo, 68
VISCOMM, 118
VISCOMM West, 51–52

Academic Programs

Academy of Art College, 37
Ampro Photo Workshops, 144
Art Center College of Design, 38
Brooks Institute of Photography, 38–39
Center for Photonics Studies, 71
Hallmark Institute of Photography, 85
High-Speed Motion Analysis Systems & Techniques, 142
International Center of Photography, 109
Maine Photographic Workshops, 79–80
New England School of Photography, 87–88
Ohio Institute of Photography and Technology, 123
Ohio University School of Visual Communication, 124
Oklahoma School of Photography, 125
Oregon School of Arts & Crafts, 125–26
PhotoCentral—Hayward Area Recreation and Park District, 46
Photographic Center School, 140–41
Portfolio Center, 67
Pratt Institute, 113–14
Rhode Island School of Design, 129
Rochester Institute of Technology, 114–15
Rocky Mountain School of Photography, 95–96
Savannah College of Art & Design, 68
School of the Art Institute of Chicago, 74
School of Visual Arts, 115
Southern Illinois University at Carbondale, 74
Tisch School of the Arts/NYU, 116
Washington University Summer Art Study in Florence, 94
Western Academy of Photography, 145

Digital Imaging Programs

American Film Institute, 38
Ampro Photo Workshops, 144
Anderson Ranch Arts Center, 54–55
Art Center College of Design, 38
Brooks Institute of Photography, 38–39
Camera & Darkroom Digital, 101
COMPrehend Computer Education Centers, 61
Creative Computer Workshop, 40
Desktop America, 106
Digital Works, 83
Dynamic Graphics Educational Foundation, 71–72
Electronic Imaging Center, 92
Fitchburg State College Photoshop Workshop, 85
Gamma Technical Institute, 72
Georgia School of Professional Photography, 66
Hill Country Arts Foundation, 131
Interactive Factory Workshops, 85
J&J Computing, 110
MAC University, 72–73
Maine Photographic Workshops, 79–80
Meteor Technology Education, 90
New England Institute of Professional Photography, 87
New England School of Photography, 87–88
New Horizons Computer Learning Center, 67
NPPA Electronic Photojournalism Workshop, 121
Ohio Institute of Photography and Technology, 123
Palm Beach Photographic Centre, 64–65
Photo Metro Digital Workshops, 46
Photographic Resource Center, 88
Photographics Unlimited, 113
Photography at the Summit & Sports Photography Workshop, 58–59
Professional Photographers of North Carolina/Summer Short Session, 122
Samy's Digital Imaging, 48
Santa Fe Workshops, 103
Technical and Education Center of the Graphic Arts and Imaging at RIT, 116
Texas School of Professional Photography, 131–32
The Darkroom, 50
Toronto Image Works, 144–45
Triangle Institute of Professional Photography, 129
United Digital Artists, 117
United Digital Artists/West, 51
VISCOMM, 118
VISCOMM West, 51–52

Visual Studies Workshop, 118–19
Winona International School of Professional Photography, 69
Wisconsin Indianhead Photographers School at Treehaven, 142–43
Zzyzx, 53

On-the-Road Programs

Al Weber, 37
Allaman's Montana Photographic Adventures, 94
Ambient Light Workshops, 70
Anchell Photography Workshops, 54
Anderson Ranch Arts Center, 54–55
Art Ketchum Workshops, 71
Birds as Art, 61
Bob Shell Photo Workshops, 136
Branson Reynolds Photographic Workshops, 55
California Natural Wonders Photographic Workshops, 39
Center for Inner Focus, 137
Center for Nature Photography, 35
Center for Photography at Woodstock, 106
Clayton Fogle's Hummingbirds, 40
Conifer Photographic Workshops, 56
Cory Nature Photography, 130
Coupeville Arts Center, 138
David Halpern Photography Workshops, 124
Dramatic Light Nature Photography, 56–57
Duckworth Forensic Photography, 125
Everglades Photo Safari, 62
Exfoditions, Journeys beyond Photography, 41
First Light Photo Workshops & Safaris, 108
First Light Photography Tours, 57
Frank Balthis Photography Workshops, 42
Gerlach Nature Photography, 89
Great American Photography Weekend, 76–77
Hidden Worlds, 43
Howard Bond Workshops, 90
Image Experience Workshops, 108
Indian River Photo Workshops, 108–9
International Model Testing Workshops, 98–99
International Wildlife Adventures, 138–39
Ireland with Ron Rosenstock, 110
Jean Michel Cousteau/Project Ocean Search, 43–44
Jim Bones Photographic Workshop, 101–2
JMC Eye Photo, 135
Joe McDonald Wildlife Photography, 127
John Sexton Photography Workshops, 44
Joseph Van Os Photo Safaris, 139
Katmai Coastal Tours, 35
Lepp & Associates, 44
Macro Tours Photographic Workshops & Tours, 45
Maine Photographic Workshops, 79–80
Maria Piscopo, 45
Mexico Photography Workshops, 141
Midwest Photographic Workshops, 90–91
Monte Zucker Portrait/Wedding Classes, 63
Natural Habitat Adventures, 58
Nature Images Workshops, 63
Nature One Photography & Wildlife Adventure, 100
Nature's Light, 123
Neversink Photo Workshops, 112
New England School of Photographic Arts, 59–60
New Vision Workshops, 63–64
Northern Exposures, 139
Northern Short Course in Photojournalism, 112–13
Northlight Photo Workshops, 113
NPPA Electronic Photojournalism Workshop, 121
NPPA Flying Short Course, 121
Osprey Photo Workshops & Tours, 82
Palm Beach Photographic Centre, 64–65
Philip Augustin Workshops, 126
Photo Explorer Tours, 91
PhotoCentral—Hayward Area Recreation and Park District, 46
Photographic Arts Workshops, 140
Photography Workshops International, 88
Proam Photo Workshops, 47
Ray McSavaney Photographic Workshops, 47
Robert Winslow Photo Tours, 59
Rocky Mountain School of Photography, 95–96
Rod Planck Presents, 91
Ron Sanford, 48
Santa Fe Workshops, 103
School of Evidence Photography, 128
Sell & ReSell Your Photos, 142
Sierra Photographic Workshops, 48–50
Steve Gilroy's Alaska Photo Tours, 36

Summit Photography Workshops, 50
Superior/Gunflint Photography Workshops, 93
Touch of Success Seminars, 65
Tuscany Color Photography Workshop, 117
Two Coyotes Workshops, 132–33
UC Santa Cruz Extension, 50
Utah Canyons Workshops, 133
Visual Journeys, 104–5
Voyagers International, 119
Washington University Summer Art Study in Florence, 94
WaterHouse Photo Tours, 65–66
Wilderness Photographic Workshops, 52–53
Wilderness Travel, 53
Workshops in the West, 133
Yankee Schooner Cruises, 81

Financial Aid

Academy of Art College, 37
Alden B. Dow Creativity Fellowships, 89
Ampro Photo Workshops, 144
Anderson Ranch Arts Center, 54–55
Arrowmont School of Arts & Crafts, 130
Art Center College of Design, 38
Atlantic Center for the Arts, 60–61
Bemis Center for Contemporary Arts, 98
Brooks Institute of Photography, 38–39
Carina House: A Monhegan Residency, 78
Center for Inner Focus, 137
Center for Photography at Woodstock, 106
Centrum Artist in Residency Program, 138
Contemporary Artists Center, 83–84
Country Photography Workshops of New Jersey, 99
Coupeville Arts Center, 138
Fabric Workshop & Museum Artist-in-Residence Program, 127
Fine Arts Work Center in Provincetown, 84
Georgia School of Professional Photography, 66
Golden Gate School Professional Photographic Workshops, 42
Hallmark Institute of Photography, 85
Headlands Center for the Arts, 42–43
Hill Country Arts Foundation, 131
Illinois Workshops, 72
International Center of Photography, 109
Kalani Honua Eco-Resort Artist-in-Residence Program, 69–70
Light Work, 111
Maine Photographic Workshops, 79–80
Mary Anderson Center for the Arts, 75
Medicine Wheel Artists' Retreat, 86
Mid-America Institute of Professional Photography, 75
Missouri Photo Workshop, 93
Mt. Carroll Center for Applied Photographic Arts, 73
Nantucket Island School of Design & the Arts, 86–87
New England School of Photography, 87–88
Ohio Institute of Photography and Technology, 123
Ohio University School of Visual Communication, 124
Oklahoma Fall Arts Institutes, 124–25
Oregon School of Arts & Crafts, 125–26
Palm Beach Photographic Centre, 64–65
Penland School of Crafts, 122
Peters Valley Craft Center, 100
Photographic Center School, 140–41
Portfolio Center, 67
Pratt Institute, 113–14
Professional Photographers Society of NY Photo Workshop, 114
Rochester Institute of Technology, 114–15
Rocky Mountain School of Photography, 95–96
Roswell Artist-in-Residence Program, 102
Santa Fe Workshops, 103
Savannah College of Art & Design, 68
School of the Art Institute of Chicago, 74
School of Visual Arts, 115
Skowhegan, 80–81
Southern Illinois University at Carbondale, 74
St. Cloud State University Summer Photo Imaging Workshop, 92
STUDIO for Creative Inquiry, 128–29
Taos Institute of Arts, 104
Texas School of Professional Photography, 131–32
Tisch School of the Arts/NYU, 116
Triangle Institute of Professional Photography, 129
Vermont Studio Center, 135–36
Villa Montalvo Artist Residency Program, 51
Washington University Summer Art Study in Florence, 94
West Coast School of Professsional Photography, 52
Western Academy of Photography, 145

Winona International School of Professional Photography, 69
Wisconsin Indianhead Photographers School at Treehaven, 142–43
Women's Studio Workshop, 119–20

Handicapped Access

American Film Institute, 38
Atlantic Center for the Arts, 60
Bemis Center for Contemporary Arts, 98
Center for Photonics Studies, 71
Dynamic Graphics Educational Foundation, 71
Fabric Workshop & Museum Artist-in-Residence Program, 127
Fitchburg State College Photoshop Workshop, 85
Gamma Technical Institute, 72
Georgia School of Professional Photography, 66
Hallmark Institute of Photography, 85
Helene Wurlitzer Foundation, 101
JMC Eye Photo, 135
Latigo Ranch Photography Workshops, 57
Light Work, 111
MAC University, 72
MacDowell Colony, 99
Mary Anderson Center for the Arts, 75
Meteor Technology Education, 90
Mid-America Institute of Professional Photography, 75
Millay Colony for the Arts, 111
Missouri Photo Workshop, 93
Monte Zucker Portrait/Wedding Classes, 63
Ohio University School of Visual Communication, 124
Oklahoma Fall Arts Institutes, 124
Palm Beach Photographic Centre, 64
Penland School of Crafts, 122
Photo Metro Digital Workshops, 46
Photographic Center School, 140
Photographics Unlimited, 113
Portfolio Center, 67
PPA Imaging Conference and Expo, 68
Professional Photographers of North Carolina/Summer Short Session, 122
Professional Photographers Society of NY Photo Workshop, 114
Roswell Artist-in-Residence Program, 102
Samy's Digital Imaging, 48
Savannah College of Art & Design, 68
School of the Art Institute of Chicago, 74
Southern Illinois University at Carbondale, 74
St. Cloud State University Summer Photo Imaging Workshop, 92
STUDIO for Creative Inquiry, 128
Texas School of Professional Photography, 131
The Darkroom, 50
Tisch School of the Arts/NYU, 116
Triangle Institute of Professional Photography, 29
UC Santa Cruz Extension, 50
United Digital Artists, 117
United Digital Artists/West, 51
VISCOMM, 118
VISCOMM West, 51
Workshops in the West, 133
Yaddo, 120

Web Sites

Preface Web site addresses with http://

Acadia National Park Artist-in-Residence Program, www.acadia.net/anp, 78
American Film Institute, www.afionline.org, 38
Ampro Photo Workshops, www.amprophoto.com, 144
Anderson Ranch Arts Center, www.apogeephoto.com/anderson_ranch.html, 54
Branson Reynolds Photographic Workshops, www.simwell.com/reynolds, 55
California Natural Wonders Photographic Workshops, www.apogeephoto.com/calwonders.html, 39
Camera & Darkroom Digital, www.camera-darkroom.com., 101
Center for Photography at Woodstock, www.users.aol.com/cpwphoto, 106
Clayton Fogle's Hummingbirds, www.apogeephoto.com/clayton_fogle.html, 40
Conifer Photographic Workshops, www.apogeephoto.com/conifer.html, 56
Digital Works, www.bostonphoto.com/bpi, 83
Djerassi Resident Artists Program, www.djerassi.org, 40
Exfoditions, Journeys beyond Photograph, www.exfoditions.com, 41
Great American Photography Weekend, www.apogeephoto.com/gapweek1, 76
Hallmark Institute of Photography, www.hallmark-institute.com, 85
Howard Bond Workshops, www.apogeephoto.com/howard_bond.html, 90

Interactive Factory Workshops, www.ifactory.com, 85
International Model Testing Workshops, www.apogeephoto.com/icms.htm, 98
International Wildlife Adventures, www.wildlifeadventures.com, 138
Ireland with Ron Rosenstock, www.gorp.com/voyagers.htm, 110
Jean Michel Cousteau/Project Ocean Search, www.jmcfir.com, 43
Jim Bones Photographic Workshop, www.rt66.com/ ~jimbones, 101
Joe McDonald Wildlife Photography, www.apogeephoto.com/joe_mcdonald.html, 127
John Sexton Photography Workshops, www.apogeephoto.com/john_sexton.html, 44
Kalani Honua Eco-Resort Artist-in-Residence Program, www.randm.com/kh.html, 69
Katmai Coastal Tours, www.alaska.net/ ~seebears/katmai.html, 35
Maine Photographic Workshops, www.MEWorkshops.com, 79
Maine Photographic Workshops/New York, www.MEWorkshops.com, 111
Meteor Technology Education, www.meteor.com, 90
Mexico Photography Workshops, www.apogeephoto.com/mexicophoto.html, 141
Nature Images Workshops, www.apogee photo.com/natureimages.html, 63
Nature's Light, www.apogeephoto.com/natures_light.html, 123
Neversink Photo Workshops, www.apogeephoto.com/neversink.html, 112
Northern Short Course in Photojournalism, www.sunsite.unc.edu/NPPA, 112
NPPA Electronic Photojournalism Workshop, www.sunsite.unc.edu/NPPA, 121
NPPA Flying Short Course, www.sunsite.unc.edu/nppa, 121
Ohio University School of Visual Communication, www.viscom.ohiou.edu, 124
Oklahoma Fall Arts Institutes, www.telepath.com/okarts, 124
Palm Beach Photographic Workshops, www.pbphoto.workshop.org, 64
Photo Metro Digital Workshops, www.photometro.com, 46
Photographic Center School, www.speakeasy.org/photocen, 140
Photographic Resource Center, www.bu/edu/trc, 88
Redwood Exposure, www.northcoast.com/ ~ redwood, 47
Rochester Institute of Technology, www.RIT.edu, 114
Rocky Mountain School of Photography, www.apogeephoto.com/rsmp.html, 95
Samy's Digital Imaging, www.net101.com/samyscamera, 48
Santa Fe Workshops, www.sfworkshop.com, 103
Savannah College of Art & Design, www.scad.edu, 68
School of the Art Institute of Chicago, www.artic.edu/saic, 74
Snake River Institute, www.wyoming.com/ ~jacksonhole/SRI, 143
Southampton College Master Photography Workshop, www.southampton.liunet.edu, 115
Southern Illinois University at Carbondale, www.siu.edu/departments/cmcma, 74
Taos Institute of Arts, www.taosnet.com/TIA, 104
Technical and Education Center of the Graphic Arts and Imaging at RIT, www.RIT.edu, 116
Tisch School of the Arts/NYU, www.nyu.edu, 116
Toronto Image Works, www.magic.ca/tiw, 144
Touch of Success Seminars, www.apogee photo.com/touch_of_success.html, 65
UC Santa Cruz Extension, www.ucsc.edu/unex, 50
United Digital Artists, www.uda.com, 117
United Digital Artists/West, www.uda.com, 51
Visual Journeys, webart.com/ visualjourneys, 104
Voyagers International, www.gorp.com/voyagers.html, 119
Wild Eyes Photo Adventure, www.apogeephoto.com/wildeyes.html, 97
Women's Studio Workshop, www.web mark.com/wsw/wswhome.htm, 119
Workshops in the West, www. apogee photo.com/winthewest.html, 133
Yankee Schooner Cruises, www.mid coast.com/ ~ rosewa, 81
Zzyzx, www.zzyzxworld.com, 53

About the Author

Stuart Cohen is a professional photographer with over 20 years' experience shooting stock and assignments for a variety of commercial and editorial clients. He has traveled extensively as the leading provider of photos to publishers of language arts educational materials. His stock photographs are distributed worldwide by Comstock. Cohen is co-author of *The Joy of Photographing People* and author of *Lenses for 35mm Cameras,* both for Eastman Kodak. He also writes extensively on ethical and professional issues for the photography trade press, including *Photo District News, Professional Photographer* and *Nature Photographer* magazines. Stuart Cohen lives in Marblehead, Massachusetts.

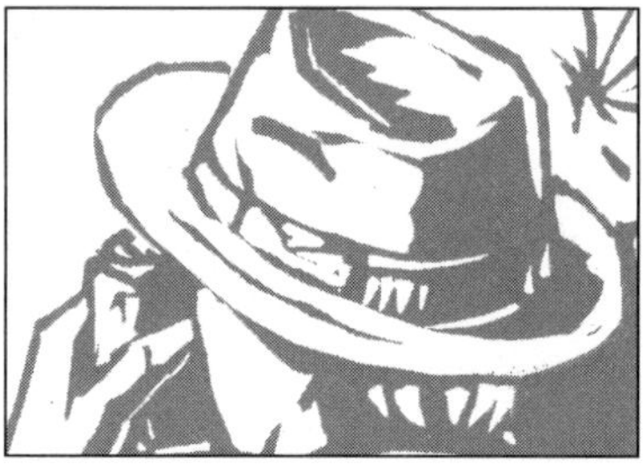

About Getting Your Act Together™

The Watson-Guptill Resource Guides to:

• Workshops • Conferences • Artists' Colonies • Academic Programs

With attendance soaring at workshops, seminars, conferences and other opportunities for continuing education, this particularly timely series presents dependable, candid resource guides tailored to meet the needs of adult artists in several specific categories.

Taking the frustration and guesswork out of the process of finding the right venue for further training, each guide offers a comprehensive and critical review of arts programs, organized alphabetically by state, covering workshops, conferences, artists' colonies and academic programs.

Each program entry provides such key information as contact name and address (plus phone and fax numbers, e-mail and Web site addresses), application requirements, financial aid opportunities and size of program. The books also cover general information on relevant associations, organizations and unions, as well as the business side of each discipline.